Ethical and Religious Thought in Analytic Philosophy of Language

Ethical and Religious Thought
in Analytic Philosophy of Language

Quentin Smith

Yale University Press   New Haven and London

Designed by Rebecca Gibb. Set in Ehrhardt type by Keystone Typsetting, Inc. Printed in the
United States of America by BookCrafters, Inc., Chelsea, Michigan.

Library of Congress Cataloging-in-Publication Data
Smith, Quentin, 1952–
Ethical and religious thought in analytic philosophy of language /
Quentin Smith.
    p.   cm.
Includes bibliographical references and index.
ISBN 0-300-06212-5 (cloth : alk. paper)
1. Analysis (Philosophy)   2. Ethics.   3. Religion—Philosophy.
I. Title
B808.5.S65   1998
146'.4—dc21
97-17476
CIP

A catalogue record for this book is available from the British Library.

The paper in this book meets the guidelines for permanence and durability of the Committee on
Production Guidelines for Book Longevity of the Council on Library Resources.

10 9 8 7 6 5 4 3 2 1

Contents

Preface

The phrase "analytic philosophy" brings to many people's minds two ideas, that linguistic analysis is a favored philosophical method and that the issue of the meaning of human life is either "senseless" or too vague to be a fitting subject of inquiry. It is thought by many that if one is interested in theories of the meaning or meaninglessness of life, then one must turn not to twentieth-century analytic philosophy, but perhaps to existentialism or even to novels or poetry.

This stereotype of analytic philosophy is exemplified by Stephen Hawking's remarks in his popular book *A Brief History of Time.* Hawking believes that even *physics* provides a more direct treatment of the topic of life's meaning than analytic philosophy. He articulates the popular view that analytic philosophers have abandoned the perennial questions, such as the "why" of it all, and have turned to linguistic analysis instead: "Philosophers reduced the scope of their inquiries so much that Wittgenstein, the most famous philosopher of this century, said 'The sole remaining task for philosophy is the analysis of language.' What a comedown from the great tradition of philosophy from Aristotle to Kant!" Physics, by contrast, aims to answer "the question of why it is that we and the universe exist."[1]

Some analytic philosophers who do explicitly discuss the meaning of life, such as E. D. Klemke, claim that they can address the issue but not as analytic philosophers. Klemke writes that "most philosophical problems are highly technical and . . . the making of minute distinctions and the employment of a specialized vocabulary are essential for the solution of such problems. . . . On the other hand, I am inclined to think that the philosopher ought to occasionally leave the study, or the philosophical association lecture hall, or even the classroom, and, having shed his aristocratic garments, speak as a man among other men."[2]

One purpose of this book is to show that this widespread interpretation of analytic philosophy is in many respects mistaken and that theories of the ethical or religious meaning (or meaninglessness) of human life follow directly from the methods of linguistic analysis used by many analytic philosophers. It will appear, contrary to what Hawking says, that analytic philosophers have always been concerned with the ultimate questions and that the concern with language is not an end in itself but a method by which these questions are approached. Many will grant that concern with ultimate questions has become widespread in analytic philosophy since the 1970s with the renewed interest in theism, normative ethics, and moral realism, but it needs to be shown that this concern has been here all along, beginning with the logical realism of the early G. E. Moore and Bertrand Russell and extending through logical positivism, ordinary language analysis, and linguistic essentialism. This concern is present in Rudolf Carnap as well as in Alvin Plantinga, despite the radically different conclusions of these two authors.

Furthermore, it will appear (contrary to Klemke's suggestion) that treatment of the issue of the meaning or lack of meaning of human life does not require a departure from the normal and technical ways of doing analytic philosophy but is itself a normal and technical way of doing analytic philosophy. Issues in the philosophy of language and their implications for the meaning or meaninglessness of human life have been treated rigorously and exactly in the analytic tradition.

My concern with the meaning or meaninglessness of human life is about objective rather than subjective meaning. Human life has an objective ethical meaning if and only if moral realism is true, that is, if and only if moral facts obtain independently of whether humans believe they obtain. Human life has an objective religious meaning if and only if theism is true. Because analytic philosophers have been concerned almost exclusively with Judeo-Christian monotheism, this type of theism will be the topic in my discussions of the philosophy of religion. In the Conclusion, I shall discuss a different kind of theism: a naturalistic pantheism.

Subjective meaning may vary from one human life to another and may be defined in terms of what a person cares about and what goals she strives for. A human's life is subjectively meaningful if and only if she cares about some things and strives for some goals. Subjective meaning is a degreed concept, its limiting case being a subjectively meaningless life, one in which a person cares about nothing and has no goals. If human life lacks both an objective ethical meaning and an objective religious meaning, there still can be subjective meanings. Indeed, the standard position of the atheist and moral antirealist is that the only meanings human life can possess are subjective meanings.

The topic of this book is objective ethical and religious meaning, and that is how I shall use the phrase "the meaning of human life." I shall discuss whether and how theses about objective ethical or religious meaning (or meaninglessness) can be known by various methods of linguistic analysis.

A *method of linguistic analysis* may be defined in a number of ways, but the definition I shall adopt implies that a philosopher uses this method if the conclusions she reaches in the discipline of the philosophy of language are premises of central arguments developed in other philosophical disciplines. This definition is not as idiosyncratic as it might appear to some at first glance, because certain other popular definitions of this method can be reduced to this definition. For example, it is often said that the method of linguistic analysis (as employed in some philosophical discipline) involves explicating the sense (meaning) of the key words pertinent to the subject matter of that discipline. (Philosophers frequently talk about the "meaning" of words, but to avoid confusing this use of "meaning" with its use in "the meaning of human life," I shall talk about the "sense" of words.) Thus, the subject matter of ethics is studied by explicating the sense of such words as "good," "right," "duty," and the like. This definition, however, is reducible to the definition I offer. For the philosopher typically explicates the sense of such words by applying to them theses about the nature of linguistic sense that belong to his philosophy of language. For example, the predominant philosophy of language in logical positivism is captured in the slogan, "The sense of a (nontautological and non–self-contradictory) sentence is the method of its verification," and this method was characterized by many positivists as an acquaintance with the relevant sense-data that confirm or disconfirm the sentence in question.

This thesis about linguistic sense is a crucial premise in the positivist ethical theory known as "emotivism." The following summary argument for some versions of emotivism may be constructed:

1. The sense of a nontautological and non–self-contradictory sentence is the method of its verification.

2. The method of verifying a sentence is a procedure for becoming acquainted with the relevant sense-data.

3. Ethical sentences, those containing words such as "good" and "right," are unverifiable because there are no sensory observations that could verify or disverify them.

4. Therefore, ethical sentences are senseless (and may be characterized as little more than expressions of the emotions or wishes of the speaker).

The conclusion implies, of course, that there is no objective ethical meaning of human life. This positivist theory will be discussed in more detail in chapter 2, but let me briefly note here that premises (1) and (2) are theses developed in the discipline of the philosophy of language, and they are premises from which key conclusions in the discipline of ethics are derived. In some respects, the discipline of the philosophy of language is more fundamental than the discipline of ethics and other disciplines, in that its conclusions serve as premises of major arguments developed in the other disciplines. The method of linguistic analysis may thus be understood as the methodological procedure of using the conclusions reached in the philosophy of language as premises of other disciplines.

This method is widely used in analytic philosophy, but, as everyone knows, it is not the only method used by analytic philosophers. For instance, the method of linguistic analysis is no more the main or only method used in John Rawls's *Theory of Justice* than it is in Aristotle's *Nicomachean Ethics*. I am concerned, however, to show that the connection between the use of this linguistic method and the perennial philosophical questions is far more intimate than is normally supposed; linguistic analysis provides no less direct a route to the perennial issues about meaning than does the phenomenological method used by the existentialists.

Many of the movements in analytic philosophy, for example, logical positivism and ordinary language analysis, may be characterized in terms of the different versions of the method of linguistic analysis they employ. By a *version* of the method of linguistic analysis I mean a use of a specific thesis about linguistic sense *as a premise* from which to derive conclusions in the various philosophical disciplines. Different versions of this method correspond to different theses about linguistic sense. In this book, I shall distinguish four movements in analytic philosophy and show that each uses a different version of the method of linguistic analysis. The relevant four theses about linguistic sense may be summarized by a certain statement or slogan about the sense of words or sentences. These four statements are as follows:

1. Logical realism: Every word in a sentence has a sense which is its referent.
2. Logical positivism: The sense of any sentence that is neither a tautology nor a contradiction is its method of verification.
3. Ordinary language analysis: The sense of an expression is its ordinary use.
4. Linguistic essentialism: The sense of most singular and general words is their rigid designatum.

It is worth emphasizing that "sense" is the generic word I use for *semantic content* and does not correspond to how members of these four movements used the word. For example, many essentialists, including Ruth Barcan Marcus, Saul Kripke, David Kaplan, Hilary Putnam, and N. Salmon, distinguish their view from earlier views by saying that the semantic content of many singular and general words is not a "Fregean sense" but is instead the direct referent of these words, this referent being the rigid designatum.

I shall argue that these four analytic movements are associated with the following theses about objective meaning:

Logical realism: Human life has an ethical meaning but no religious
   meaning.
Logical positivism: Human life is ethically and religiously meaningless.
Ordinary language analysis: Human life is ethically and religiously
   meaningless.
Linguistic essentialism: (For some essentialists) human life has an ethical and
   religious meaning.

Linguistic essentialism (Marcus, Kripke, Plantinga, Robert Adams, David Brink, Thomas Hurka, and others) differs from the other three movements in that it embraces a wide divergence of views about life's meaning or meaninglessness. I shall concentrate on the theories that imply there is objective meaning.

The versions of the method of linguistic analysis encapsulated by these slogans are historically sequential, beginning with logical realism and ending with linguistic essentialism, a current phase. But these are not the only phases of analytic philosophy. For example, such analysts as Richard Swinburne and John Rawls are not members of any of these four movements. Furthermore, these are not the only versions of the linguistic method used by analytic philosophers; for example, there is a tradition associated with the causal theory of reference. My treatment of analytic philosophy in this book is selective and is meant to illustrate my thesis about linguistic analysis and ethical and religious meaning. This book is not intended as a history of analytic philosophy; Gottlob Frege, W. V. O. Quine, Carl Hempel, and other major figures are not discussed, and the topics discussed are confined to some themes in the philosophy of language, ethics, and the philosophy of religion.

Chapter 1 is devoted to logical realism, and the subsequent chapters to the other three movements. The book is structured in such a way that the discussions of the four analytic movements are not of equal length, but of progressively increasing length. The discussion of logical realism is the shortest, and the discussion of linguistic essentialism the longest. Part I is about logical realism, logical positivism, and ordinary language analysis, and part II is about linguistic essentialism. Linguistic essentialism is given the most lengthy treatment because its history is the least known (and the most inaccurately represented in the current literature), and the movement has the greatest relevance to contemporary philosophical debates.

The discussion of these four movements includes as much critical evaluation as exposition. I shall argue that the respective theses about objective meaning of the four movements are not adequately justified by the arguments offered by members of these movements, and I shall work toward a positive theory of objective meaning, which shall be a version of naturalist moral realism (in the perfectionist tradition of ethics) and naturalist pantheism. My criticisms of these four movements will prepare the ground for the main positive part of this book, which mostly appears in chapter 6 (my argument for perfectionism) and the Conclusion (my argument for pantheism). My arguments for a novel version of naturalist perfectionism and pantheism are the most important *philosophical* (as distinct from historical) aspects of this book. From this philosophical perspective, my analyses and criticisms of the four analytic movements may be viewed as means to the end of developing these new theories in metaethics, ethics, and philosophy of religion.

This book was written in the years 1988–96. I should like to thank Kristin Andrews, Kent Baldner, David Brink, Panayot Butchvarov, Nino Cocchiarella, Michael Devitt, Joseph Ellin, Arthur Falk, Thomas Hurka, David Kaplan, Laurie Paul, Alvin Plantinga, Michael Pritchard, David Schenk, William F. Vallicella, and two referees for Yale University Press for helpful comments about some of the ideas in various drafts of the book. I am grateful to the American Council of Learned Societies for a 1996 Fellowship and to the National Endowment for the Humanities for a 1995 Summer Stipend, which enabled me to complete the book.

Part I
Logical Realism, Logical Positivism, and Ordinary Language Analysis

1 Logical Realism

1. The Logical Realists' Method of Linguistic Analysis

The first phase of analytic philosophy is sometimes called the phase of logical realism and is characterized by a platonic theory of universals, direct realism in perceptual theory (we directly perceive physical objects), and intuitionism in ethics (ethical values are directly intuited). It is arguable that the three most definitive works in this phase all appeared in 1903, Bertrand Russell's *Principles of Mathematics* and G. E. Moore's "Refutation of Idealism" and *Principia Ethica*. Because this is the first phase of analytic philosophy, there is a sense in which 1903 is the beginning of the movement known as analytic philosophy. In other senses, this movement began earlier; for example, it might be said that it began on the evening in late 1898 when Moore convinced Russell (in conversation) that monism and idealism are mistaken and logical realism is true. It is also justifiable to say that in terms of recorded evidence the movement began a few months earlier in August 1898, when Moore first conceived its basic ideas and expressed them in an exultant letter to Desmond MacCarthy that began, "I have arrived at a perfectly staggering doctrine."[1] However, the first *published* expression of the theory was Moore's "Nature of Judgement" (1899).[2] But in still another sense, the analytic movement began in 1879 with the publication of Frege's *Begriffsschrift*, in which appeared the first characteristic doctrine of analytic philosophy, quantification theory (Frege's logical analysis of "some," "all," and related expressions), although Frege (unlike Moore and Russell) was not sufficiently influential during his lifetime to begin a movement.

My initial concern is with the particular version of the method of linguistic analysis that was used by many of the main representatives of logical realism. This version is well summarized in the following passage from Russell's *Principles of Mathematics:*

> In the present chapter, certain questions are to be discussed belonging to what may be called philosophical grammar. The study of grammar, in my opinion, is capable of throwing far more light on philosophical questions than is commonly supposed by philosophers. Although a grammatical distinction cannot be uncritically assumed to correspond to a genuine philosophical difference, yet the one is *prima facie* evidence of the other, and may often be most usefully employed as a source of discovery. Moreover, it must be admitted, I think, that every word occurring in a sentence must have *some* meaning: a perfectly meaningless sound could not be employed in the more or less fixed way in which language employs words. The correctness of our philosophical analysis of a proposition may therefore be usefully checked by the exercise of assigning the meaning of each word in the sentence expressing the proposition. On the whole, grammar seems to me to bring us much nearer to a correct logic than the current opinions of philosophers; and in what follows, grammar, though not our master, will yet be taken as our guide.[3]

This paragraph evinces the most methodologically influential tenet in the philosophy of language pertinent to logical realism, the tenet that *to every word in a sentence there correlates a sense* (what Russell calls a "meaning"). Russell calls each of these senses a *term,* and terms divide into things, such as persons or trees, and concepts, such as properties or relations. This tenet about sense uses "sense" to mean *referent,* such that the senses of concrete names are the things to which they refer, and the senses of adjectives and verbs are the concepts to which they refer.[4] (Russell talks of "indication" rather than reference, but I shall treat these two words as being synonymous.)[5] The tenet appeared in an earlier form in Moore's "Nature of Judgement," where the correlated senses are called not terms but concepts. This tenet is used in a methodological sense by logical realists (as their "method of linguistic analysis") in that it is both a major thesis in their philosophy of language and a premise of significant arguments in other disciplines. For example, it is a crucial premise in Russell's metaphysical argument that there are things that do not exist. This argument may be illustrated as follows: If all words have referents, and the referents of concrete names are things, then "Pegasus" refers to a certain thing, namely, Pegasus, the flying horse. This implies there *is* a referent of "Pegasus," even if this referent does not exist. This argument generalizes to any A of which there is a name or definite description. As Russell writes, "For if A were nothing, it could not be said not to be [that is, A could not be the referent of 'A' in the sentence 'A is not']; 'A is not' implies that there is a term A whose being is denied, and hence that A is. Thus unless 'A is not' be an empty sound, it must be false—whatever A may be, it certainly is."[6] This thesis about linguistic sense can also be used to justify theses in other disciplines, such as ethics. It can be argued that the adjective "good" does not refer to any natural property and therefore—because every adjective refers to some property—"good" must refer to some nonnatural property, some property that we grasp by a special sort of intuition. The alternative that "good" refers to no property but merely expresses the speaker's approval is tacitly ruled out by the tenet that every word has a sense and its sense is its referent.

2. The Logical Realists' Theory of the Religious Meaninglessness of Human Life

This example leads us directly to the theory of the objective meaning or meaninglessness of human life implicit in some of the ideas of the logical realists. According to the logical realists, God cannot be known to exist, but we do know there is a good in itself. The objective meaning of human life involves the referents of certain ethical adjectives; this meaning is knowable given the linguistic thesis that there are referents of ethical adjectives, a thesis the realists derived from their more general linguistic thesis that every word has a sense which is its referent. If this linguistic thesis is false and ethical adjectives merely express emotions, then these adjectives do not refer to anything, and human life thereby does not have the objective meaning the realists ascribed to it.

This theory of ethical meaning and religious meaninglessness is given a poetic expression in Russell's essay "A Free Man's Worship" (1903), which states that there exists no God meant by human acts of worship but that there is a good in itself meant by acts of valuation. Russell writes,

> purposeless, . . . void of meaning, is the world which science presents for our belief. Amid such a world, if anywhere, our ideals henceforward must find a home. That man is the product of causes which had no prevision of the end they were achieving; that his origin, his growth, his hopes and fears, his loves and his beliefs, are but the outcome of accidental collocations of atoms; that no fire, no heroism, no intensity of thought and feeling, can preserve an individual life beyond the grave; that all the labors of the ages, all the devotion, all the inspiration, all the noonday brightness of human genius, are destined to extinction in the vast death of the solar system, and that the whole temple of man's achievement must inevitably be buried beneath the debris of a universe in ruins—all these things, if not quite beyond dispute, are yet so nearly certain that no philosophy which rejects them can hope to stand. Only within the scaffolding of these truths, only in the firm foundation of unyielding despair, can the soul's habitation henceforth be safely built.

How, in such an alien and inhuman world, can so powerless a creature as man preserve his aspirations untarnished? A strange mystery it is that nature, omnipotent but blind, in the revolutions of her secular hurryings through the abysses of space, has brought forth a child, subject still to her power, *but gifted with sight, with knowledge of good and evil, with the capacity of judging all the works of his unthinking mother.*[7]

There is no God but "the God created by our own love of the good" (57), and thus the locus of objective meaning in our lives must reside in "that energy of faith which enables us to live constantly in the vision of the good" (58). Thus, Russell suggests that the desire for an objective religious meaning is unsatisfied and that in this respect human lives must be devoid of fulfillment. But there are moral ideals of which we have knowledge, and whatever fulfillment, regarding objective meaning, we are capable of achieving must involve the valuation of these ideals.

Russell offered little by way of argument for these claims about objective meaning and meaninglessness, and one must turn to the writings of Moore to find a more precise and well-argued statement. Another reason for redirecting our attention to Moore is that Russell's views on the objective meaning / meaninglessness of human life (like his basic metaphysical and linguistic positions) were largely shaped by earlier writings of Moore, which makes Moore the original figure in this connection. Moore's essay "The Value of Religion" (1901) determined the main contours of the logical realist theory of the meaning / meaninglessness of human life, much as his article "The Nature of Judgement" (1899) determined its basic metaphysical and linguistic positions. In the later essay, Moore avows that human life is religiously meaningless because "there is *no* probability that God exists," but that objective meaning can be found in ethical ways of life, and therefore we should "divert the feeling which the religious wish to spend on him [God], towards those of our own kind, who . . . are worthy of all the affection we can feel."[8]

Before examining Moore's arguments for these theses, one might ask whether he is right in implicitly suggesting that an objective ethical meaning can satisfy desires not only for ethical meaning but also for religious meaning. This suggestion seems to me dubious. For one thing, it may be questioned whether humans are worthy of *all* the affection we can feel and whether "we might perhaps with advantage *worship* the real creature a little more, and his hypothetical Creator a good deal less" (120, my emphasis). It is arguable contra Moore that humans are *not* appropriate objects of worship or of such other religious emotions as piety, adoration, awe, and reverence. This is connected with the notion of metaphysical worth and of great-making properties. Humans are simply not *great* enough beings to be worthy of worship. Perhaps they are deserving of respect and in some cases even admiration, but worship is inappropriate. Humans are not all-knowing, all-powerful, perfectly free, perfectly happy, perfectly good, and permanent beings, and they are not the cause of the universe, and thereby do not deserve the religious emotions that are appropriately directed to such a being. If there is no God, then certain emotions in the repertoire of human emotions cannot be appropriately felt, and the aspect of human nature that desires to relate emotionally to a metaphysically perfect being must remain unfulfilled.

If Russell's and Moore's position is correct, namely, that human life is religiously meaningless but ethically meaningful, then only part of the human desire for objective meaning can be fulfilled. We should side with Russell rather than Moore and hold that the emotional fulfillment of an ethically meaningful way of life should be built on "the firm foundation of unyielding despair" about religious meaning. But this also is not quite accurate, because the desire or need for religious meaning is not universal; if somebody has no desire for religious meaning, then God's nonexistence will not produce despair in him. Accordingly, we should say that for any person who has a desire for a religious and an ethical meaning of life, the happiness he attains through his ethically meaningful life should coexist with his despair at the lack of a religious meaning. This appeared to be Russell's attitude at the time he wrote "A Free Man's Worship."

What arguments does Moore give for the claim that human life is religiously meaningless but ethically meaningful? Regarding the religious question, Moore begins by assuming that "all the arguments to prove the existence of God rest upon evidence like this" (110), namely, statements about daily facts such as "This hand moves." The question is whether the existence of God can be inferred from such facts about the world. According to Moore, the crucial argument is the so-called argument from design, which goes as follows: "From the nature of the world, as it appears on observation, we can infer that it or parts of it were or are caused by a being immensely intelligent, wise or good" (111). The argument (as Moore states it) goes,

1. Certain useful and beautiful things in the world were caused by humans.
Therefore,
2. "Anything useful or good we find in the world, that is not a work of man's designing—man himself, above all, the most useful and beautiful of all—had also for its cause a person of intelligence and goodness [viz., God]" (11).

Moore claims that there is reason to believe (1) only if it is necessarily true that "every natural event has a natural cause" (112), which Moore takes to have the force of

3. Necessarily, every natural event has only a natural cause (and no supernatural cause).

Now (3) is clearly inconsistent with (2) because (2) implies that some natural events, the beginning of the existence of some useful or good things, have a supernatural cause. If (3) is true, then God, since he is not a natural cause, "is not a cause of anything at all" (112), which, given the definition of God as the cause of the universe, is tantamount to the claim that God does not exist. Consequently, Moore concludes, the argument from design fails.

But Moore's reasoning here is open to several objections. I shall consider one problem, his failure to distinguish adequately between principles of deductive and of probabilistic inference. Moore on the one hand treats the argument from (1) to (2) as a probabilistic argument, as an attempt to answer the question, "Have we any evidence rendering it probable that God exists? . . . Is his existence at all probable?" (108–09). But Moore's objection to the argument from (1) to (2) is that we "cannot be sure of" (112) (1) unless (3) is true; if (3) were not true, it would be *possible* that the good and useful things we believe are caused by humans are caused not by humans but supernaturally—"the hospital might have been made by miracle and not made by man" (112). We might well respond to Moore that an argument for the probable existence of God requires only that its premises be probably true, and that the possibility of their falsity is consistent with the argument being successful. And (1) is probably true. We observe hospitals and the like to be caused by humans, and we have no reason to think they are not. Thus, if we take (1) as meaning

    1′. It is probable that some useful and beautiful things in the world were

              caused by humans (but possible that they are instead miraculously caused),

we need not assume (3), and Moore's objection to the argument from design can be met.

But this is not to say, of course, that the probabilistic argument from design is successful, that (1′) makes (2) probably true. This argument encounters a host of other problems; for example, it fails to include in its premises all relevant information. Some relevant information is that there is observational evidence that the useful and good things in the world that are not caused by humans have other natural causes, for example, of the sort specified in the Darwinian theory of evolution and the big bang cosmological theory. For instance, we have observational evidence that human beings are caused by a process of natural selection operating upon our prehuman ancestors, and that these ancestors in turn have other natural causes.[9] The addition of this information to the premises of the argument blocks the probabilistic inference to (2) or at least renders it seriously problematic.[10]

But in the earlier essay, "The Nature of Judgement," Moore offers what may be taken as a backup argument for (3), namely, that it is one among the synthetic a priori principles about existents that are intuitively or immediately evident. The justification for believing (3) does not reside solely or even primarily in the fact that it is (allegedly) presupposed by (1) or other empirical statements, but in its self-evidence. Synthetic a priori propositions about existents "would, in fact, be true, whether any such propositions [empirical propositions such as (1) or "This hand moves"] were true or not. Kant has only taught us that, if any of them are true, it must be so likewise. He failed to see that its truth may be asserted immediately on the same ground as theirs."[11] But this argument—or rather, assertion—runs into problems of its own. Many people, theists in particular, find (3) to be intuitively false, and many others who are agnostics or who do not share Moore's brand of atheism[12] would disagree with Moore's claim that (3) is intuitively self-evident. If we accept Moore's contention that intuition is to be taken as a justification for belief or disbelief in (3), then the occurrence of conflicting intuitions suggests that it is justified to believe (3) and justified to disbelieve (3). Consequently, there is no means of knowing whether (3) is true or not, because there is no method of deciding between the conflicting intuitions. An impasse such as this raises fundamental questions about the adequacy of Moore's intuitionism and the linguistic method upon which his intuitionism is based, questions that will arise again over Moore's ethical theory.

It is admittedly not clear from the above discussion how Moore's theory of the religious meaninglessness of human life is based on his method of linguistic analysis, specifically, upon the logical realist tenet that every word has a sense which is its referent. But there is a connection, as I shall make apparent after I discuss Moore's theory of the ethical meaning of human life. The relation between the linguistic method and the theory of life's meaning/meaninglessness is most explicitly manifest in the ethical writings of Moore, which constituted the focus of his concern with objective meaning or meaninglessness. Moore wrote one article on religion but four articles and two books on ethics.[13]

3. The Logical Realists' Theory of the Ethical Meaning of Human Life

A suitable transition from the logical realists' philosophy of religion to their ethics is best made by showing how the logical realist method of linguistic analysis determined different conclusions to be reached in each of these disciplines. This difference arises from a common position they take about God and the good in itself. Our attention shall remain with Moore's statement of this theory, given that he originated and developed it to the greatest degree. As we have seen, Moore argues that God's existence cannot be inferred from facts about the world, but he goes on to say the same about the good in itself: "Our religious belief stands in the same position as our moral beliefs. These moral judgements, too, it may be said, are independent of beliefs about the world: their truth also can never be inferred from that of daily facts."[14] Given this claim, one might question why Moore draws different conclusions about the good in itself and God. We may ask, if we can infer the existence neither of God nor of the good from "daily facts," should we not in fairness adopt a skepticism about the good as well as about God?

The answer to this question pertains directly to the method of linguistic analysis the logical realists used. The thesis that every word has a referent that constitutes its sense entails that both "God" and "goodness" have referents. If we adopt Russell's and Moore's terminology, this means that the referents of "God" and "the good" are *beings*.[15] But Pegasus is also a being, and the religious question is whether God is not merely a being, but also an *existent*, something that (for example) enters into causal relations with the universe. Moore's position is that the principle of causality (3) precludes any inference from natural events to a non-natural cause, but the situation with the good in itself is different, because the good in itself is defined not as an existent individual that has causal relations with other existents, but as something that has the ontological status merely of *being*. Thus, the fact that we cannot infer the existence of the good from natural events does not count against the truth of our moral beliefs, for these beliefs presuppose not that the good exists but merely that it has being. And that the good has being follows from the thesis about linguistic sense that is definitive of logical realism; if every word has a referent, ethical adjectives have referents, namely, the ethical properties in the class of properties that belong to the class of intrinsic goods.

But one should not pretend that Moore's distinction between existents and mere beings has a clarity that it does not in fact possess. According to Moore's theory in *Principia Ethica*, something's being located in time is a sufficient condition of it having existence. If, however, there is something not located in time, it does not follow that it is a mere being. Moore holds that there are many timeless beings—numbers, propositions, and the like—that are mere beings, but he also allows that there may be atemporal beings that exist (110–12). A prime example is God. But Moore believes there is no proof of such atemporal existents and no reason to believe there are any. Unfortunately, however, Moore is less than clear about the distinctions involved. His theory would be tolerably clear if "exists" meant or implied "has being and is located in time" and if "has mere being" meant or implied "has being and is not located in time." But once timeless existents are allowed as possible, the distinction between existence and mere being becomes blurred. In fact, Moore never says exactly what the distinction between a mere being and a timeless existent comes to. Perhaps one could say that a mere being is a universal and a timeless existent an individual, but such a statement would be an addition to, rather than an explication of, Moore's philosophy.

I shall reconstruct in some detail Moore's argument for the being of the good in itself. To begin with, consider the property of goodness that all intrinsic goods possess. Moore holds that goodness is not a natural property. Examples of natural properties are mental and physical properties such as pleasure and roundness. A natural property is located in time and is part of the object of which it is a property, whereas a nonnatural property is timeless and is not a part of the objects to which it belongs (41). One might wish that Moore would elaborate further upon this distinction, but we may assume for purposes of argument that this distinction is tolerably clear.[16] Moore wants to argue that "good" does not refer to a natural property and that goodness is a nonnatural property and has mere being rather than existence. His argument has this structure:

4. Every word has a sense, which is its referent.

5. The sense of adjectives is a property to which they refer.

6. "Good" is an adjective.

7. "Good" does not refer to a natural property.

Therefore,

8. "Good" refers to a nonnatural property.

Clearly, the linguistic theses about sense, (4) and (5), are crucial to the conclusion, (8), because without them one cannot derive (8) from (6) and (7). As I mentioned earlier, one could instead infer from (6) and (7) that "good" does not refer to anything at all but merely expresses the speaker's emotion or approval.

Also crucial to this argument is (7). Moore supports (7) by noting that if "good" referred to a natural property, such as pleasure, then certain sentences which are clearly not tautologies would be tautologies. For instance, "Pleasure is good" would be a mere tautology, meaning pleasure is pleasant, whereas "Pleasure is good" is clearly not a tautology but a synthetic assertion, an assertion whose denial is neither implicitly nor explicitly self-contradictory. "Pleasure is good" is synonymous with the synthetic assertion "Pleasure ought to exist."[17] A similar argument may be constructed against any other attempt to define "good" in terms of a natural property.

But the conclusion that "good" refers to a nonnatural property is not sufficient to establish that human life has an objective ethical meaning. For the fact that there is such a property does not entail it is exemplified, that is, that there is anything that possesses goodness. If human life has an objective ethical meaning, then there is a class of intrinsic goods, a class of properties and relations that possess the property of goodness. Moore believes that there is such a class and that the two greatest goods that we can know to belong to it are *aesthetic enjoyment* and *personal affection.* The endeavor to instantiate these complex properties or relations is the focus of the ethical purpose of our lives. Thus, Moore writes,

> That it is only for the sake of these things [aesthetic enjoyments and personal affections]—in order that as much of them as possible may at some time exist—that any one can be justified in performing any public or private duty; that they are the *raison d'etre* of virtue; that it is they—these complex wholes *themselves,* and not any constituent or characteristic of them—that form the rational ultimate end of human action and the sole criterion of social progress: these appear to be truths which have been generally overlooked. (189)

Moore's argument that goodness is possessed by aesthetic enjoyment and personal affection is not straightforward, but it may be reconstructed in part as follows. We begin with thesis (8), which is based on the logical realist theory of linguistic sense:

8. "Good" refers to a nonnatural property.

9. "Aesthetic enjoyment" has a referent, a certain complex property.

Therefore,

10. The ethical words in the sentence "Aesthetic enjoyment is good" (along with the copula "is") guarantee that this sentence's parts have sense and that the sentence expresses a proposition.

11. Every proposition is either true or false.

Therefore,

12. The proposition expressed by "Aesthetic enjoyment is good" is either true or false.

According to Moore, propositional truths or falsehoods are mere beings and obtain nondependently upon humans (111). Thus, if there are ethical truths and falsehoods, then there is a class of intrinsic goods, even if we do not know them.

But this thesis is only halfway to Moore's position that aesthetic enjoyment is a member of this class, that is, that the proposition in question is true. How do we know that the proposition expressed by "Aesthetic enjoyment is good" is true? According to Moore, we know this simply through intuition; by grasping the proposition the sentence expresses, we understand that it is true. In other words, the reason we believe the proposition to be true is that it appears to be true. In answer to the obvious objection that there is a diversity of opinions and "appearings to be true" about ethical matters, Moore refers to his linguistic method as a means of solving such conflicts. He notes that "in all those cases where we found a difference of opinion, we found also that the question had not been clearly understood" (145). Moore is implying that if we clearly distinguish the different senses of words we shall clearly grasp the relevant ethical propositions and thereby achieve a uniform belief in their truth or falsity. This intuitionist theory is based on the thesis that the sense of adjectives is their referent. This thesis is taken to imply that adjectives have a semantic reference that is distinguishable from the speaker's reference. "Aesthetic enjoyment" stands in a semantic relation to the property of aesthetic enjoyment of referring to it, and the speaker who utters this expression (with a clear understanding of its sense) stands in a psychological relation to this property of referring to it. The psychological relation is an act of consciousness but the semantic relation is not. When Moore gives an example of a deliberate case of a divergence between speaker's and semantic reference, namely, that it would be foolish if "I were to announce that, whenever I used the word 'good,' I must be understood to be thinking of that object which is usually denoted by the word 'table'" (6), he is using "thinking" to mean speaker's reference and "denoted" to mean semantic reference. Moore's contention is that once we distinguish clearly the senses (semantic referents) of different words or of different uses of the same word, then the speaker's referents will be intuitively clear, and we will thereby be able to recognize and agree about which propositions are true or false. This gives us the additional premises needed to establish the conclusion that the objective ethical meaning of human life involves valuing aesthetic enjoyment as one of the greatest intrinsic goods. Let us follow Moore and call the speaker's apprehension of the proposition expressed by "Aesthetic enjoyment is good" (which includes the speaker's reference to the properties of aesthetic enjoyment and goodness) an "intuition." The additional premises are

13. The intuition of a proposition as being true is a justification for believing the proposition to be true.
14. Disagreements about the truth or falsity of the sentence "Aesthetic enjoyment is good" are due to different propositions being associated with this sentence (which is itself a consequence of the words being assigned different referents).
15. If people use the sentence "Aesthetic enjoyment is good" to express the same proposition, they will share the same intuition.
16. If this sentence is used to express the proposition Moore argues that it properly does express, then there will be an intuition of this proposition as true.

Therefore,

17. The belief that the mentioned proposition is true is justified.

It follows from (17) that we are justified in believing that valuing the goodness of aesthetic enjoyment is a part of the objective ethical meaning of human life.

Premise (15) may be taken as following from (14). Given that Moore reports that he has the intuition that the mentioned proposition is true, (16) and (17) are true if (14) and (15) are true. So the crucial issue comes down to whether (13) and (14) are true. In effect, Moore's theory that aesthetic enjoyment is part of the objective ethical meaning of human life hinges upon whether intuition is a justification for ethical belief and whether people will share the same intuition if they assign the same ethical proposition to the sentence.

4. The Implication of Logical Realism that Life is Meaningful but Absurd

It is very difficult to accept that people have the same intuitions about the same ethical propositions. Moore writes,

> No one, probably, who has asked himself the question, has ever doubted that personal affection and the appreciation of what is beautiful in Art or Nature, are good in themselves; nor, if we consider strictly what things are worth having *purely for their own sakes,* does it appear probable that any one will

think that anything else has *nearly* so great a value as the things which are included under these two heads. (188–89).

Yet other examples of great goods in themselves come to mind, such as an act of
philosophical understanding. Now Moore intuitively finds it false that

18. Philosophical understanding is at least as valuable as aesthetic
     enjoyment,

but there is a long tradition in Western philosophy that is based on the intuition
that (18) is true. Plato, Aristotle, and many other traditional philosophers find (18)
true, as do such twentieth-century ethical intuitionists as Max Scheler and Panayot
Butchvarov.[18] Other counterexamples to Moore's claim about the uniformity of
ethical intuitions can be found. So (14) is false. This also casts doubt on (13), the
claim that the intuition of an ethical proposition as being true is a justification for
believing it to be true. For if Moore intuits (18) as true and Plato intuits (18) as
false, then it is justified to believe (18) is true and justified to believe it is false.
Because there is no known method of deciding which of these conflicting intuitions
is the correct one, it is difficult to see how knowledge of such ethical propositions is
possible at all.

Note that if we are to distinguish the intuition from the belief and regard the
intuition as an alleged justification for the belief, then by "intuition" we must mean
the *appearing to be true of the proposition.* This would allegedly justify the belief in
that the proposition's *appearing* to be true would justify the belief that it *is* true. But
given the conflict among the various intuitive appearances, these appearances cannot justify the beliefs.

The problem of conflicting ethical intuitions cannot be solved by introducing
the concept of *relative ethical justification,* which represents ethical justification as
relative to a particular person. If Moore is justified by his intuition in believing (18)
to be false and Plato by his intuition in believing (18) to be true, then each is
justified in taking himself to know the truth-value of (18). But this solution does
not solve the problem of the unknowability of ethical propositions because it
merely entails that Moore and Plato are each *justified in believing* that he knows the
truth-value of (18); it does not entail that Moore *knows* the truth-value of (18), and
it does not entail that Plato *knows* this truth-value. We are still in the dark about
who knows (18) and about whether (18) is true or false. We are also in the dark
about whether or not any ethical proposition about which there are conflicting
intuitions is true or not; we merely know that the people with the conflicting
intuitions are relatively justified in believing themselves to know the truth-value of
the proposition. In a word, the irresolvable conflict among the ethical intuitions
entails that these intuitions cannot be *absolute* justifications for the ethical beliefs, and absolute justifications are required if there is to be *knowledge* of ethical

propositions and not merely relatively justified beliefs that one has a knowledge of ethical propositions.

Perhaps a suggestion by H. A. Prichard might solve this problem and provide us with the absolute justifications that are needed. Prichard is the second most influential ethical philosopher among the logical realists (after Moore), primarily owing to his classic article "Does Moral Philosophy Rest on a Mistake?" published in 1912. Prichard argues that moral philosophy rests on a mistake because it assumes that there needs to be a proof that we ought to do what in our nonreflective ethical consciousness we immediately apprehend as our obligations. There needs to be no proof, Prichard contends, because our nonreflective ethical consciousness is an intuitive knowledge of self-evident obligations.

Prichard responds to the objection that "obligation cannot be self-evident, since many actions regarded as obligations by some are not so regarded by others," by asserting that "the appreciation of an obligation is, of course, only possible for a developed moral being, and . . . different degrees of development are possible."[19] But this brief response won't do because it involves a vicious circularity. How do we know which persons are more morally developed than others? Is the person who intuits capital punishment to be immoral more morally developed than the person who intuits it to be morally permissible in some cases? How can we decide without knowing which intuitions are true? It seems we have a vicious circle: the criterion for determining which of two conflicting moral intuitions is true is that the intuition held by the more morally developed person is true, but the criterion for determining which of the two persons is morally developed is that the more morally developed one is the person with the true intuition. It does not appear, then, that Prichard has offered us a means of solving the problem of conflicting intuitions.

The above considerations about the unknowability of ethical truths suggest that human life is *objectively meaningful but absurd.* Human life is objectively meaningful because there is a good in itself, and some of our beliefs about the good in itself are true, but human life is absurd because we cannot know which of our beliefs are true.

This conclusion hinges in part upon the definition of "absurdity." Generally speaking, something is absurd if it is grossly disproportionate with what it is supposed to be, such that this disproportionateness renders the thing or activity clearly contrary to reason. The notion of absurdity as applied to human life implies that human life is grossly disproportionate (in a way that is clearly contrary to reason) to what it is supposed to be. There are at least two ways that human life can be absurd, namely, through being *objectively meaningless and absurd* or through being *objectively meaningful and absurd.* In the philosophical literature, only the first sort of absurdity has been discussed, for example, by Albert Camus and

Thomas Nagel. I shall illustrate the first sort of absurdity in terms of Nagel's theory because he discusses a specifically ethical sort of absurdity, and this is directly relevant to our present concerns (Camus's theory is of a religious absurdity). I shall then explore the meaningful absurdity that is arguably implied by the logical realist ethical philosophy.

In his essay "The Absurd," Nagel suggests that an absurd situation involves a discrepancy between reality and the pretension and aspiration of the people in that situation. He regards our lives as absurd because we value our plans and projects (the pretension) and on this basis strive to realize them (the aspiration), and yet in reality our plans and projects have no value. We normally adopt an internal perspective in which our plans and projects *seem* to have value, but when we adopt an external perspective and see that nothing really has value we recognize our lives to be absurd. Nagel assumes that there are no intrinsic values of things and that there are no necessary or synthetic a priori ethical truths; he assumes our value-presuppositions are "arbitrary" and reflect "all the contingency and specificity of our [individual] aims and pursuits."[20] The absurdity is that from the internal perspective these presuppositions do not seem arbitrary, contingent, and subjectively relative, and this seeming is indispensable to our normal endeavors and passions.

This sort of absurdity, the conjunction of objective meaninglessness and the normal but tacit pretension that there is objective meaning, could be alleviated if we ceased to pretend there is objective meaning. Our situation then would be not an absurd one but a *nihilistic* one: there is nothing worth striving for and there would seem to us to be nothing worth striving for. Nagel believes a sustained nihilistic attitude is impossible for humans—we are valuing creatures by nature— and hence that we are doomed to absurdity.

This is not, however, the sort of absurdity in which we are interested at present. (Meaningless absurdity shall be examined in later chapters.) Rather, we are assuming the logical realist view that there are synthetic a priori ethical truths and hence that some value-presuppositions are necessary and nonarbitrary and that they manifest an intrinsic moral order of reality. We are also assuming the general linguistic and epistemological framework of logical realism, that there are intrinsic value-properties of things designated by "goodness" and "evilness" in relation to which we are (or at least seem to be) in intuitive contact. Given these assumptions, life is objectively meaningful. But it is nonetheless absurd because *we cannot know this objective meaning, despite the fact that we normally if tacitly assume we do know it.* Normally, we tacitly take our value-intuitions as absolute justifications for our beliefs about what is good or evil, as giving us *knowledge* of good and evil, but these value-intuitions are not in reality absolute justifications for these beliefs. The tacit "pretension" is that the value-intuitions are absolute justifications, and the "aspiration" is to instantiate the ethical principles about which we have intuitions, but the "reality" is that these pretensions and aspirations involve a delusion. In this respect, the reality of human life is grossly disproportionate to what it is tacitly supposed to be and this disproportionateness is clearly contrary to reason, for it is clearly irrational to live on the basis of a tacit and false assumption that we have knowledge about which moral beliefs are true.

This conclusion about life's absurd meaningfulness is partially implicit in the premises of the logical realist ethics. One premise is that there are ethical truths. This premise is based on the logical realist theory that "good" refers to a property and the associated claim that ethical sentences express propositions, construed platonically (so that they possess their truth or falsity nondependently upon their being believed or disbelieved by humans). A second premise is that if our ethical beliefs are absolutely justified, they are justified by our intuitions, that is, by ethical propositions intuitively appearing to us to be true. These two premises are implicit in logical realism. The third premise comes from our own observation that there are conflicting value-intuitions even after the sense of the words in the relevant ethical sentences has been clearly understood by the parties in the dispute (something Moore denied). The fourth premise is that this conflict entails that value-intuitions do not absolutely justify our beliefs in ethical propositions, from whence it follows (given the second premise that our ethical beliefs, *if* absolutely justified at all, are justified by value-intuitions) that our ethical beliefs are absolutely unjustified. This gives rise to an absurdly meaningful situation given the fact that we normally if tacitly take our value-intuitions *as* absolutely justifying our ethical beliefs and aspire to realize various goals based on this false assumption.

The idea that human life is meaningful but absurd can be made more understandable if we make some related distinctions. One is that life is meaningful but absurd only if it is not *meaningful but tragic.* Life would be tragic if evil triumphed over good and we knew this. Our lives cannot be tragic because even if evil triumphed over good we could not know this, given that we do not know what is good and what is evil. The Jews could not say with truth that life was tragic as they were being imprisoned in labor camps and exterminated by the Germans, because (1) it appeared to the Jews that the German treatment of the Jews was evil, (2) it appeared to the relevant Germans that the German treatment of the Jews was good ("because necessary for the purification of Aryan Europe"), and (3) there is in principle no means to decide which of these appearances is the veridical one. The Jews and Germans, had they been aware of the true situation, would have lived and died in the full knowledge of the absurdity of their lives.

Of course I am not to be understand as making definitive ethical conclusions here. At present, I am merely drawing out some of the implications of logical realist ethical theory. But I would point out that if it appears intuitively obvious to the reader *that the Germans were doing evil to the Jews*, then that does not refute the argument presented in this section for the meaningful absurdity of life, because the fact that there are such intuitive appearances is one of the very premises of the argument.

A distinction essential to the theory of meaningful absurdity is that between first-level ethical beliefs and second-level ethical beliefs. A first-level ethical belief is that something is good or evil or that something is of equal or greater value than something else, for example, that *philosophical understanding is at least as valuable as aesthetic enjoyment*. A second-level ethical belief is about some or all first-level ethical beliefs. The belief that "the intuition that the proposition *that philosophical understanding is at least as valuable as aesthetic enjoyment* is true does not absolutely justify belief in this proposition" is an example of a particular second-level ethical belief, and the belief that "life is meaningful but absurd" is an example of a general second-level ethical belief. If logical realism is true, then some of our first-level ethical beliefs are true; for example, either it is true that philosophical understanding is at least as valuable as aesthetic enjoyment or it is true that philosophical understanding is less valuable than aesthetic enjoyment. But none of these beliefs is absolutely justified, and consequently we do not know which are true; that is, we do not have a second-level knowledge of which first-level beliefs are true. The absurdity of life does not *appear* as long as we experience first-level ethical beliefs. Rather, the absurdity of life *consists in* having first-level ethical beliefs and tacitly and falsely assuming they are absolutely justified by our intuitions. In contrast, the absurdity of life does not *consist in* our second-level ethical beliefs, but it *appears to us* once we experience the relevant second-level beliefs. Most of the people most of the time are not disturbed by this absurdity because most people most of the time remain on the first level of ethical beliefs.

But what should we do once we recognize our lives to be absurd?

The answer can only be, *we do not know what we should do* because if we did know, we would have ethical knowledge after all. We know the fact that our lives are absurd, but we do not know whether as a consequence we ought to commit suicide or trust blindly in whatever first-level ethical beliefs we happen to have or doubt all our first-level beliefs and try not to act or respond to anything on the basis of them or ignore the whole problem and play backgammon.

But we cannot ameliorate our situation by saying that it does not matter what we do or how we respond to our absurd situation because *it does objectively matter;* some responses are objectively right and others objectively wrong, even though we do not know which are which. It may be a synthetic a priori truth that we ought to trust our first-level ethical beliefs or it may be a synthetic a priori truth that we ought not to, and if we make the wrong decision here, then we will be living as we ought not to.

Our situation, then, is one of darkness and ignorance. The air of brightness, sunny optimism, and confidence exuded in Moore's *Principia Ethica* is unwarranted because we do not in fact know the ethical truths Moore believes we know. Our situation is dramatically typified by two warring nations whose soldiers are killing one another on the basis of their passionately held intuitions that *they are right* and not the other side, whereas the reality is that neither side knows who is right or is even capable of knowing who is right. The soldiers live, kill, and die in ignorance and illusion. The sunniness of Moore's book should be replaced by the night of Matthew Arnold's poem:

> the world, which seems
> To lie before us like a land of dreams,
> So various, so beautiful, so new,
> Hath really neither joy, nor love, nor light,
> Nor certitude, nor peace, nor help for pain;
> And we are here as on a darkling plain
> Swept with confused alarms of struggle and flight,
> Where ignorant armies clash by night.[21]

2 Logical Positivism

5. The Logical Positivists' Method of Linguistic Analysis

The movement known as logical positivism reached full flower in the 1920s but was based on ideas going back to 1905 and earlier. At least four major developments in analytic philosophy served as catalysts of the logical positivist movement. The first occurred in 1905 with the publication of Russell's "On Denoting," which showed how sentences with proper names or definite descriptions can be translated into sentences with bound variables and predicates. This enabled Russell to reject his early logical realist tenet that the sense of proper names is their referent and the associated implication that there are things that do not exist. If the sense of "Pegasus" is not its referent, we do not need to assume there is some nonexistent being *Pegasus* in order to explain how this name has a sense. A second major impetus was Russell's paper of 1908 on the theory of types, in which he argued that sentences that violated the type-restrictions are senseless. "The property of triangularity is female" is senseless because being female is restricted to individuals, not universals. This doctrine exemplifies a procedure for discrediting certain sentences not as false but as senseless, a procedure that would play a central role in positivist theories. A third impetus was manifest in Alfred North Whitehead's and Russell's *Principia Mathematica*, in which mathematical concepts were argued to be logical constructions from logical concepts. A number could be defined in terms of sets and such logical concepts as identity. This introduced the important notion of logical construction, a notion that was also used in an influential way in Russell's *Our*

Knowledge of the External World, which endeavored to show that physical things were logical constructions from sensory experiences. A fourth influence appeared in 1921 with Ludwig Wittgenstein's *Tractatus Logico-Philosophicus,* which argued that all sentences that have sense are elementary sentences or truth-functions of elementary sentences and that metaphysical sentences have no sense.

These influences motivated the positivist movement, which by 1926 had materialized in the Vienna circle, including Moritz Schlick, Friedrich Waismann, Rudolf Carnap, Herbert Feigl, Otto Neurath, and others, and in the Berlin circle, which included Hans Reichenbach, Richard von Mises, Kurt Grelling, and others. The main English proponents were A. J. Ayer, F. P. Ramsey, and Susan Stebbing, and some Americans influenced by the movement included Charles Stevenson and Nelson Goodman. The linguistic thesis definitive of the positivists' method of linguistic analysis is captured in the famous slogan that the sense ("meaning") of sentences other than tautologies and contradictions is the method of their verification. This slogan achieved wide currency late in the positivist movement and was first published in Waismann's article in *Erkenntnis* (1930), although it appears to have originated at least a year earlier in a then-unpublished writing of Wittgenstein, subsequently published as *Philosophical Remarks.*[1] One way to formulate the slogan is to say that the sense of a nontautological and noncontradictory sentence is the observational conditions that have to be met in order to determine whether the sentence is true or false. The senses of the words in a sentence may be definable in terms of other words, but ultimately we reach words that cannot be defined in terms of other words but whose sense must be shown. As Schlick puts it, "In order to find the meaning of a [sentence], we must transform it by successive definitions until finally only such words occur in it as can no longer be defined but whose meaning can only be directly pointed out."[2] Different explications of this slogan resulted in different versions of verificationism, such as the strong (conclusive) verificationism of Schlick and Ramsey, the weak (probabilistic) verificationism of Neurath, and the position of Carnap and Ayer that allowed some verifications to be strong and others weak.

Other differences appeared in the conceptions of the basic observational sentences. Schlick, Ayer, and others conceived of the basic sentences (the protocol or elementary or observational sentences) as referring to sense-data and their properties, whereas Neurath argued that they referred to publicly observable physical objects and their physical properties. Carnap was in a sense neutral between these two positions, but in his *Logical Structure of the World* he adopted the phenomenalist rather than physicalist position as epistemologically primary. In one of his later works Carnap offers as an example of a phenomenalist protocol sentence, "Now I see a red square on a blue ground,"[3] and Neurath gives the physicalist example, "Otto's protocol at 3:17 o'clock: [At 3:16 o'clock Otto said to himself: (at 3:15 there was a table in the room perceived by Otto)]."[4]

A further difference in the explications of the slogan about linguistic meaning concerned the senses in which theoretical terms were held to be definable in observational terms. For most of the 1920s and 1930s, beginning with Carnap's article of 1923 in *Kant-Studien*, theoretical terms were believed to be correlated with observational sentences by explicit definitions (material equivalences of the form $Tx \equiv Ox$, where "T" is a theoretical term and "O" an observational term).[5] But by the time of Carnap's essay "Testability and Meaning" in 1936–37, partial definitions had been introduced to accommodate dispositional terms such as "soluble in water" (the partial definitions being of the form $O_1x \supset [Tx \equiv O_2x]$, which state that if x satisfies the observational predicate O_1, then, if x satisfies the theoretical predicate T, x satisfies the observational predicate O_2, and if x does not satisfy T, then it does not satisfy O_2).[6] For the sake of simplifying my discussion of positivism, I shall treat it as committed to the pre-1936 thesis of explicit definability.

The positivists employed a method of linguistic analysis in the sense that they deduced important conclusions in other disciplines from premises involving their theory of linguistic sense. Many of their negative conclusions in metaphysics, the philosophy of mind, aesthetics, ethics, and the philosophy of religion were reached by arguing that the relevant sentences, though neither tautological nor contradictory, do not report observable states of affairs and thereby are cognitively senseless. A case in point is their argument in the discipline of metaphysics for the thesis that monism (the doctrine that there is only one substance, the Absolute, of which everything else is a property) is senseless. Let us adopt for simplicity's sake the phenomenalist version of positivism and assume that the observational sentences are about sense-data and their properties (where "sense-data" is used in the wide sense to refer to phenomena of inner sense as well as outer sense). It is a claim of the phenomenalist positivists that monism is incompatible with this conception of linguistic sense and should be judged to be senseless. According to these positivists, the monist typically claims that Reality is One and that this One Reality is not one among many sense-data or one among many properties of sense-data but instead transcends the field of the sensory given. The monist is represented as asserting that the sensory field is an illusion in the sense that it appears to be something it is not, namely, a field of distinct particulars, each of which has its own sensory properties. For the monist, these apparent "sense-data" and "properties of sense-data" are nothing but properties or parts of properties of the transcendent substance, the One Reality.

Now the phenomenalist positivists hold that this monist assertion about the One Reality is senseless. This assertion is neither a tautology nor a contradiction and hence a necessary condition of it having sense is that it be either an observational sentence or transformable by explicit definitions into some observational sentence(s). This condition includes the requirement that it imply a proper subset of the observational sentences, such that if these observational sentences are true, then certain other observational sentences are false. But because this monist sentence asserts the existence of something that transcends the field of the observable and that is compatible with any sensory appearance, it fails to meet this condition. As Ayer remarks, "The assertion that Reality is One, which is characteristic of a monist to make and a pluralist to controvert, is nonsensical, since no empirical situation could have any bearing on its truth."[7] Furthermore, Ayer continues, "it is plain that no conceivable observation, or series of observations, could have any tendency to show that the world revealed to us by sense-experience was unreal. Consequently, anyone who condemns the sensible world as a world of mere appearance, as opposed to reality, is saying something which, according to our criterion of significance, is literally nonsensical" (39). The various specific claims about reality that the monist is wont to make are one and all unverifiable; for example, "Such a metaphysical pseudo-proposition as 'the Absolute enters into, but is itself incapable of, evolution and progress' (a remark taken at random from *Appearance and Reality,* by F. H. Bradley), is not even in principle verifiable. For one cannot conceive of an observation which would enable one to determine whether the Absolute did, or did not, enter into evolution and progress" (36).

The structure of this positivist argument against monism may be summarized as follows:

1. The sense of any sentence that is not a tautology or contradiction is the method of verifying it.
2. The method of verifying a sentence is a procedure for becoming acquainted with the sense-data and sense-data properties the sentence is ultimately about.
3. The pertinent monist sentences are neither tautologies nor contradictions.
4. These monist sentences are not ultimately about sense-data and their properties.
5. Therefore, there is no method of verifying these monist sentences.
6. Therefore, these sentences have no sense.

The positivist argument in the philosophy of religion that there is no objective religious meaning of human life is parallel to this argument in metaphysics against monism, as we shall now see.

6. The Logical Positivists' Theory of the Religious Meaninglessness of Human Life

In my discussion of logical realism I said that Moore's position in the philosophy of religion was based in large part on his position that the sentence "No natural event is caused by God" expresses an intuitively self-evident proposition and therefore that atheism is true. The problem with this position is that the negation of this proposition seems intuitively self-evident to theists, and there is no means of verifying which of these "intuitions" is the correct one. This seems to have the consequence that religious sentences, be they atheistic or theistic, express something that is impossible in principle to know. But how could there be a proposition that we all understand, that has truth (or falsity), and yet cannot possibly be known by us?

One way to escape from this difficulty is to cut the Gordian knot, to deny that religious sentences *express propositions*. One may argue that atheistic and theistic religious sentences, like monist sentences, are senseless. Religious sentences such as "No natural event is caused by God" and "Every natural event is caused by God" are not tautologies or contradictions, and they are not verifiable by any sensory observations.

In order to understand this position more clearly, let us consider a parable developed by John Wisdom in which "the invisible gardener" has a role analogous to that of "God."[8]

Once upon a time two explorers came upon a clearing in the jungle. In the clearing were growing many flowers and many weeds. One explorer says, "Some gardener must tend this plot." The other disagrees: "There is no gardener." So they pitch their tents and set a watch. No gardener is ever seen. "But perhaps he is an invisible gardener," the Believer says. So they set up a barbed-wire fence. They electrify it. They patrol with bloodhounds. But they hear no shrieks that would suggest some intruder has received a shock. No movements of the wire ever betray an invisible climber. The bloodhounds never give cry. Yet still the Believer is not convinced: "But there is a gardener, invisible, intangible, insensible to electric shocks, a gardener who comes secretly to look after the garden which he loves." At last the Skeptic despairs: "But what remains of your original assertion? Just how does what you call an invisible, intangible, eternally elusive gardener differ from an imaginary gardener or even from no gardener at all?"

What the Skeptic, or positivist, is suggesting is that the sentences about the invisible gardener "make no difference in the given," that the observable world remains just the same regardless of whether there is such a gardener or there is not. No conceivable observation could verify either that the invisible gardener exists or does not exist. The Skeptic cannot say, "I can verify that there is no invisible gardener, since I have looked everywhere and cannot find him" because the Believer would reply that the invisible gardener by his very nature is invisible and thus cannot in principle be seen. Not being able to see something that by its very nature is invisible cannot count as evidence that the thing in question does not exist. But the positivist will reply that if there is no possible evidence for or against the existence of the invisible gardener, then the claim that there is such a gardener is devoid of sense. The Believer cannot explain what he means by "the invisible gardener" by defining it in terms of anything that could possibly be observed, and so the positivist concludes that this phrase is in fact senseless. The phrase may be emotionally significant to the Believer, but it is not cognitively significant. In sense-data terminology, one may say that "the invisible gardener" is not definable in terms of possible sense-data and thus is an empty expression.

The same holds true of "God." The positivists hold that the person who believes that "God exists" or "God is the cause of natural events" would not regard anything that conceivably could occur as counting against or being incompatible with this assertion. Anthony Flew characterizes an assertion by saying that "anything which would count against the assertion, or which would induce the speaker to withdraw it and to admit that it had been mistaken, must be part of (or the whole of) the meaning of the negation of that assertion" (267). If nothing at all would count against it, then the negation of the assertion has no "meaning" or sense, from which it follows that the assertion itself has no sense.

References to mystical experiences do not provide the needed verification, for the mystic is not asserting merely that she is experiencing a certain sense-datum, say a religious emotion of ecstatic pleasure, but that there is some transcendent being that is the object of this emotion. Assertions that the mystic experiences an ecstatic emotion are verifiable, but the assertion that there is a God who is the object of her emotional sensations is not verifiable.

Some theists are wont to maintain that the existence of God can be deduced from a priori sentences. But the positivists argue that all a priori sentences are either tautologies ("An unmarried man is an unmarried man") or analytic sentences that are reducible to tautologies by substitutions of synonyms for the relevant words ("An unmarried man is a bachelor"). From such sentences nothing about reality can be deduced. This follows from the conventionalism adopted by many of the positivists. An a priori truth enlightens us only by indicating the linguistic conventions governing our uses of words. "An unmarried man is a bachelor" records the linguistic convention that "an unmarried man" is used as a synonym of "bachelor." But no recording of a conventional decision to use words in a certain way can show that there exists something, a God or a bachelor, that corresponds to the words governed by the convention. If the theist objects to this characterization of a priori truths and introduces some alleged synthetic a priori proposition, such as the proposition that God is the cause of the universe, the positivist will reply that theists and atheists have conflicting intuitions about such alleged propositions and that there is no possible method of deciding which intuitions are correct. If what these sentences express cannot possibly be verified, then they do not express propositions at all and in reality are cognitively senseless, having emotional significance at best.

If the relevant religious sentences (for example, "The universe was created by

God") are neither verifiable nor tautological, then they are cognitively senseless. They are not true and they are not false. But as R. B. Braithwaite argues, they may have an emotive sense; their sense may be to express the intention of the utterer to follow a specified policy of behavior, such as a "Christian way of life."[9] Whereas moral assertions indicate specific patterns of conduct, a religious assertion is more general. A given religious assertion ("Jesus is your redeemer") belongs to a religious tradition, and the body of assertions in this tradition is what specifies the way of life. Whereas "You ought not to lie" specifies a particular course of action, "Jesus is your redeemer" specifies a general way of life by belonging to the entire body of Christian discourse, which as a whole specifies the Christian way of life. The utterer of "Jesus is your redeemer" indicates by his utterance that he intends to follow the way of life implied by the entire body of Christian discourse. Religious utterances are also typified by the fact that they express the person's intention to *feel* a certain way (and not just act in a certain way) and by the illustration of his intentions by parables or stories.

This philosophy of religion in effect reduces religion to a possible subjective meaning of human life. Religious sentences do not report facts about reality but (if uttered with the requisite conviction) evince that a certain way of life is a subjective meaning of the speaker's life; they evince, say, that living in a Christian way is something the person passionately wants to do and that this way of life greatly matters to her. The very idea that religious attitudes could relate to an objective meaning of human life is argued to be based on a faulty understanding of the sense of religious expressions; they are falsely assumed to have cognitive sense (to be verifiable or tautological) whereas they merely have emotive sense. Braithwaite recognizes an objection that may be made to this account: "If a man's religion is all a matter of following the way of life he sets before himself and of strengthening his determination to follow it by imagining exemplary fairy-tales, it is purely subjective: his religion is all in terms of his own private ideals and of his own private imagination. How can he even try to convert others to his religion if there is nothing objective to convert them to?" (162). Braithwaite suggests that the point of religious conversion is to pass on information about how to persevere in a way of life that the people may want to follow. The point of religious conversion may *seem* to be something else, to reorient a person so that she becomes related to something objectively holy, but in fact the real point is a change in the person's merely *subjective* attitude to life.

An implication of the positivist's philosophy of religion is that religious nihilism is no less senseless than the piety and ecstasy of the believer. The positivist's philosophy does not warrant the response of Nietzsche to the "death of God." There occurs this passage in Nietzsche's *The Gay Science:*

"Whither is God" he cried. "I shall tell you. *We have killed him*—you and I. All of us are his murderers. But how have we done this? How were we able to drink up the sea? Who gave us the sponge to wipe away the entire horizon? What did we do when we unchained this earth from its sun? Whither is it moving now? Whither are we moving now? Away from all suns? Are we not plunging continually? Backward, sideward, forward, in all directions? Is there any up or down left? Are we not straying as through an infinite noth- ing? Do we not feel the breath of empty space? Has it not become colder? Is not night and more night coming on all the while?" (aphorism 125)

Let us consider one possible way to interpret this passage. By "God is dead" Nietzsche means to suggest that humans (at least in large part) have stopped believing in God and that the sense of there being an objective religious meaning to life has ceased to be the guiding factor in human life and culture. Can the positiv- ist's philosophy of religion be interpreted in this light? Can it be said that positiv- ism, by maintaining that the existence of God is unverifiable in principle, has promoted the loss of belief in God and the sense that we are now "straying as through an infinite nothing"?

This would be a mistaken interpretation of positivism because positivists reject religious nihilism as well as theism. Positivists would say that Nietzsche is no less deluded than St. Thomas Aquinas or St. Teresa. Let us define religious nihilism as the combination of the belief that the concept of God is uninstantiated and an emotional response of despair at this fact. Nietzsche evokes this despair in his comment that we are moving "away from all suns. . . . Has it not become colder? Is not night and more night coming on all the while?" There is despair because although it might have been the case that there is a god warming us with rays of infinite love and providing a direction to our lives, there is in fact no universal love at the bottom of things but rather the desolateness and loneliness of an impersonal cosmos.

Such feelings are based on a senseless attitude, the positivists would say, because *there is no concept of God* and therefore no concept that either is instantiated or that fails to be instantiated. If "God" or "the divinity" expresses a concept, then these words have sense, and assertions involving these words can be verified or falsified. The case is rather that the word "God" or "divinity" is associated with imagery and emotions and expresses no concept. The positivist would point out that there is no further content to "God" than such emotionally tinged images as are expressed in the passage from Nietzsche's book. The word "God" is associated (for example) with the image of a sun, the phrase "God loves us" with an image of the bright and warming rays of a sun, and "the nonexistence of God" with images of darkness, coldness, and empty space.

In mystical ecstasy, there is an intensely pleasurable emotional sense-datum and perhaps also images of white light or a fuzzy image of a radiant face or a ghostlike presence, but there is no external reality in which one is in contact. Likewise, in religious despair there is a painful emotional sense-datum and perhaps images of darkness and gloom and of a vast empty space, but there is no *concept* that one is comprehending or believing to be uninstantiated.

Carnap says that "God" as used by metaphysicians fails to meet the two criteria of having sense. The first criterion is that the syntax of the word be fixed, which is done by specifying the word's mode of occurrence in the simplest sentence-form in which it is capable of occurring. The elementary sentence-form for the word "stone" is "x is a stone," where some designation from the category of things (for example, "this diamond") occupies the place of the variable "x." The second criterion is that the method of verifying elementary sentences containing the word be specified. This second criterion is tantamount to showing how the word can be reduced ultimately to the words which occur in observation sentences, which describe sensory experience (phenomenalism) or observable things (physicalism).

Carnap states that metaphysicians have not specified the elementary sentence-form for "God": "An elementary sentence would here have to be of the form 'x is a God'; yet, the metaphysician either rejects this form entirely without substituting another, or if he accepts it he neglects to indicate the syntactical category of the variable x. (Categories are, for example, material things, properties of things, relations between things, numbers, etc.)" (66). What Carnap calls a "syntactical category" is what philosophers, including Carnap himself, would later call a "semantic category."

The metaphysician might respond to Carnap that he has indicated the syntactical category, namely, *immaterial thing* or *disembodied person*, but Carnap would deny that there is any such category, which pertains to his second criticism of the metaphysician's use of "God." Carnap claims this word has not been reduced to words in observation sentences, sentences which report sensory data or observable physical things. The metaphysician would respond to this by questioning the adequacy of this criterion of linguistic sense, but I shall postpone considering this question until a later section.

For now, I want to draw the full consequences of the positivist critique of both religion and nihilism. Because "God" is irreducible to observation words, this word is uttered with "associated images and feelings," but these "do not bestow a meaning on the word" (67). Consequently, the very question about whether human life has an objective religious meaning is senseless; it is senseless to assert that it has an objective religious meaning and senseless to assert with Nietzsche that it is religiously meaningless. Our very concern with this question is but an utterance of senseless sequences of words that are associated with images and feelings of the sort expressed in the passage from Nietzsche's book.

Accordingly, my classification of the positivist philosophy of religion as a theory "of the religious meaninglessness of human life" must be understood in a special way. It should not be understood as imputing to positivists the belief that "human life has an objective religious meaning" is false. Rather, it should be understood as imputing to them the belief that this sentence lacks cognitive sense.

The positivist would say that the rational response to the realization of the cognitive senselessness of theism and atheism is to give up concern about religious meaning or at least to attempt to free ourselves from any need or wish for such meaning or regret that there is none. If we feel religious emotions and imagery and mistake these as having cognitive import, then we are deluded, and the rational ideal is to escape delusion. Even if religious ecstasy or despair is felt to be our deepest emotion, that only goes to show that the emotional side of the human personality is susceptible to radical delusion and that we ought to avoid these deeper feelings if we are to remain on a clear and steady kilter.

Now this result of Carnap and Ayer cannot properly be said to confirm the widespread view that logical positivists have "ignored the question about the meaning of life," for they have not ignored it but instead have offered an original diagnosis of it. They argue not that life is meaningless or that we cannot know the answer to this question but that the question itself is senseless. Moreover, they offer an explanation of why this question has seemed to make sense to people and has attracted intense emotion.

Carnap subsumes under metaphysics the purported theories of objective religious meaning of human life. Carnap suggests that the urge for metaphysics has its ultimate roots in ancient mythology, in which primitive humans personified natural phenomena in order to give expression to their emotional relationship to their natural environment. Thus, primitive humans' fear of earthquakes gives rise to the need to express this fear by personifying earthquakes and endeavoring to conciliate the "threatening demon of earthquakes." In the metaphysical theories of a transcendent god that were associated with the Judeo-Christian-Islamic and Hindu traditions, among others, this *need to give expressions to one's basic attitude to life* persisted and motivated the various metaphysical constructions. Carnap writes that, like mythology,

> metaphysics also arises from the need to give expression to a man's attitude
> in life, his emotional and volitional reaction to the environment, to society, to
> the tasks to which he devotes himself, to the misfortunes that befall him.
> This attitude manifests itself, unconsciously as a rule, in everything a man
> does or says. It also impresses itself on his facial features, perhaps even on the

character of his gait. Many people, now, feel a desire to create over and above these manifestations a special expression of their attitude, through which it might become visible in a more succinct and penetrating way. (79)

This desire to create a special expression of one's attitude may lead to artistic creation or to metaphysics. But the metaphysical expression is misleading, Carnap contends, because through the form of its' works it pretends to be something that it is not, namely, something with theoretical sense that is true or false and that purports to describe states of affairs in the world. The metaphysician creates a system of statements that are apparently related as premises and conclusions and thus give the impression that the metaphysician is similar to the scientist in endeavoring to provide knowledge of reality. Carnap writes, "The metaphysician believes that he travels in territory in which truth and falsehood are at stake. In reality, however, he has not asserted anything, but only expressed something, like an artist [namely, his personal attitude to life]" (79).

The important idea behind these remarks of Carnap is that the theoretical articulation of an objective religious meaning of life is in fact the *expression of one's subjective meaning of life.* It is far from true that Carnap is oblivious to the question of life's meaning; he is concerned about this issue, and his novel contribution to the debate is the idea that humans have a strong need to create a *special expression* of the subjective meaning of their life and that metaphysical representations of objective meaning (or objective meaninglessness) are (unlike artistic representations) *misleading forms* of these special expressions.

Accordingly, we need to distinguish between the normal and unconscious expressions of the subjective meaning of one's life (for example, in one's facial features) and the special conscious expressions, which occur in art and metaphysics. The latter expressions occur in those people to whom *expressing in a special (artistic or metaphysical) form* the subjective meaning of their life is itself a subjective meaning of their lives, indeed, perhaps the most important subjective meaning. In artists this need is expressed in a proper form but in metaphysics it is not.

How does the metaphysical delusion about objective meaning or meaninglessness come about? Why should not the need to express subjective meaning take the form only of religious paintings, the music of Palestrina and Bach, and the like? One reason is temperamental; people who form philosophical beliefs about theism or atheism have a desire to express themselves in the medium of concepts rather than images. This desire, coupled with the misleading surface forms of ordinary language, leads the person to formulate sentences that seem to express concepts (senses) about objective meaning or meaninglessness but which in reality do not. The misleading forms of linguistic locutions thus are partly responsible for the delusion that there is a philosophy of objective meaning or meaninglessness. A central origin of this linguistic delusion is the use of a word that once had a sense but no longer does. Indeed, this is the case with the word "God." Originally this word had a sense and referred to a more or less humanlike being that lived on Mount Olympus, in Hades, or the like or else referred to a spiritual being immanent in nature, for example, as Oceanus is immanent in the ocean. Used in this original mythological sense, "God" was a part of meaningful sentences, sentences that are falsifiable by the relevant observations (for example, of the summit of Mount Olympus). But this word came to be used to refer to something entirely beyond sensory experience and thereby became deprived of its original sense without being given a new sense. It retained an association with images and feelings, but not with any concept. It thereby became suitable for expressions of one's subjective meaning of life but in a misleading way, since people who used it mistakenly believed they were referring to something with this word or at least expressing some concept.

The positivist theory of religious sentences hinges on the assumption that sentences such as "God causes the universe" and "God does not cause the universe" must be tautologies or verifiable in terms of sensory observations if they are to make sense. But why should we suppose that the nontautological and nonverifiable nature of these sentences deprives them of cognitive sense? Further, is it really the case that such religious sentences are not verifiable or falsifiable?

7. Is Religious Meaning Unverifiable?
At least two lines of criticism may be leveled against the positivist philosophy of religion, that theism is indeed a verifiable or falsifiable hypothesis and that the verificationist criterion of linguistic sense is false. I shall discuss the first line of criticism in this section and the second in section 9, where I evaluate the positivist ethical theory.

If theism is falsifiable by sense experience, then it has sense. I think there is an argument that it is falsifiable by sense experience. If there is a perfectly good, wise, and powerful person who is continuously creating the universe, then this person will permit no gratuitous evil, that is, evil that is necessary for the existence of some equal or greater good. Accordingly, if we can observe gratuitous evil, then we will have falsified the hypothesis that there is such a creator.

One difficulty with this argument is that "good" and "evil" are maintained by the positivists to be cognitively senseless terms, and hence to claim that it is observably true or false that "there is gratuitous evil intrinsic to the universe" is to beg the question against positivism.

However, theism can be defined in a way that avoids this ethical problem. Certain observable and factual states of affairs are relevant to the problem of evil, states of affairs that the theist regards as good or evil. We may confine our attention to these factual states of affairs, without mentioning their moral value. For example, we can talk about suffering in a purely factual way. Certain of these factual states of affairs may be argued to be inconsistent with theism. If there were cases of intense and prolonged suffering or premature death and these instances were not required for *compensating or outweighing* cases of happiness, life, knowledge, free choices, sympathetic behavior, or the like, then we could say that there is no god.

Let us say that any suffering that is required for these compensating or outweighing states of affairs is *required suffering,* that is, suffering that is required in the sense that it is necessary for the existence of the compensating or outweighing states of affairs. Any suffering that is not required in this sense is a case of *gratuitous suffering.* On this reading, "God is the creator of the universe" would have a sense in that this sentence would be reducible, at least in part, to possible sensory experiences of human happiness, wisdom, free choices, and so forth and to cases of required suffering. This sentence would also be reducible to other possible sensory experiences, such as experiences of a universe that is suitable for humans to inhabit and achieve happiness. "God is the creator of the universe" is verifiable by such sensory experiences and is falsifiable by sensory experiences of instances of gratuitous suffering. This sentence would entail "Some human experiences are happy, wise, free, and so on; all instances of intense and prolonged human suffering are required; and the universe is suited for human habitation and happiness," and this sentence would in turn entail more specific sentences.

Responding to the positivist in this way will make atheism and theism meaningful (that is, it will make them *have sense*). However, this formulation will not give equal advantage to the theist and the atheist. The atheist might well argue that this formulation of theism makes atheism the *verified* theory. The fact that many instances of suffering we observe are not observed to be required by compensating factors supports the atheist's case. We all have many sensory experiences of human suffering (or premature death) that are not required for any compensating or outweighing states of affairs, at least not as far as we can tell. For example, human diseases such as cancer, AIDS, schizophrenia, and bipolar disorder often involve intense, prolonged suffering and premature death, and yet nobody can point to any series of sensory experiences that *compensate for* or *outweigh* these instances of suffering and premature death. It would be preposterous to say, for example, that the suffering and premature death of millions of AIDS patients are compensated for by the increase in our knowledge of how the AIDS virus works. Nor are they compensated for by the experiences of sympathy and caring that some people show toward AIDS patients. There appears to be nothing at all that compensates for this suffering and early death.[10] The atheist will grant that it is logically possible that there may be in the future or elsewhere in the universe a series of sensory experiences of happiness, knowledge, freedom, that compensate for these instances of suffering and early death. But the atheist will point out that this shows merely that it is logically possible that theism is true. It would not refute the argument that *the available evidence* counts against theism. It would not provide a counterargument to the inductive atheistic argument, namely, the argument that there are observations of suffering and no observations of phenomena that compensate for these sufferings, and therefore that theism is probably false.

The theist may attempt to find some loophole in this inductive argument from needless suffering.[11] But the theist is not well advised to defend her theism simply by trying to refute this atheistic argument. For even if the theist were successful in countering this argument, the other tenets of positivism would preclude the theist from having a justified or true belief that God created the universe. Even if the observational evidence is that all sufferings and premature deaths are required for outweighing states of affairs, that would not verify *the special sort of belief* that the theists want verified. The falsifiable version of theism I have outlined is a much-truncated version of theism. If the sense of "God created the universe" is reducible to possible sensory observations of human happiness, knowledge, free choices, required suffering, an inhabitable universe, and the like, *and this sentence is verified*, that would not provide the theist with what she wants, namely, an *irreducible* belief in a disembodied person that is all-wise, all-powerful, and all-good and that cannot be sensorily observed. Believing in the existence of this person is not the same thing as believing in the existence of human happiness, required suffering, and an inhabitable universe. But according to the positivist criterion of sense, the only sense that belief *in the existence of God* can possess is the belief *in the existence of happiness, required suffering, an inhabitable universe, and so on.* For the positivist, everything but these mundane observational data constitutes mere emotional associations, imagery, and the like. Consequently, the theist can maintain that her distinctive irreducible beliefs make sense only if she can show the positivist criterion of sense is mistaken.

Yet there may be a way that the theist can maintain her distinctively theistic beliefs without rejecting the positivist criterion of linguistic sense. Instead of including the relevant theistic sentences in the class of verifiable sentences, the theist may include them in the class of tautologies. Because tautologies have sense, according to the positivists, theism would then have sense by positivist standards. Moreover, because the sense of tautologies is not reducible to possible sensory observations, the theist need not reduce her theses to claims about sensory data.

Positivists, of course, hold that theistic sentences such as "God exists" are *not* tautologies. Note that "tautologies" is here used in Ayer's wide sense. For Ayer, all true nonempirical sentences are a priori sentences and are tautologies. The current distinction between tautologies and analytic sentences is not made by Ayer. For him, "A bachelor is an unmarried man" and "A bachelor is a bachelor" are both called tautologies and are both called analytic sentences. Furthermore, they are also both called a priori sentences, for there is no true a priori sentence that is not a tautology.

Ayer claims that "God exists" is not a tautology and therefore cannot be deduced from premises all of which are tautologies. The theist, however, may reject the idea that "God exists" is not a tautology. Some philosophers, such as Bonaventura, have held that "God exists" is a tautology and is synonymous with the obviously tautological sentence "God is God." And some philosophers, such as Aquinas, have held that God is identical with existence.[12] This may suggest the following tautological proof of God's existence:

1. If God is God, then God exists.
2. God is God

Therefore

3. God exists.

Alternatively, we may argue

4. God is identical with existence
5. Existence exists

Therefore

6. God exists.

The difficulty with this line of argument is that no theist has succeeded in demonstrating by "natural reason" that (1) or (4) are tautologies, and the prospects do not look bright that this may one day be demonstrated. Accordingly, the theist is best advised to argue against the positivist criterion of linguistic sense, rather than attempt to accommodate her theism to this criterion.

8. The Logical Positivists' Theory of the Ethical Meaninglessness of Human Life

Moore's logical realist theory of the ethical meaning of human life hinged upon his contention that propositions about the good in itself are synthetic a priori propositions, such as the proposition expressed by "Aesthetic enjoyment is good." The positivists would note that synthetic sentences have sense if and only if they are verifiable, and synthetic a priori sentences have sense if and only if they are verifiable by means of some a priori cognition. The relevant cognitions here would be the "intuitions" that Moore talks about. The problem, however, is that people have different intuitions, and there is no criterion for deciding among these intuitions. Thus, a given sentence cannot be verified by noting that there is an intuitive belief that it is true, for in cases of dispute one person will have an intuitive belief that it is true and a second will have an intuitive belief that it is false. The positivists conclude that because there is no method of verifying these synthetic assertions, it follows that they are cognitively senseless.

But ethical sentences do serve a function, the positivists point out. They evince a person's moral approval of something (they express his or her moral emotions) and also aim to elicit a similar attitude in the listener. This implies that ethical assertions are neither true nor false; they are no more true or false than "Ouch!" or "Hurrah!" The sentence "Stealing is wrong" serves to express my negative attitude toward stealing and to elicit a similar attitude in others. But there is no property of evilness or ought not to be that this sentence ascribes to stealing. To think that "wrong" refers to such a property because it is an adjective and the sense of every adjective is its referent is to presuppose the problematic linguistic thesis of the logical realists.

One implication of this doctrine is that there really are no moral disputes or arguments, strictly speaking. Or rather, the moral arguments that are possible are not about the values of actions but about the facts of the case. We can argue about whether John did or did not take the money, but there is no argument possible about whether his stealing is right or wrong. Either we both have an attitude of disapproval toward his stealing or we do not. But if you disagree with me, it is not the case that your moral belief is false and mine true, or vice versa, because truth and falsity are not applicable to moral attitudes. There remains just a difference in attitude. Ayer comments that "it is because argument fails us when we come to deal with pure questions of value, as distinct from questions of fact, that we finally resort to mere abuse."[13]

The most important theory of ethical sentences developed within the logical positivist tradition is Charles Stevenson's, which he presented in his article "The Emotive Meaning of Ethical Terms" (1937) and developed at length in his book *Ethics and Language* (1944). Stevenson claims he is analyzing "good" in one of its leading ordinary uses, namely, its moral use. In "The Emotive Meaning of Ethical Terms" Stevenson lists three characteristics that an adequate definition of "good" must possess. These three requirements must "appeal strongly to our common sense," that is, they must conform to what we all normally understand by "good" in its typical ethical use. The three requirements are:

1. The definition must explain how we can sensibly disagree about whether something is "good."
2. "Goodness" must have a "magnetism"; that is, a person who recognized that "x is good" must have a stronger tendency to act in its favor than he would otherwise have had.
3. The "goodness" of something must not be verifiable solely by the use of the scientific method.

Stevenson suggests that "I approve of this; do so as well" is the nearest analogue to a definition of "This is good" that we possess. Stevenson notes that strictly speaking "good" cannot be defined, although its emotive sense can be described. It is impossible to define "good" without distorting its emotive sense. The emotive sense of "good" is its tendency to produce a favorable attitude in the listener and to express a favorable attitude of the speaker. The nearest analogue, "I approve of this; do so as well" has a different emotive sense and so does not perfectly capture "This is good." For one thing, "good" has a subtly suggestive emotive sense; it suggests to the listener that she approve of the thing as well. But "I approve of this; do so as well" is instead a command for the other to approve of it, not a subtle suggestion. Second, "This is good" expresses my approval, but "I approve of this" reports the fact of my approval, rather than expresses it. Third, "good" centers the attention of the listener on the thing being talked about, but "I approve of this" centers the attention of the listener on the speaker. Thus we cannot define the emotive sense of "good," but we can describe it, just as I have done.

Stevenson claims that this meets the three conditions he laid down. First, it explains disagreement. Moral disagreement is disagreement in interest, not disagreement in belief. Disagreement in interest is when John favors A and Jane favors B instead.

Second, it explains the magnetic connection between goodness and action; "I approve of an action; do so as well" expresses my inclination to do it or the suggestion that somebody else do it.

Third, it cannot be verified by science because the scientific method cannot be used to resolve a disagreement between two people about whether something x is good.

Stevenson's theory implies that whatever ethical meaning human life possesses is a subjective meaning. If I believe something is good, this is equivalent to the fact that I approve of it and that I recommend that others approve of it as well. If I approve of something, then I am appreciating something that matters to me, and I want others to appreciate it as well. Likewise, if I approve of a course of action that is open to me, I will be motivated to perform this action, and this action may be performed as a part of my larger life plan. My life may thus come to possess a subjective ethical meaning. But human life cannot have an objective ethical meaning because such meaning contradicts the definition of "good." The sense of "good" is an emotive sense, rather than cognitive sense, and this emotive sense involves an expression of the speaker's emotional approval; thus "good" by its very sense is dependent upon human attitudes for its existence.

It remains to be seen if there are ground to reject this definitional exclusion of the possibility that human life has an objective ethical meaning.

Stevenson argues that his definition of "good" is adequate because it meets his three conditions and, more generally, because it captures how we ordinarily use "good" in its moral sense. Accordingly, Stevenson will not have succeeded in his purpose if his definition does not meet all of these three conditions or if it does not capture our ordinary moral use of "good." There are good reasons to think that

Stevenson's theory does not meet all of these conditions (specifically, 1 and 2) and does not capture how "good" is ordinarily used in the moral sense.

Let us begin with some general points about how "good" in its ordinary usage is not equivalent to "I approve of this; do so as well!" There are at least ten respects in which Stevenson's definition fails to cohere with our commonsense moral attitudes:

1. One problem with Stevenson's definition is that it is inconsistent with our ascription of "good" and "bad" to things or events that are not in fact objects of our emotional attitudes. The moral value of things is *counterfactually independent* of emotional attitudes to it. It is part of our ordinary moral thinking that actions would be right or wrong even if these actions were not objects of the appropriate attitudes. For example, suppose a stranger breaks into somebody's house at night and murders the occupant in her sleep. Suppose we were in fact present and felt horror at the murderer's act. We believe the murder is wrong. But now change the situation so that we are not present at the murder and that nobody ever disapproves of the murder. We believe that this murderous act still would be morally evil, even if nobody had ever disapproved of it. The murder victim is killed in her sleep and so she does not disapprove it. The murderer approves of his own action, so as far as he is concerned the murder is good. And nobody else, we will suppose, ever finds out about this murder. We would nonetheless regard the murder as wrong. Here "wrong" cannot imply that somebody disapproves of it, because there is nobody to disapprove of it. The wrongness of the act belongs to the act, independently of whether the act is an object of disapproval.

2. Actions are also *temporarily independent* of our emotional attitudes. Suppose somebody discovers the murder a week later and is horrified at it. We do not believe that the moral wrongness of the murderous act comes into existence one week later, when somebody first disapproves of it. But this would be the case if the positivist doctrine were true, because the wrongness of the act would consist in somebody's disapproval of it and this disapproval comes into existence one week after the act was committed.

   What is common to both the counterfactual and temporal version of this argument is that we do not believe whether an act is wrong is dependent on the chance event that somebody happens to be aware of it and disapproves of it. We believe the wrongness to be inherent in the act itself. What is dependent on the chance event of somebody being aware of it is the recognition and appreciation of its wrongness.

3. A third problem with the positivist definition is that it builds into the

sense of moral terms an expression of our emotions of approval or disapproval. We often make moral judgments, however, without expressing any emotional attitude. Suppose I feel emotionally enchanted with a sunrise over the ocean and exclaim, "That is beautiful!" Here I make my judgment with an accompanying emotion. But if somebody asks me a week later if the sunrise was beautiful, I would say, "Yes, the sunrise was beautiful" without expressing any enchantment or any other emotion. Nonetheless, I mean the same by my assertion; I still mean (apart from tense distinctions) what I originally meant when I was feeling enchanted. This shows that the expression of emotion is not part of the sense of my assertion. The sense remains the same when the emotion changes from being present to being absent, and therefore the sense does not include the emotion or its expression.

Likewise, I can report my moral views to somebody without expressing emotion or without intending the other person to share my attitude. If somebody asks me what I believe to be good, I can respond, "The pursuit of philosophy is good, the pursuit of science is good, and so on" without expressing any emotion or without wanting the other person to approve of the pursuit of philosophy or science.

4. The positivist theory also has the following implausible consequence. Positivist doctrine implies that something is bad if and only if it is disapproved of, and something is good if and only if it is approved of. This implies that everything in the world would be good if we all approved of it! Because it is our moral duty to make the world a better place, this implies that we should approve of everything! By virtue of approving of things we formerly regarded as evil, we make them become good. If I am disturbed by the evil in human history, for example, by the Nazis' extermination of the Jews, I can easily eliminate the moral horrors of history by changing my disapproval to approval. But this consequence contradicts our ordinary moral thinking. It is built into our moral thinking that we can make bad things become good by our *changing the bad things*, not by *changing our attitude* toward them.

5. Another problem with the positivist theory is that it fails to account for the ordinary distinction between *belief and truth* when it comes to moral attitudes. We distinguish between a person's belief that something is good and whether his belief is true or false. This distinction is not the same distinction we make when we note merely that two people have *different beliefs*, for example, that Jane's belief differs from my belief. For example, we would say of the lone murderer mentioned above that his belief that his murder was good is a false belief. This does not mean

merely that he has a different moral belief than we do. And we would say that if the Nazis had won World War II and had succeeded in indoctrinating all subsequent generations with the belief that the extermination of the Jews was good, we would say that in this case the moral beliefs of all humans would be mistaken. This moral criticism of the beliefs is different from the anthropological observation that the moral beliefs of subsequent generations are different from our moral beliefs.

6. A further implausible consequence of the positivist theory is that there can be no contradictions between my moral beliefs. It is not a logical contradiction to have two different emotional attitudes to the same thing, but I am involved in a logical contradiction if I have two inconsistent beliefs about the same thing. Suppose, for example, that I believe both that "killing is never morally justified, no matter what the circumstance" and "sometimes war (and the killing it involves) is justified." Normally, we would say that my moral beliefs are logically contradictory. But the positivist theory implies merely that I have ambivalent feelings toward the same thing, without committing any contradiction.

7. A further problem with the positivist theory is that it fails to reflect the distinction we make between *moral ignorance and moral knowledge.* We often say that somebody simply does not know or realize that a certain action is wrong. If we see a young boy torturing a cat, we would say that the child is too young to realize this act is morally wrong, and we want to teach the child this piece of moral knowledge.

8. Furthermore, *moral deliberation* would make no sense. I may believe that a certain action is the one I ought to take, but may not be entirely certain and may think about the issue, discuss it with others, and try to arrive at the correct answer. But the positivist's theory implies that I already have the "correct answer" in the only sense possible, namely, that I already approve of the action. If whatever I approve of at the outset of my deliberation is right (it is right in the only sense that it can be right, that I approve of it), then there is no point in engaging in deliberation and no progress that I could possibly make in my moral thinking. If I change my attitude to disapproval, that is not arriving at a correct answer but simply changing one equally valid attitude for another.

9. An additional discrepancy between the positivist definition and ordinary moral experience is that "good" does not include Stevenson's "magnetizing" element within its sense. According to the Stevenson definition presented earlier, the definition of "good" must satisfy three

conditions, and one of these conditions is that it imply that goodness has a magnetism. But Stevenson seems mistaken on this account because magnetism does not belong to the sense of "good." I can ascribe goodness to something and not feel magnetized by it. For example, I can lie in bed in the morning and believe that I ought to get up and write philosophy but nonetheless remain unmoved; I may turn over and go back to sleep. We are not always magnetized by what we believe is good.

10. Moreover, in cases in which we find goodness magnetizing, Stevenson's account of the magnetism is inconsistent with the phenomenological facts. Stevenson's locution, "I approve of this; do so as well!" does not express the *magnetism* of some course of action but the *result* of this magnetism. That is, my approval of something and my hope that you approve of it as well is not what magnetizes me; rather, I approve of something *because* it magnetizes me. This reflects the fact that "goodness" does not express an internal condition of myself but an external feature of the world that elicits my internal condition.

For these ten reasons, the positivist theory of ethics fails to meet one of its own conditions, that of correctly analyzing our commonsense moral attitudes. Because the positivist theory includes as a condition of its truth that it correctly analyze our commonsense moral attitudes, we may conclude that it is not true.

The results I have reached are consistent with the results of my discussion of logical realist ethics, namely, that human life possesses an objective ethical meaning. My criticisms of positivism suggest that we experience things to possess intrinsic moral values, values which are not dependent upon our attitudes. Nothing I have said, however, solves the problem we encountered with logical realism, namely, that there is no apparent means of resolving conflicting moral intuitions or beliefs. I have rebuffed the positivist attack on the theory of objective ethical meaning, but my criticism of positivism does nothing to solve the problem of absurdity. As far as we know at present, our ethical life is objectively meaningful but absurd. Whether this problem can be resolved is discussed in chapter 6.

9. The Inadequacy of the Principle of Verification

The fact that the positivist ethical theory is at odds with our ordinary moral experience at so many points suggests that there may be a deeper problem underlying the construction of this theory. The philosophical method the positivist employed may itself be fundamentally defective. The method of linguistic analysis, based on the verification principle, shall be argued in this section to be flawed at its very core.

I shall begin with the familiar argument that the principle of verification (PV) is self-referentially incoherent because it is senseless if true.

PV. A sentence has cognitive sense if and only if it is verifiable by sense-data
   or is a tautology or contradiction.

1. The PV is not verifiable by any sense-data.
2. The PV is not a tautology.

Therefore,

3. The PV is cognitively senseless if it is true.

Therefore,

4. The PV is not true.

How might the positivist respond to this? In Ayer's debate about positivism with
Frederick Copelston, Ayer states that he derives "this principle from an analysis of
understanding. I should say that a statement meant knowing what would be the
case if it were true. Knowing what would be the case if it were true means knowing
what observations would verify it, and that in turn means being disposed to accept
certain situations as warranting the acceptance or rejection of the statement in
question."[14] By "observations" he means sense observations and by "situations" he
means series of sense-data. This passage might suggest that the PV is a tautology,
an analytic principle, since it is derived from an "analysis of understanding."
By "understanding" Ayer means the understanding that belongs to "ordinary
common-sense statements and to scientific statements" (104). Thus, it seems the
positivist may respond to my argument by rejecting premise (2). The PV has
cognitive sense because it is a tautology.

But what justifies the belief that the PV is a tautology? Ayer suggests the justification is that the PV is derived by analysis from the concept of commonsense and
scientific understanding. Accordingly, if Ayer's position is to be rejected, it needs to
be shown that the PV is not derived from an analysis of commonsense and scientific
understanding.

To begin with, it does not seem plausible that the PV belongs to the commonsense concept of understanding. If we examine common sense, we will find that it
regards as having cognitive sense many sentences that the PV implies are cognitively senseless. Clearly, "God exists" is a commonsense statement that many
people believe to be true and many others believe to be false. Because being true
or false implies having a cognitive sense, the evidence is that common sense regards "God exists" as having cognitive sense and therefore that the PV is not
implied by commonsense understanding. This is also true of ethical sentences, as
we have seen. "It is wrong to steal" is regarded as true and thus as having cognitive
sense, thus again disconfirming Ayer's contention that the PV belongs to commonsense understanding.

Ayer may retort that *he* at least is not able to understand these religious and
ethical sentences. He asserts, "Someone may say he understands them, in some
sense of understanding other than the one I've defined. I reply, It's not clear to me

what this sense of understanding is, nor, *a fortiori* of course, what it is he under-stands (104). Ayer is suggesting that he cannot understand any synthetic sentence unless it reports possible sense-data. One problem might be that Ayer is tacitly supposing that understanding something empirical requires imagining it, imagina-tion being understood as imaging possible sense-data (the Humean fallacy). If this is his mistake, he can easily be shown to be incorrect, for we can understand the empirical sentence "An extraterrestrial organism has a sixth sense organ different from ours" or "The universe contains an infinite number of galaxies." We cannot imagine these states of affairs, but we can understand them. Alternatively, Ayer may be presupposing a metaphysics of phenomenalism, that, necessarily, what exists are sense-data and nothing else. But this is an extremely contentious meta-physical assumption and is hardly warranted as a premise of an a priori analysis of the concept of understanding.

If Ayer denies that he is making these mistakes and insists that he is simply unable to grasp a cognitive sense of "God exists" or "Stealing is wrong," then, if we are to take his failure to understand at face value, we should have to conclude that Ayer is mentally abnormal. But I do not think it is rational to take his protestations of inability to understand at face value. A more plausible interpretation of Ayer's protestations is that he has tacitly stipulated in his own mind that the phrase "to understand" means to comprehend possible sense-data, and he refuses to countenance as *understanding* what we normally count as understanding (even though he in fact *understands*, in the normal sense, what we all normally understand). In short, Ayer is in the grip of a false theory, and what he says is dictated not by the obvious facts but by the constraints of his theory.

The PV is also inconsistent with scientific understanding. As a case in point, consider Ayer's assumption that "X exists" means that "it is possible to have sensory experiences of a certain sort." For example, "The table exists" means it is possible to have certain visual and tactile experiences. It is part of the methodology of science, however, to allow that some things may exist of which it is not possible to have sensory experiences. This is clearly the case in physical cosmology, where it is frequently asserted that "there exist other universes than our own, and many of these universes are uninhabitable by any possible intelligent organism." This sen-tence manifestly does not mean it is possible to have sensory experiences of these other universes. Indeed, it is impossible to have such experiences. Thus, the PV is inconsistent with science no less than with common sense.[15]

The conclusion of this chapter, then, is that the logical positivists have not succeeded in showing that human life lacks an objective ethical or religious mean-ing. The tentative results of the critical arguments in this chapter and chapter 1 are that human life has an objective ethical meaning, but that our ethical life is none-theless absurd because there is apparently no method of resolving ethical disagreement. Whether there is such a method will be further discussed in the chapters on essentialism. The conclusions I have reached about religion are that theism and atheism both make sense and that whether God exists is a legitimate issue. I have pointed to an apparent difficulty confronting theism, namely, the fact that there appears to be gratuitous suffering and premature death ("the problem of evil"), but I shall not attempt a more definitive argument in this area until the chapters on essentialism.

But before embarking on these tasks, I must confront another, very different challenge to the assumption that it makes cognitive sense to talk about objective ethical and religious meaning: the challenge mounted by the ordinary language movement.

3   Ordinary Language Analysis

10. The Ordinary Language Analysts' Method of Linguistic Analysis

The ordinary language movement had surplanted the positivist movement in England by the 1940s and reached its zenith during the 1950s. Its two main bases were at Oxford, which was associated with J. L. Austin, Gilbert Ryle, Waismann, J. O. Urmson, R. M. Hare, P. H. Nowell-Smith, P. F. Strawson, and others, and at Cambridge was associated with Wittgenstein and John Wisdom, among others. Americans such as Alice Ambrose, Norman Malcolm, Max Black, John Searle, and Paul Edwards also made substantial contributions to this movement. The origin of the ordinary language movement can be traced to some developments in linguistic analysis that motivated a dissatisfaction with the positivists' assumptions about linguistic sense and the turn to an "ordinary use" conception of linguistic sense.

One of these developments was the increased critical scrutiny directed upon the verification principle and the dissatisfaction with any of the extant formulations of it as either excluding as senseless too much (some scientific sentences) or including as sensible too much (some speculative metaphysical sentences).[1] But more important than the dissatisfaction with the various formulations of it was the growing suspicion that the verification principle was itself "senseless" by its own standard. According to the positivist conception of linguistic sense, the verification principle has sense if it is either a tautology or an empirical statement. But both suggestions seemed dubious. I presented my criticisms of the verification principle in chapter 2, and here I need only note that a number of partly similar criticisms of this principle were presented in the late 1930s and 1940s as positivism saw its decline. Some analysts noted that if the principle was not based on ordinary or scientific use, it was a stipulative definition, an arbitrary convention about the use of "sense," and could be rejected complacently by those interested in speculative metaphysics, who could continue to use "sense" in a nonpositivist way and remain immune from criticism. But the verification principle also did not seem to be an empirical generalization from criteria of linguistic sense in natural languages because in natural languages "God gave his only son to us," "Lying is evil," and other sentences that the positivist wanted to call cognitively senseless are accepted as having cognitive sense. Wisdom and Stevenson were the first to publish criticisms of this principle, arguing that the verification criterion of linguistic sense is itself cognitively senseless. In an article in *Mind*[2] (1938) Wisdom argued that the verification principle was neither a tautology nor an empirical generalization but was itself a bit of speculative metaphysics, and in the same volume of *Mind* Stevenson suggested that "sense" or "meaning" as used in the verification principle expressed a merely emotive or "*persuasive*" definition of 'meaning.' "[3]

Other developments in linguistic analysis led philosophers in the direction of ordinary language analysis in the hope of solving some of the problems facing the positivists' method. These developments pertained to the relation of the "artificial" observation language systems to natural or ordinary language. One problem concerned the fact that the observation language systems were supposed to capture the cognitive sense not only of scientific theories but also of empirical ordinary language sentences. Of course some positivists, such as Carnap, defined philosophy as the analysis of the "language of science," but by this phrase they typically meant "all statements (i.e. theoretical sentences as distinguished from emotional expressions, commands, lyrics, etc.) used for scientific purposes *or in everyday life*."[4] But it gradually became apparent that the artificial observation languages of the positivists' devising were too inflexible and narrow to accommodate the wide variety of ordinary sentences or even of the ordinary "theoretical" sentences that Carnap mentioned. Indeed, it became a question whether the exact, technical sentences needed for the observational reduction base of natural and formal scientific sentences were able to reproduce, or be equivalent to, any of the ordinary, nonscientific kinds of discourse. As Strawson later remarked, using "scientific concepts" to refer to the linguistic expressions that included the reduction base expressions for the natural and formal sciences, "it seems in general evident that the concepts used in non-scientific kinds of discourse could not literally be *replaced* by scientific concepts serving just the same purpose."[5]

Yet there seemed to be a problem even more fundamental than this, namely, that the observational languages constructed by the positivists ultimately rested upon ordinary usage for their sense. Ordinary locutions served as the material from which the technical observational locutions were constructed by a process of refinement. Now it seems that in order to produce exact observational locutions by refining or altering certain ordinary locutions it is first necessary to know exactly what is being refined or altered. Austin recommends, accordingly, that "before indulging in any tampering [with ordinary locutions] on our own account, we need to find out what it is that we have to deal with."[6] The problem touched upon here pertains to the fact that the observational language systems, such as the one Carnap developed in *The Logical Structure of the World,* themselves relied on ordinary language as the *metalanguage* in terms of which the technical observational language was discussed and explained. It seemed to Austin, Strawson, Ryle, and others that an indisputable consequence of this fact is that a knowledge of the basic or irreducible sense of any observational language requires a study of the metalanguage in terms of which the sense of the observational language is explained. And this suggests that an analysis of ordinary usage is philosophically more fundamental than the construction of the observational language because, as Strawson observes, "clarity about the metaconcepts themselves will be achieved only by attending to the [ordinary] use that is made of them."[7]

The recognition that the sense of ordinary locutions is more fundamental than the sense of the observational locutions suggested to linguistic analysts that linguistic sense is not ultimately to be defined in terms of observational verifications but in terms of *ordinary use.* This key "redefinition" of linguistic sense had its first published appearance in Wisdom's article "Philosophical Perplexity" (1936–37), which is often regarded as the first publication that falls squarely within the ordinary language movement.[8] This article, which Wisdom acknowledges is strongly influenced by Wittgenstein's lectures at Cambridge in the 1930s, puts forth the first published characterization of linguistic sense as "ordinary usage." Wisdom makes the claim that if a sentence "lacks a conventional usage" or is "in conflict with conventional use" then it is "nonsensical."[9] Wisdom, however, did not originate this slogan. A testimony to the influence of Wittgenstein upon the philosophers of the 1920s and 1930s is that he originated not only the positivists' slogan about verification but also the slogan about ordinary use: in his essay *Philosophical Grammar,* written in 1932–34, Wittgenstein says, "The use of a word in the language is its meaning."[10] Our real interest is in the implications of this new slogan. One important implication, developed by Wisdom in the above-mentioned article, concerns the evaluation of many traditional philosophical theories. The implication is that these theories expressed a mostly unconscious misuse of ordinary language and therefore failed to express meaningful statements. Wisdom suggests two specific patterns of this misuse of ordinary locutions: "Philosophical statements mislead when by the use of like expressions for different cases, they suggest likenesses which do not exist, and by the use of different expressions for like cases, they conceal likenesses which do exist."[11] These sorts of confusions should be cleared up by the ordinary language analyst, whose task is to clarify the likenesses and differences that in fact obtain among expressions in ordinary language.

These remarks suggest a new way of doing linguistic analysis. Instead of offering definitions of locutions, as the positivists did, the ordinary language analyst *describes the uses* of locutions. Instead of giving a definitional substitute for an expression such as "thing" or "person," the analyst describes the rules governing its everyday use. This implies that philosophical statements are not tautologies, statements of equivalences, as the positivists thought, but descriptions, empirical generalizations about how ordinary expressions are used. This indicates how the new "method of linguistic analysis" is to be understood. A method of linguistic analysis, as I defined it earlier, is a procedure for deducing conclusions in some philosophical discipline from the crucial theses about the nature of linguistic sense that belong to one's philosophy of language. The method of ordinary language analysis is a procedure for deducing conclusions from the linguistic thesis that *the sense of an expression is its ordinary use.*

This claim about ordinary language analysis requires some clarification and substantiation. The use of ordinary language analysis to derive positive conclusions in the various philosophical disciplines was more common to the Oxford school (of Ryle, Austin, and others) than to the Cambridge school (Wittgenstein, Wisdom, and others), for the Cambridge analysts tended to emphasize the dissolution of traditional philosophical problems by ordinary language analysis rather than their resolution. I shall take one of Ryle's works as an example of the positive use of this method.

Ryle writes of his book *The Concept of Mind* that "as a whole [it] is a discussion of the logical behavior of some of the cardinal terms, dispositional and occurrent, in which we talk about minds."[12] Specifically, the aim of the book is to state the rules governing the use of "the verbs, nouns and adjectives, with which in ordinary life we describe the wits, characters and higher-grade performances of the people with whom we have to do" (15). Ryle argues that these rules are widely misunderstood in that they are mistakenly represented as implying that these words are used to signify private inner episodes or tendencies for such episodes to occur; in fact, Ryle claims, these rules imply that these mental words are used to refer to overt, publicly observable behaviors of people or their dispositions to engage in such behaviors. The conclusion Ryle draws from this is that a person's mind is not a private, unextended sphere in which there occur mental episodes, but instead consists of "the person's abilities, liabilities and inclinations to do and undergo certain sorts of things, and of the doing and undergoing of these things in the ordinary world" (199).

I believe Ryle's project can be interpreted as involving an argument from theses in the philosophy of language to theses in the philosophy of mind. Ryle begins by developing certain theses about language;[13] he distinguishes between what it is "proper" to say in ordinary life and what it is "improper" to say.[14] If it is not proper to say something, then the sentence in question "makes no sense" (23). An expression is improper if it violates the rules of ordinary use or, in Ryle's terminology, if it violates "the logical regulations governing their [the expressions'] use" (7). Thus Ryle may be understood as adopting the following premises about the sense or meaning of expressions:

  1. The sense of an expression is its ordinary use.
  2. An expression is senseless if it violates ordinary usage.

From these premises, which belong to the philosophy of language, Ryle implicitly draws the inferences that

  3. The senses of mental words are their ordinary use.
  4. Sentences about minds that violate ordinary use are senseless.

From here, Ryle proceeds to dismiss Cartesian dualism (understood in a broad sense) and conclude that logical behaviorism (which may be used to describe Ryle's theory) is true. His argument is that

  5. Sentences that imply the Cartesian thesis that the mind is a series of private and unextended episodes or tendencies for such episodes to occur violate the rules of ordinary use and therefore are senseless.
  6. Sensible sentences about minds imply instead that the mind is primarily a set of publicly observable behaviors or dispositions to engage in such behaviors.

Given the additional premise that many of our utterances about minds that conform to the rules of ordinary use are true (such as, for example, the utterance "She is awake now"), it follows that minds are primarily sets of public behaviors and dispositions.

Note here both the analogy and disanalogy between the methodological principles of logical positivism and ordinary language analysis. Both hold that many traditional philosophical sentences, the so-called metaphysical sentences, are not false but senseless, although their justifications for this assertion are different. For the positivists, metaphysical sentences are senseless because unverifiable in principle, whereas for the ordinary language analysts, they are senseless because they violate ordinary use. The positivist is able to salvage some locutions traditionally used for metaphysical purposes by using them in a verifiable or tautological manner, but the ordinary language analyst salvages these locutions by "giving them back" their ordinary use. Wittgenstein, speaking for the ordinary language analysts, articulates this purpose when he says, "What *we* do is to bring words back from their metaphysical to their everyday use."[15]

But the idea that ordinary language philosophy should involve only words as ordinarily used is not strictly accurate. Philosophy does not add to or "go behind" the worldview implicit in ordinary usage but is a theory *about* ordinary usage. As a theory about ordinary usage, philosophy need not contain locutions all of which belong or conform to ordinary use but may contain technical expressions that formulate the rules of ordinary use and the implications of these rules. The introduction of technical expressions to formulate ordinary rules of use is commonplace among the ordinary language analysts. For example, Austin introduces such terms as "illocutionary expressions," "performative expressions," and "constative expressions." Likewise, Ryle makes such technical assertions as, "When two terms belong to the same category, it is proper to construct conjunctive propositions embodying them" (22). It is true that Wittgenstein says that "when I talk about language (words, sentences, etc.) I must speak the language of every day," but if we interpret this strictly to mean that the analyst cannot introduce any technical language, then we must say that Wittgenstein does not follow his own recommendation.[16] For example, Wittgenstein is not speaking the language of every day when he talks of "language-games" and suggests that language is a game. Indeed, it is a violation of ordinary use to say that "language is a game"; it is "correct" to say that chess is a game and football is a game but not that *language* is a game. Thus, to preserve the coherency of Wittgenstein's own philosophy we must allow some philosophical technicalities to be used in the analysis of ordinary language.

It is important to note in this context that the linguistic thesis that is definitive of ordinary language analysis—"the sense of a word or sentence is its ordinary use"— itself lacks an ordinary use, and thus ordinary language analysts, on pain of self-referential incoherence, must admit of a category of sensible *nonordinary* uses of language. The problem faced here is somewhat analogous to the problem faced by the logical positivists with their verification principle. The principle of verification (the sense of the nonanalytic sentences is the method of their verification) seems self-referentially incoherent since it is neither analytic nor verifiable. But the positivists are perhaps in worse straits because the principle of verification in its originally intended sense arguably seems to be a synthetic a priori statement, and the admission of this category of sense wrecks the case of the positivists against the "metaphysicians." The ordinary language analysts encounter fewer problems because they can equanimously assume a *second-order category of linguistic sense,* the category of formulations or characterizations of the senses in the first-order category of sense, the first-order senses being the *ordinary uses* of locutions. "Language-game" and "illocutionary acts" are not senseless because they belong to the characterization of ordinary uses. The admission of this second-order category of sense does not, however, give the game away to the "metaphysicians" because the metaphysicians represented themselves as characterizing not ordinary usage but a reality that was "behind" the commonsense world presupposed by ordinary usage.

This solution to the problem of nonordinary uses of words suggests how the philosophy of religion and ethics can be developed in a way that is compatible with the method of ordinary language analysis. The philosophy of religion and ethics consists of *formulations* of the rules of use of ordinary sentences and the implications of these formulations.

11. The Ordinary Language Analysts' Theory of the Religious Meaninglessness of Human Life

(i) Basic Religious Sentences as Framework Sentences

The positivists claimed that religious sentences lacked sense because they are unverifiable; these sentences merely express emotions and are associated with imagery (the religious myths). The rejection of the verification theory of sense and the acceptance of the ordinary use theory led to the idea that religious sentences did have a sense (even if unverifiable) because they had an ordinary use. The positivists classified both metaphysical and religious sentences as senseless because both are unverifiable, but the ordinary language analyst classified only metaphysical sentences as senseless because only they lacked an ordinary use. The purpose of the ordinary language philosophy of religion is to formulate the rules of use of ordinary religious sentences. This purpose animated the writings of Wittgenstein, D. Z. Phillips, Peter Winch, Hare, Rush Rhees, Ilham Dilham, O. C. Drury, and other developers of the ordinary language philosophy of religion. As Phillips writes, "Instead of stipulating [with the positivist] what *must* constitute intelligible use of language, one should look to see how language is in fact used. If one does, one comes across the use of language found in magical and religious rites and rituals. . . . [The philosopher's] tool is a descriptive one; he gives an account of the use of language involved. He can only say that these language-games are played."[17]

If religious sentences are not ordinarily used to express verifiable propositions, for what purpose are they used? Consider the sentence "God always cares for us." This cannot be falsified, Phillips contends, because "the faithful speak of God's care even in adversity [and] there seems to be no possibility of securing evidence of God not caring" (106). But so far from the unverifiability of this sentence rendering it senseless, the unverifiability is necessary for its sense. Indeed, "if there were evidence, this would in fact destroy the whole business," as Wittgenstein emphasizes.[18] This religious sentence is a *framework sentence* (which expresses what Wittgenstein calls a "picture," Hare a *blik*, and Malcolm a fundamental "groundless belief"). The positivists allowed as sentences with sense only verifiable sentences and analytic sentences and failed to recognize other varieties of meaningful sentences, such as framework sentences. Framework sentences do not possess a truth value and are not based on reasoning or grounds. Rather, they articulate the criteria of what counts or does not count as an explanation or evidence, the criteria of justification, the criteria of good or bad reasoning, and so on within some particular language-game. In *On Certainty* Wittgenstein describes five characteristics of these sentences: (1) they are accepted as not possibly in error, (2) they are not based on experience, (3) cultural changes can bring about changes in which framework principles are accepted, (4) people "cut off" from these principles are said not to be in error but to be joking or insane, and (5) these principles are rarely formulated. Framework principles are not something we *decide* to accept or reject; rather, we are taught or absorb these principles as children as "common ways of speaking and thinking that are pressed on us by our human community."[19] Acceptance of these principles is the condition of learning how to talk or acquire a language-game; framework principles are the foundational rules of use of the language-game that is practiced.

Consider an example of a nonreligious framework sentence. Norman Malcolm gives the example, "Familiar material things (watches, shoes, chairs) do not cease to exist without some physical explanation."[20] This is not an analytic sentence but it is not verifiable or falsifiable either. According to Malcolm, there is no possible observation that could falsify this sentence because in any case in which there is no apparent explanation we may assume that there is some explanation that we have not (yet) been able to discover. Rather, this sentence expresses the framework within which we interpret occurrences in daily life and the sciences; for example, if we cannot find our watch, we do not assume as a possibility that it disappeared without explanation. The framework sentence expresses the criterion by which we take ourselves to be justified in believing that something caused the disappearance of a familiar material thing; for example, if John was the only person in the room where my watch was and my watch has disappeared, then this criterion (ordinary things do not disappear without explanation) justifies my belief that John took my watch.

"God always cares for us" and "God exists" are framework religious sentences in that they serve as justifications of other religious sentences. In order for there to be framework religious sentences, there must be other religious sentences that occur within the framework and that do possess truth values and for which there is evidence (of the sort specifiable by the framework sentences). These sentences express "doctrinal beliefs," as Malcolm calls them (186). There is evidence or argument for these beliefs of the sort specified by the relevant framework sentences; for example, in the Christian religion the framework sentences "God exists" and "The Bible is the revealed word of God" show that evidence for a doctrinal belief is found in what the Bible says and that a valid argument form is, "The Bible says such-and-such; therefore, such-and-such is true." An example of a doctrinal sentence is, "The Bishop of Rome has supreme authority," and the relevant framework sentences tell us that evidence for this doctrinal belief (if there is any evidence) may be found in the Bible, perhaps in the passage where Jesus says to Peter that he is the rock of the church. Analogously, framework principles of Hinayana Buddhism would be that "there is Nirvana" and that the criterion of truth is conformity to the Dhammapada and other Buddhist scriptures that report the infallible word of Gautama Buddha.

This account of religious sentences (framework and doctrinal) suggests the following critique of the positivists' philosophy of religion. The positivists assumed there was only one language-game and only one set of framework principles, that of the sciences and the factually descriptive core of common sense. The principle of verifiability via sense-data and the principles of inductive reasoning are scientific framework principles, and the positivists measured every other framework by the principles of this framework. This is why religion turns out to be senseless. But we may quote Wittgenstein to the effect that there is religious reasoning, but it "is an entirely different kind of reasoning" from scientific reasoning (279). It is irrational within the scientific framework to adopt a theory about the nature of combustion that conflicts with experimental evidence, but we encounter a different kind of irrationality when we consider that it is irrational within Catholicism to conduct a Black Mass rather than a proper Mass. Criteria of evidence are also different. If "The Bishop of Rome has supreme authority" is asserted to be true on the basis of a passage in Genesis, this is a blunder, but it is a blunder not because one appeals to the Bible rather than to, say, sensory evidence, but because one appeals to Genesis rather than to the New Testament, where the relevant evidence (if any) can be found. As Wittgenstein writes, "Whether a thing is a blunder or not—it is a blunder in a particular system. Just as something is a blunder in a particular game and not in another" (279). The positivists rejected mystical experience because it could not be verified by sensory evidence, but this is a "category mistake" because mystical experiences are verified or falsified by virtue of being compatible or incompatible with religious doctrine. Phillips says, "If Paul claims on the road to Damascus he saw the heavens open and heard a voice telling him of his error in persecuting the Christians, the meaning of calling the vision divine [rather than a hallucination] depends on [and is verified in terms of] the religious beliefs held at that time."[21]

Now this new ordinary language philosophy of religion seems to rescue religion from the attack mounted by the positivists; it seems to show that religion makes sense and that human life has an objective religious meaning. But does it show this?

(ii) The Alleged Denial but Real Implication of Religious Meaninglessness

The philosophy of religion espoused by Wittgenstein, Phillips, and others entails that human life lacks a religious meaning, even for the believer, although they would vehemently deny this implication. Their philosophy of religion does not meet a criterion that I stated in the Preface for there being an objective religious meaning of human life, namely, that God exist or that some accurate concept of God be instantiated by some human-independent reality. One way to state this is to say that human life has a religious meaning if "God exists" is true. The ordinary language analysts hold that this sentence is not true; it is not false either but has no truth value. To say that it is not true is to say there is no reality to which this sentence corresponds. But at the same time we cannot say that it purports to correspond to reality but fails to do so (and is false) because its ordinary use is to express a framework principle.

The reality of God on this view is the reality of a certain picture or framework that humans accept and whose existence is dependent on the humans who adopt this framework. Phillips remarks that "religious expressions which involve talk of God are not referring expressions . . . no object corresponds to such talk. . . . [They] are expressive in character, and what they express is called the worship of God. . . . What is meant by the reality of God is to be found in certain pictures which say themselves."[22] Rhees comments that " 'God exists' is not a statement of fact. You might say also that it is not in the indicative mood. It is a confession—or expression—of faith."[23] If we adopt the logical behaviorism of Wittgenstein, Ryle, and others, we may analyze this faith in God, not in terms of a mental act of believing (without justification) in a certain proposition, but in terms of a set of religious practices and dispositions to engage in such practices. To believe in God or to have faith in God is to engage in the behaviors of worship, prayer, and the like.

This is not to say that the reality of God is that of a human framework or world-conception *in contrast* to the reality of the law-governed physical objects studied by the sciences. It is false that there is a given world that is independent of human language and concepts and that our language may come to correspond to. Rather, there is a world or reality only relative to some language-game and world-picture, for what counts as real or unreal is itself relative to a world-picture. The world of science is no more the "true world" than the world of religion because there is no "true world" in relation to which different world-pictures can be compared to see which one "corresponds" to it.

The ordinary language philosophers of religion would say that "God is the creator of the heaven and the earth" is a framework religious sentence and has no truth value; it simply states part of the framework within which the religious form of life is conducted. But if we adopt the second-order language that articulates the rules of use of this sentence within religious language, then we may say that it is not the case that God is a creator of some language-independent universe. God is a part of a world-picture, and a world-picture or concept cannot create anything. There is no "universe in itself" that could be created anyway because there are merely different forms of life of humans, each embodying a certain world-picture, and

God qua world-picture does not create other world-pictures or forms of life. The given is not the universe or God but *forms of life* (equivalently, frameworks, world-pictures, basic language-games). Wittgenstein states, "What has to be accepted, the given, is—so one could say—*forms of life.*"[24] We may compare this with the phenomenalist positivists, for whom the given was not forms of life but *sense-data,* and with the logical realists, for whom the given was the ensemble of all existents and beings.

The idea of the ordinary language philosophers of religion is that if "God is the creator of the universe" is analyzed to mean that there is some "universe in itself" that is created by a god that is the referent of "God," then the formulation of this analysis is a piece of metaphysical nonsense. In this respect, these philosophers are fully in line with the positivists. If this position is correct, then the need to mean (refer to) something holy and to mean it in an objective way that involves transcendence of the self and the human community cannot be satisfied. Consider, for example, this passage from the Islamic philosopher and mystic Al Ghazzali: "When the worshipper thinks no longer of his worship or himself, but is altogether absorbed in Him whom he worships, that state, by gnostics, is called the passing away of mortality, when a person so passed away from himself feels nothing of his bodily members, nor of what is passing without, not what passes within his own mind. . . . He is journeying first *to* his Lord, and then at the end, *in* his Lord."[25]

The person is here aiming for radical self-transcendence, to be in touch with something maximally great that is not a mere concept or picture in his own mind; he aims for some transcendent reality he "discovers" in his mystic flight and that is not "invented" by himself or his religious community. But the ordinary language philosophers of religion would discount this aim as a product of metaphysical confusion. All we can really mean in religious attitudes is a part of a picture that belongs to and is dependent upon a form of human life. To requote Phillips, "The reality of God is to be found in certain pictures which say themselves." The urge to experience *objective* meaning is thwarted from the start.

Consider Ghazzali's statement "The worshipper thinks no longer of his worship or himself" but solely of God. Phillips, Wittgenstein, Malcolm, and the like hold that the reality of God is the reality of a concept integral to a world-picture, and that a concept is to be analyzed in logical behaviorist terms as an ability or disposition to behave in certain ways. Thus, the concept of God is the ability to engage in such religious practices as prayer and worship. There is no sense in the attempt to transcend the worship toward some referent of the worship because the worship is all there is.

Consider further the condition of an *intrinsic purpose* of human existence that belongs to the notion of objective meaning. The intrinsic purpose pertinent to religious meaning may be a functional purpose, a purpose which humans were designed to fulfill by a cosmic designer. But if the designer himself is but a part of a human conceptual framework, then the functional purpose is not something that is intrinsic to human existence (something that is built into human existence and is not a mere invention of humans) but is invented by humans in the sense that it is a part of a conceptual framework they construct and adopt. It is a purpose that humans assign themselves, as it were, by virtue of constructing and living by the religious framework. The religious meaning of human life in effect reduces to a subjective meaning of life.

Given this, should we say that the ordinary language philosophy of religion (if true) justifies a religious despair, at least for those who desire an objective religious meaning? To consider a concrete example, let us turn to the religious despair expressed by T. S. Eliot in "The Hollow Men." Eliot writes in one stanza of the absent "eyes" of a watching and providential god:

> The eyes are not here
> There are no eyes here
> In this valley of dying stars
> In this hollow valley
> This broken jaw of our lost kingdoms
>
> In this last of meeting places
> We grope together
> And avoid speech
> Gathered on this beach of the tumid river
>
> Sightless, unless
> The eyes reappear
> As the perpetual star
> Multifoliate rose
> Of death's twilight kingdom
> The hope only
> Of empty men.

The ordinary language philosophers of religion would say that Eliot's attitude makes sense, but only as a first-level attitude; it is senseless if it is a second-level attitude that takes as its justification the ordinary language philosophy of religion. That is, this religious despair makes sense within the religious framework *broadly construed*, so as to encompass not only belief but also doubt, rebellion, and despair at the absence of God. It is a move within the religious language-game, a negative move, one that belongs to the decline of religious faith and to the situation of the "death of God." But it is a piece of metaphysical nonsense if it purports to be a second-level attitude that is motivated by the ordinary language philosophy of religion. In this case, it would amount to the metaphysical (not religious) assertion that *there is a framework concept of God, but God does not exist; there is nothing to which the concept refers and therefore religious despair is warranted.* This sentence makes no sense because it neither has an ordinary use nor is a formulation of a rule of ordinary use. It is an attempt to say something that cannot be said, to go beyond the boundaries of sense.

But the feeling persists that this sentence does make sense and that if the reality of God is but the reality of a picture or a conceptual component of a framework, then religious despair is warranted for the person who desires an objective religious meaning. Whether this feeling is justified or not depends on the extent to which a criticism of the ordinary language philosophy of religion can be successfully mounted.

(iii) Problems with the Ordinary Language Philosophy of Religion

There are at least two problems with the ordinary language philosophy of religion: (a) it fails to describe accurately ordinary usage, and (b) it is self-referentially incoherent.

(a) The ordinary language philosophy of religion makes a pretense of capturing religious language as it is ordinarily used, but this pretense is empty because ordinary religious sentences are not used in the manner specified. Specifically, sentences like "God exists," "God is always caring for us," and "The Bible is the revealed word of God" are not used as framework sentences but as sentences with a truth value that are capable of being argued for or against on the basis of reasons. Consider the sentence "I believe that God exists." This is ordinarily used on some occasions to express the utterer's commitment and practice of a religious way of life, worship, prayer, and the like. But this is not its only ordinary use; it is also used to express the conviction that there exists a transcendent Creator of the universe, that the concept of God is not uninstantiated but in fact has an instantiation. The suggestion that the reality of God is but the reality of a picture that says itself is a blatant violation of ordinary use; no ordinary language user (but an eccentric) would say that "God exists" carries no more existential import than that there is a concept of God that belongs to a conceptual framework some people adopt (and that it does not assert that there exists, transcendent to all human frameworks, a creator of the universe). Of course, formulations of the rules of ordinary usage need not themselves have an ordinary usage, but they must not be in contradiction with the ordinary uses of which they purport to be rules. A rule must be such that an ordinary speaker would be able to recognize it if confronted with its explicit formulation and explanation, and say, "Yes, that is what I implicitly meant by saying 'God exists.'" But it is preposterous to think that if we interrupted a person praying to God and asked him if the reality of God is nothing but the reality of a concept or set of religious practices he would say, "Yes, I am not really praying to any transcendent entity to intercede on my behalf; I am merely expressing a concept that refers to nothing." The statement " 'God' is used to express a framework concept rather than to refer to a transcendent creator" *is not* a formulation of a rule of ordinary usage.

Wittgenstein asserts about religion that

> the point is that if there were evidence, this would in fact destroy the whole business.
>
> Anything that I normally call evidence wouldn't in the slightest influence me.
>
> Suppose, for instance, we knew people who foresaw the future; make forecasts for years and years ahead; and they described some sort of a Judgement Day. Queerly enough, even if there were such a thing, and even if it were more convincing than I have described it, belief in this happening wouldn't be at all a religious belief.[26]

Wittgenstein is mistaken here; if such an event occurred, Christians (or at least fundamentalist Christians) would regard it as a confirmation of their beliefs. "You see," they would say to the "secular humanists," "I told you there would be a Judgment Day." Christians (or fundamentalist Christians) believe quite literally that at some time in the future an empirically ascertainable event will occur in which people are judged and sent to heaven or hell; that they believe this is evident from listening to them talk about their beliefs. Christians also appeal to evidence to support the contention that the Bible is the revealed word of God: "The Bible predicted that certain things would happen in the future and these things did happen. Surely that is evidence that the Bible is the revealed word of God." (This was once said to me by an ordinary Christian.) Likewise, "God exists" is regarded both as being a true statement and as having evidence to support it. A farmer once told me that "life comes only from life" and regarded this as the evidence that God exists (all life on earth must have come from some other Living Being, God), and another ordinary believer put her argument in the form of a rhetorical question: "If God did not create the Earth, then who did?" (she was appealing imprecisely to a certain principle of causality, that everything that begins to exist has a cause). A member of the Hare Krishna sect of Hinduism once offered me as evidence for the existence of his god that people experienced the presence of the deity when chanting "Hare Krishna," which is an appeal to mystical experience of a sort as evidence for the existence of a deity. The ordinary view on this matter is not that mystical experiences are true because they conform to religious doctrine, but that the fundamental tenets of religion are themselves verified by religious experience. Examples could be multiplied, but the point is that there is abundant evidence that the religious sentences in question are used to express a proposition the speakers take to be *true* and that they are ordinarily regarded as having *evidence* that supports them.

The ordinary language philosophy of religion is so far off the mark in its description of the rules of use of ordinary religious language that one wonders how such an implausible theory could have originated in the first place. I believe this philosophy is an ill-matched conjunction of the logical positivist philosophy of religion with the "ordinary use" philosophy of language. The positivists held that (i) evidence is irrelevant to basic religious sentences, (ii) religious sentences are not in the indicative mood and do not have a truth-value, and (iii) religious sentences merely express emotions or attitudes. These three theses were adopted by the ordinary language philosophers of religion but were given a new derivation; instead of being derived from the verificationist theory of linguistic sense, they were derived from the ordinary usage theory. The evidence given for (i)–(iii) is now that *this is how religious sentences are ordinarily used.* The prevalence of the positivist bias was so deep that they simply failed to note the seemingly obvious fact that this is not how religious sentences are ordinarily used.

(b) A second main problem with the ordinary language philosophy of religion concerns the threat of self-referential incoherence. It asserts that no system of linguistic rules or statements within this system corresponds to reality, that there is no reality to which any such language-game could or could not correspond, and that no language-game is any more "accurate" or "justified" than another. "Grammar is not accountable to any reality," Wittgenstein asserts in *Philosophical Grammar;*[27] indeed, reality is accountable to grammar, at least in the sense that the distinction between reality and unreality is made within a language-game and is relative to that language-game. Talk about an independent reality in relation to which different language-games can be compared is metaphysical nonsense. But are these various claims self-referentially coherent or is it the case that a contradiction results if they are applied to themselves? Let us consider a particular quotation from Peter Winch's widely heralded (by ordinary language philosophers) essay "Understanding a Primitive Society," in which Winch compares the Zande language-game with that of Western science. Winch criticizes metaphysical talk about "agreement with reality" as nonsense:

> [A science-based metaphysician], although he emphasizes that a member of scientific culture has a different conception of reality from that of a Zande believer in magic, wants to go beyond merely registering this fact and making the differences explicit, and to say, finally, *that the scientific conception agrees with what reality actually is like, whereas the magical conception does not.* . . . He wants to go further and say: *our [scientific] concept of reality is the*

correct one, the Azande are mistaken. But the difficulty is to see what 'correct' and 'mistaken' can mean in this context.[28]

As a convenient summary of the theory that appears self-referentially incoherent, we shall use the sentence (A):

  A. There is no independent reality to which any language-game could
       correspond and which could make it "the correct" language-game;
       reality is relative to and dependent upon a particular language-game.

The problem with (A) is that it seems to be senseless according to the criteria of linguistic sense adopted by the ordinary language philosophers. They assume that all sentences that have a sense occur either within a language-game or are framework sentences stating the rules of use of sentences within a specific language-game. But the sentence (A) seems to be neither a sentence within a specific language-game nor a framework sentence that states the basic principles or rules of use of some specific language-game. In order to be true, (A) must be not a framework sentence (since framework sentences have no truth values) but a sentence within a framework, a move within some specific language-game. But if so, it cannot pretend to be an absolutely true assertion about all language-games because language-games are incommensurable; sense, justification, and truth are relative to a specific language-game. But if (A) is a framework sentence it is neither true nor false and thus cannot be said to characterize truly the nature of all language-games. In any case, it cannot be a framework sentence because such sentences articulate the rules of some specific language-game, and (A) purports to be about all language-games.

According to the ordinary language analysts, there are no criteria of evidence, reasoning, sense and nonsense, truth and falsity, real and unreal that are common to all language-games. Winch writes in *The Idea of a Social Science* that

> criteria of logic are not a direct gift of God, but arise out of, and are only in-
> telligible in the context of, ways of living or modes of social life. It follows
> that one cannot apply criteria of logic to modes of social life as such. For in-
> stance, science is one such mode and religion is another; and each has criteria
> of intelligibility peculiar to itself. So within science or religion actions can be
> logical or illogical: in science, for example, it would be illogical to refuse to
> be bound by the results of a properly carried out experiment; in religion it
> would be illogical to suppose that one could pit one's strength against God's
> and so on. But we cannot sensibly say that either the practice of science itself
> or that of religion is either illogical or logical; both are non-logical.[29]

But what criteria of intelligibility and logic does this very passage instantiate? If the criteria are those of some specific mode of social life, then the assertions in this passage cannot purport to be true absolutely, to be absolute truths about all modes of social life. But if these assertions are meant to be truths about all modes of social life, then there must be some absolute standpoint that transcends the modes of social life and from which features of these modes of life can be described. But in this latter case, there are criteria of logic and intelligibility that are not merely relative to some given social life, but are absolute and apply to all modes of social life.

The ordinary language analysts do seem to be committed to a body of absolute truths. For example, "The sense of an expression is its ordinary use in some specific language-game," "Evidence for the truth or falsity of a certain view is determined by 'what we would say' in the relevant circumstances," "The purpose of philosophy is to formulate the rules of use of the various language-games," "Religion and science are two different and incommensurable frameworks," "Sentences are either framework sentences or are sentences within a certain framework," and so on are all assertions that are neither framework sentences of some particular mode of social life nor sentences within such a framework; they are sentences that purport to transcend all social frameworks and describe some features common to them all or to describe absolute differences between two frameworks. These assertions purport to be true (absolutely) and to correspond to all language-games. But if this is the case, then all language-games become the *independent reality,* and the sentences that describe these games are *the body of absolute truths* that correspond to the independent reality. These sentences then would no longer be part of any language-game because they would "correspond to absolute reality" and would not share the merely relative truth of the sentences within a specific language-game. But how is this possible if the very theses of ordinary language philosophy are true? How can we transcend all language-games and adopt some absolute viewpoint on reality if reality itself is relative to a given language-game?

Milton Munitz has recently espoused a version of this "language-game relativism" theory in his *The Question of Reality:*

> Wherever we find a metaphysician declaring he has succeeded in uncovering and conveying the essence of the world, we can be sure that he is suffering from a pathological illusion endemic to all such forms of inquiry and speculation. This consists in taking as real what is at best only the projection onto reality of the system of concepts, of grammatical connections, stipulations, and conventions of a network of forms of representation. To overcome this illusion, we must rid ourselves of the belief that any grammar corresponds to an essential structure inherent in the world, that there is a unique and absolute truth of a metaphysical sort awaiting discovery by human beings.[30]

But does not this passage instantiate the very "illusion" that the "language-game relativists" are supposed to overcome? Are not the ordinary language philosophers offering us their purported discovery of the essence of the world—that this essence is *human beings playing language-games?* If so, cannot we say of the ordinary language philosophers what they say of the metaphysicians, that they err in "taking as real" a mere projection of their forms of representations—the representations constitutive of ordinary language philosophy, such as the thesis (A) given above? If these philosophers are to follow their own advice and rid themselves of the belief that "any grammar corresponds to an essential structure inherent in the world," they must rid themselves of the belief that *the grammar of their ordinary language philosophy* corresponds to the essential structure inherent in the world. But if they rid themselves of this belief and assert that their philosophy is a mere projection that is no more "accurate" or "justified" than any other philosophy, then they must rid themselves of the belief that their philosophy, and not some other philosophy, is the true philosophy.

One may attempt to avoid this difficulty by asserting that *there is* an absolute standpoint from which one can survey and describe all language-games and that absolute reality or the world in itself consists of all the linguistic practices of all humans. This would be a version of subjective idealism, that reality is just human reality. The phenomenalism of some of the logical positivists implies that reality is just human reality and that human reality is reducible to a series of sense-data; the ordinary language analyst may be taken as implying that reality is just human reality and as reducing human reality to the set of linguistic behaviors of humans.

But if we adopt this way of resolving the difficulty, we may ask if there is any reason to believe that the philosophy resulting from this resolution is true. I would suggest that there is no reason to believe that absolute reality consists only of humans engaged in linguistic activities. If it is true that absolute reality consists of these linguistic practices, then presumably there is some means of finding out that this is true or some way of justifying this belief. Presumably, this is through observation; we observe humans engaged in various language-games. Indeed, this is a method the ordinary language philosophers use to establish their various claims; they observe people talking in certain ways in certain circumstances and generalize from these observations about the rules of use of the relevant expressions. This is a method of *observation and induction.* Moreover, the analysts typically use rules of deductive inference, such as *modus ponens,* in constructing arguments for their theses. The absolute standpoint adopted by the ordinary language analysts is just that of "Western science and logic." Given that this is the case, we may next ask, If observation, induction, and deduction can establish that the linguistic behavior of humans belongs to absolute reality, why cannot they establish that other components also belong to absolute reality, such as tables, mountains, and stars? If observation, induction, and logic provide knowledge that language-users exist, surely they also provide knowledge that chimpanzees, ants, flowers, galaxies, and the like also exist. And once we establish this, cannot we go on to show that Western science and not Zande magic is a true theory of absolute reality? The issue between the theists and atheists would also be a matter that can be decided absolutely; for example, we may establish that there is some principle of causality at work in absolute reality and then construct some relevant argument for or against the thesis that there is some cause of the whole universe.

A second way to avoid the problem of self-referential incoherence that threatens ordinary language philosophy is to claim that the standpoint from which statements like (A) above and those of Winch and Munitz are made is itself a certain language-game, namely, a game played (for the most part) by certain ordinary language philosophers at Oxford and Cambridge during the mid-twentieth century. These various statements would be moves within this language-game and would be true relative to it. (Or else they would be framework sentences of this language-game.) In this case, ordinary language philosophy would not purport to characterize (with absolute truth) the nature of other language-games or indeed the nature of anything. Neither would it purport to claim that it is true (absolutely) that there is no independent reality and no body of absolute truths that correspond to this reality. It would merely stipulate some arbitrary conventions and make assertions that are true merely relative to these conventions. But the ordinary language position would then lose any substantive interest; it could be rejected with impunity by the formulators of absolute truths, who could go on to philosophize about the nature of absolute reality without fear of attack from the "language-game relativists." (A relative assertion by its very nature cannot oppose an absolute assertion because "It is relatively true that there are no absolute truths" is consistent with "It is absolutely true that there are absolute truths.")

In sum, the ordinary language philosophy of religion has not provided us with the means to determine whether or not human life has an objective religious meaning. The claim that "God" is used not to refer to a transcendent entity but merely to express a picture or concept is a misrepresentation of the ordinary rule of use of this word and indeed entails that human life lacks an objective religious meaning in the ordinary sense of "religious." Furthermore, the "language-game relativity theory of reality" that underpins the ordinary language philosophy of religion cannot be justifiably taken to be an absolutely true theory of reality.

12. The Ordinary Language Analysts' Theory of Ethical Meaninglessness

It is possible to consider and evaluate the ordinary language analysts' ethical philosophy independently of the problematic "language-game relativism" that underpins their philosophy of religion. The logical independence of their ethics from "language-game relativism" results from the independence of nonnormative facts and values; one can consider a theory of values without explicitly bringing in a theory that nonnormative facts are absolute or relative to a language-game. Of course, there is an important connection between the analysts' "language-game relativism" and their ethics (as we shall see), but it is possible to ignore or bypass this connection in the main part of the discussion.

The four most important books in the ordinary language ethical philosophy are Stephen Toulmin's *An Examination of the Place of Reason in Ethics* (written in 1946–47 but published in 1950; this is the first systematic application of the ordinary language method to ethics); Hare's *The Language of Morals* (1952) and *Freedom and Reason* (1963); and P. H. Nowell-Smith's *Ethics* (1954). The most influential of these books have been Hare's, and his theory of "prescriptivism" is often taken to be the ethical theory that supplanted the "emotivism" of the logical positivists.

The ethical theories of these thinkers shall be examined from four perspectives. I begin by explaining their criticism of the positivists' ethics, a criticism I take to be basically sound. I will then argue that the ordinary language ethical theories imply that human life is ethically meaningless, despite the analysts' strong denials of this implication. Following this, I show that their arguments for the part of their theories that implies life is ethically meaningless are unsound. Finally, I evaluate the soundness of the ordinary language method in connection with the question of whether life has an ethical meaning; I shall argue that it may contribute evidence relevant to answering this question, but that by itself it is insufficient to answer it.

12.1 The Critique of Positivist Ethics

The ordinary language analysts took a step away from the complete ethical nihilism of the positivists and toward (but did not reach) a theory of positive ethical meaning. The history of analytic ethics may be looked at in the following way. In the beginning there is the optimistic theory that life has an objective ethical meaning (Moore, Prichard, Russell). This extreme optimism led to its polar opposite, the total pessimism of the positivists. From this negative extreme, subsequent movements began working their way back to a more optimistic theory. The ordinary language analysts took one step in this direction and the essentialists another, so that with some essentialists we have what may be called a cautious or qualified optimism about life's objective ethical meaning. The step away from the positivists' pessimism taken by the ordinary language analysts shall be discussed in this section. My two main examples will be Toulmin's and Hare's theories.

(iv) Stephen Toulmin's "Good Reasons" Theory of Ethics

Toulmin originated the ordinary language ethical philosophy with his 1950 book but acknowledges his indebtedness to the lectures of Wittgenstein and Wisdom in 1946 (although they did not lecture on ethical matters). The method Toulmin uses is familiar to us: "The only facts, upon which the truth of what we have to say will depend, are those more familiar, unquestionable facts of usage [of ethical language]."[31] From this starting point, Toulmin effectively criticizes positivist ethics as being inconsistent with the facts of ordinary usage.

The positivists, we recall, claimed that ethical sentences lacked a truth-value. For Carnap, "A value-statement is nothing else than a command in a misleading grammatical form. . . . it is neither true nor false."[32] Toulmin points out that this theory is inconsistent with the rules of use of value-statements and compares a command as ordinarily used with a value-statement as ordinarily used:

> If, when the sergeant-major has bellowed his order ["Stand to attention!"], I
> go up to a private and say to him, "D'you know; the R.S.M. wasn't telling
> the truth", he may stare at me or laugh, but he will certainly not understand.
> But if the sergeant-major has only said to him, "You ought to be standing at
> attention", and I do the same, he will agree, ask for my reasons, or begin to
> argue with me. He will not regard my statement as strange or unintelligible,
> for he will be thoroughly familiar with such discussions. That being so, it is
> quite wrong to call it nonsense. (53)

Toulmin seems right here; we do ordinarily accept value-statements as having truth or falsity, and in this respect they are dissimilar to commands.

Positivists also claimed that ethical agreement among disputants is obtained by mere persuasion, but Toulmin correctly notes that we ordinarily distinguish agreement obtained in this way from agreement obtained by valid reasoning. We do offer rational justification for ethical judgments and do reason about ethical matters:

> questions of truth, falsity and rational justification (or verification, in a broad
> sense of the term) do continually arise in ethics. If you tell a child, "You
> ought to take off your dirty shoes before going into the drawing room", and
> he asks "Why?", then the answers, "Because your Mama does not like you to
> dirty the carpet" and "Because it makes unnecessary work", are reasons—
> and pretty good ones, too—while the answer, "Because it's the third Tuesday
> before Pentecost", seems a poor one. (52–53)

The method Toulmin is using here is Wisdom's, as described in his essay "Philosophical Perplexity," which I discussed in an earlier section; Wisdom noted a central pattern of misuse of ordinary locutions, namely, "when by the use of like expressions for different cases, they [the philosophers] suggest likenesses which do not exist." By calling both commands and ethical sentences "commands," they used a like expression for different cases and suggested a likeness which did not exist, namely, that both lacked truth-values. And by calling both expressions such as "Hurrah!" and "That is good" emotional exclamations and means of persuasion, they suggested a likeness that does not exist, namely, that expressions of both sorts fail to obey rules of reasoning. It is the task of the ordinary language analyst to clear up confusions of this sort by clarifying the likenesses and differences that in fact obtain among expressions in ordinary language.

Toulmin regards the conflict between the positivists' theory and ordinary usage to be sufficient reason to reject the former: by dismissing evaluative reasoning, the positivist's "argument runs counter to common sense and common usage, *and can be rejected*" (47; emphasis added). I shall later give reason to doubt that "S runs counter to common usage" entails "S is false or senseless" when I examine the ordinary language method in general, but for the present I shall merely acknowledge that Toulmin and other ordinary language analysts do seem to be correct at least in their claims about ordinary usage in their dispute with the positivists. This is a marked contrast with their claims about ordinary religious sentences, which seemed far off the mark, as we saw in the last section.

To proceed further with the ordinary language analysts' description of ordinary ethical sentences, Toulmin maintains that ordinary ethical discourse evinces two sorts of reasoning. The first is deontological, in which a good reason for a particular action's being moral is that it instantiates a general principle that is accepted by the community to which one belongs. (Consistent with his ordinary language method, Toulmin effortlessly slides from "R is accepted as a good reason for the morality of the action A in a certain community" to "R is a good reason for the morality of the action A." This slide is invalid, as I shall later show.)

The second sort of reasoning is teleological, in which reasons are offered for the morality of some general principles or social practices of a community. Such a principle or social practice is ordinarily accepted as good if it leads to certain results, namely, the avoidance of unnecessary suffering and inconvenience. For example, it is ordinarily said that a "good reason" for the general principle that one ought to keep one's promises is that following this principle results in less suffering and conflict of interest than not following it.

I think we may concede that these two sorts of ethical reasoning are present in ordinary ethical thinking, at least in our culture, although we do not need to commit ourselves to the further claim that these are the only sorts of ethical reasoning in which we engage. The question that naturally arises at this point is whether Toulmin's theory carries the entailment that there is an objective ethical meaning of human life. But before I address this question, it will be helpful to compare Toulmin's theory with Hare's more influential theory of "prescriptivism."

(v) Hare's Prescriptivism

Hare begins with the same criticism of the positivists with which Toulmin began and that also underlay the ordinary language analysts' defense of the sense of religious sentences, namely, that the verification criterion of linguistic sense is too narrow to capture all that is ordinarily said to have linguistic sense. Hare says of prescriptive sentences such as imperatives and moral sentences,

> Imperative sentences do not satisfy this criterion [the verificationist criterion], and it may be that sentences expressing moral judgements do not either; but this only shows that they do not express statements in the sense defined by the criterion; and *this sense may be a narrower one than that of normal usage.* It does not mean that they are meaningless, or even that their meaning is of such a character that no logical rules can be given for their employment.[33]

The general criticism that the ordinary language analysts leveled against the positivists is perhaps best explained by P. H. Nowell-Smith, who noted that the positivists assumed that "the logic of every type of discourse must be identical"[34] and that this logic is the logic of the indicative or descriptive sentence, which ascribes a property to something. If a sentence fails to ascribe a property to something (and be verifiable by observing something's possession of that property), then it is "illogical" and senseless. Because commands and ethical sentences both fail to meet this requirement, they are senseless. However, an inspection of ordinary usage shows (Nowell-Smith continues) that commands and ethical sentences have their own logic.

Toulmin emphasized the difference between imperative and ethical sentences, but it is integral to Hare's prescriptivism to emphasize their similarity and indeed to say that an ethical sentence differs from an imperative by virtue of being universalizable. It is worth exploring this difference because I shall argue that in spite of it both Hare and Toulmin end up with the same implicit result (a result denied by both), that human life is ethically meaningless.

Hare wants to say that ethical sentences have sense, express statements (propositions), and a first step in his argument is to show that imperatives or commands express statements. As we saw, positivists such as Ayer, Carnap, and Stevenson held that ethical sentences express emotions and are intended to influence causally one's audiences by arousing their emotions and so stimulating them to action. Stevenson alleges that if you say that somebody ought not do something, "you are attempting . . . to get him to disapprove of it."[35] They assimilated ethical sentences to commands and commands to causal influences. The command "Do this!" is regarded as an instrument to influence the actions of another. But instead of denying the similarity between commands and ethical sentences, as Toulmin does, Hare challenges the positivist theory of commands. He makes the plausible observation that there is a difference between *telling someone to do something* and *getting him to do it.* In the first case, the sentence expresses a proposition—we are *telling someone something* (namely, telling him to do something)—but in the second the sentence-utterance is an instrument to act on the other's feelings, much as hollering, "Hey!" in a loud and threatening tone of voice may be an attempt to cause the other person to feel intimidated and so do as one wishes.

The point becomes clear when we compare the common semantic content of a command and an indicative sentence, say, "Shut the door!" and "You are going to shut the door." These sentences have in common the propositional content *your shutting the door in the immediate future*, and they differ in what Austin would call their "illocutionary force"; in one case, the speaker *commands* the listener to make the proposition true and in the other the speaker *asserts* it to be true. By failing to grasp adequately this distinction between semantic content and illocutionary force, positivists failed to see that commands and ethical sentences have a propositional content no less than do indicatives.

Ethical sentences differ from commands, according to Hare, in that they are universalizable. The ethical sentence "You ought not to smoke in this compartment" entails not only the singular imperative "Do not smoke in this compartment," but also the universal imperative "Do not smoke in any compartment exactly like this one." By contrast, this universal imperative is not entailed by "Do not smoke in this compartment." In fact, Hare claims, universal ethical sentences are equivalent in sense to universal imperatives.

But Hare's point is more subtle than this. He claims that in ordinary language it is "almost impossible" (177) to formulate a *proper* universal imperative because the typical so-called universal imperative (for example, "No smoking") contains an implicit reference to an individual (for example, "No smoking" may mean no smoking in this compartment). But in the cases in which there occur proper universal imperatives, they are "equivalent in meaning" (178) to universal ethical sentences; for example, "*Render to* no man evil for evil" is equivalent in meaning to "*One ought to render to* no man evil for evil" (178).

One may respond to this prescriptivist thesis that the universal ethical sentence differs from the properly universal imperative in that the former ascribes the value-property of *ought to* and the latter does not, but Hare denies there is any such property (for reasons I shall evaluate in a later section). A person who believes there is such a property would say that Hare has reduced universal ethical sentences to properly universal imperatives and thereby omitted their distinctively ethical component.

Is the prescriptive sense that Hare assigns to ethical sentences sufficient to enable human life to be objectively meaningful? I shall argue that neither Hare's, Toulmin's, nor Nowell-Smith's doctrine is consistent with the belief that life is objectively ethically meaningful.

12.2. The Alleged Denial but Real Implication of Ethical Meaninglessness

Ethical Relativism

Hare's, Toulmin's, and Nowell-Smith's theories imply that ethical sentences have sense; but this does not imply that human life has an objective ethical meaning. Indeed, the implication of their theory is that life is ethically meaningless, although they resist strongly this implication.

The important point is that for the ordinary language analysts ultimate ethical principles are neither true nor false. I said earlier that Toulmin, Hare, and Nowell-Smith disagreed with the positivists by asserting that ordinary ethical sentences are true or false. But these analysts have in mind with this claim only the usual or typical ordinary ethical sentences, the *nonbasic ones*. Nonbasic ethical sentences are true or false and can be verified or falsified; Hare observes that " 'ought'-sentences . . . can only be verified by reference to a standard or set of principles which we have by our own decisions accepted and made our own" (78). But these basic principles are not themselves true or false, unless "true" means "relatively true," where a principle is "true relative to John" in the sense that John decides to accept and live by the principle.

Hare observes that the complete justification of a nonbasic ethical decision is the description of the way of life of which the decision is a part. But if I then ask the basic question, "Why ought I live like that?" no further answer is possible. We can only ask the interlocutor to *decide* about which way she ought to live, "for in the end everything rests upon such a decision of principle" (69). Everything rests upon a personal decision because moral sentences do not correspond to any moral facts any more than commands do. For Hare, descriptive sentences such as "The door is shut" correspond to a fact, but "Shut the door!" and "You ought to shut the door" do not.

This antirealism about moral facts is connected with Hare's idea that ethical adjectives like "good" and "ought" do not refer (contra the logical realists) to value-properties of things. Neither do they merely express emotion and serve to influence causally others' emotions and actions. Rather, they express the speaker's *decision* to adhere to (to act and live by) the principle that is expressed by the sentence to which the adjective belongs. More exactly, they express the speaker's commitment to act by the principle and his prescription or recommendation that all others in similar circumstances act by the principle.

The same sort of ethical relativism, antirealism, and noncognitivism is implied by Toulmin's theory. As noted, Toulmin admits two sorts of ethical reasoning, the deduction of a moral sentence from a general principle accepted by one's community and the justification of a general communal principle by showing that it avoids suffering and inconvenience. Thus a particular moral sentence is true if it is deduced from a communal principle, and a communal principle is true if it results in preventing suffering. But the way of life of the community as a whole cannot be justified, and a sentence describing this way of life is not (absolutely) true or false; rather, it is something the person must decide to accept or reject, to conform to or not. The comparison between two communal ways of life, for example, the Muslim and Christian, is "a private one: which is to say, not that it *cannot* be reasoned about, but that, reason as you may, the final decision is personal" (153). It is not (absolutely) true or false that one communal way of life is morally better than another one and so a person must decide for herself whether to adopt the one way of life or the other.

At this point the distinction between framework sentences and sentences within a framework becomes relevant. The ultimate ethical principles are like the framework sentences discussed in section 11 in that they have sense but no truth-value and provide the criteria by which sentences within the framework are verified as true or false. The ethical sentences that have truth-values are the ones within a framework, and they are true merely relative to that framework. (Strictly speaking, then, these nonbasic sentences do not have truth-values either, if a truth-value means—as it normally does—an *absolute* truth-value.) In these and other respects, the "language-game relativism" that applies to nonethical discourse, such as religious and scientific discourse, also applies to ethical discourse.

Now if it is not the case that some ultimate ethical propositions are true and others false (for example, *that constitutional democracy is better than communism* or *that living by the law of the jungle is better than living by Christian standards*), then in this respect it is *arbitrary* which ultimate ethical propositions I decide to adhere to and live by. It is ultimately arbitrary how I choose to live, whether I choose to advance scientific knowledge or join a criminal subculture, whether I choose to pursue dictatorial power or democratic coexistence. And this means human life is pointless: it has no objective ethical meaning. Life has an objective ethical meaning only if there are absolutely true ethical principles (according to my definition of "objective" in the Preface), and this necessary condition is not met by the relativism of the ordinary language analysts.

(vi) Arbitrariness and Apathy

The nihilistic implication that human life is ethically meaningless is not appreciated or even admitted by the ordinary language analysts, so it is worth explaining it at some length. Toward this end, it would be helpful to compare the position implicitly reached by Hare, Toulmin, and Nowell-Smith with the largely similar position of the existentialists, particularly Sartre. But this is not to say that Sartre fully realized the nihilistic implications of ethical relativism. Sartre writes in *Being and Nothingness* that "my freedom is the unique foundation of values and that *nothing*, absolutely nothing, justifies me in adopting this or that particular value, this or that particular scale of values. As a being by whom values exist, I am unjustifiable. My freedom is anguished at being the foundation of values while itself being without foundation."[36] Sartre talks about anguish in this context, but it may well be doubted if anguish is a rational or realistic response to the unjustifiability of value-choices. I think a person who truly realized this ethical situation would become *apathetic*, because he would no longer be able to take his goals or way of life seriously. What is there to be anguished about if there is no possibility of making a mistake or making the wrong choice? And there is no such possibility because what counts as a mistake and wrong choice is itself an arbitrary matter (which is tantamount to saying that there are no mistakes, for a mistake by its very nature is nonarbitrary). To be in anguish implies that I am terribly concerned that I might go (absolutely) wrong, and such a concern is an expression of self-deception (bad faith) or error if there is no absolute right and wrong. Anguish implies an attitude of utmost seriousness and earnestness, but this attitude is not a realistic attitude if value-choices are completely arbitrary. In order to take my choices and endeavors seriously, *I cannot believe that it is arbitrary whether I choose to pursue A rather than not-A.* If it is arbitrary whether I struggle to advance communism or democracy, or environmental conservation or industrial exploitation, and I realize this, how can I pursue either alternative with passion or conviction? It is impossible to imagine that a Robespierre, Lenin, Gandhi, or others with a passionate revolutionary purpose in life held before their minds throughout their lives that "it is arbitrary whether one chooses to pursue the revolution rather than preserve the status quo."

Before dealing with what the ordinary language analysts have to say about this question, I want to pursue the Sartre connection a little further. About three or four years after writing *Being and Nothingness,* Sartre came to realize that apathy and despair are indeed more appropriate responses to the unjustifiability of value-decisions than anguish. He comments in his essay on *Baudelaire* that

> if you have begun by sampling to the point of nausea this consciousness, which has neither rhyme nor reason and which has to invent the rules which it proposes to obey, usefulness ceases to have any meaning at all. Life is nothing more than a game; man has to choose his own end without waiting for orders, notice or advice. Once a man has grasped this truth—that there is no other end in this life except the one that he had deliberately chosen, he no longer feels any great desire to look for one. . . . If we are to believe in an enterprise we need in the first place to be pitched into it; we have to ask ourselves what is the best method of bringing it to a successful conclusion; we must not ask ourselves what its object is. For a thoughtful person every enterprise is absurd. Baudelaire could not "take" his enterprises "seriously." He realized only too well that one only found in them what one had oneself

begun putting in them. . . . Nothing had any meaning except the meaning which consciousness gave it. This accounts for Baudelaire's profound sense of his own uselessness.[37]

Baudelaire felt useless because there is no intrinsic ethical purpose of human existence, if by "intrinsic ethical purpose" is meant one that is not invented but discovered by humans and that obtains regardless of whether people recognize or pursue it. There would be an intrinsic ethical purpose if it were true *that humans ought to live in such and such a way* and this truth obtained regardless of whether humans were aware of it. This would be a purpose built into the furniture of reality, so to speak. If there were such a purpose, we could "put ourselves to use" by endeavoring to realize it, but because there is no such purpose, "usefulness ceases to have any meaning at all[;] life is nothing more than a game." The expression "game" is indeed appropriate in the context of the present discussion because according to the ordinary language analysts life is at bottom just a *language-game* we arbitrarily invent and play.

(vii) Hare and the Ordinary Senses of "Arbitrary"

Yet the attitude of ethical despair is entirely foreign to Hare, Toulmin, Nowell-Smith, and the other ordinary language analysts. For them, such despair or nihilistic apathy is a result of linguistic confusion. Hare is very exercised to make this point. To begin with, he asserts, it is nonsense to say that ultimate ethical decisions are arbitrary or unfounded *because it is a misuse of ordinary language to describe them as arbitrary:* "This is not how we use the words 'arbitrary' and 'unfounded' " (69). Everything that could possibly be taken into account in justifying the decision has been taken into account, so it would instead be correct to say that it is the most well founded of decisions.

If Hare is right, then it would be misplaced to feel the malaise of life felt by Sartre's Baudelaire. His despair would be based on a linguistic confusion, a misunderstanding of the rules of ordinary use of such words as "arbitrary" and "unjustified." If he correctly understood the sense of these words, his malaise would disappear, and he would be able to live a "normal" and "well-adjusted" life.

But this "solution" to the problem of despair over the lack of objective ethical meaning is unsuccessful for two reasons: (i) it incorrectly describes the rules of the ordinary use of "arbitrary" and (ii) even if it correctly described them, it is invalid to infer from the claim that *it is not ordinarily correct to say that ultimate ethical decisions are arbitrary* to the conclusion that *it is not true to say these decisions are arbitrary.*

The second reason pertains to the problematic nature of the method of linguistic analysis that defines the ordinary language movement, and I shall postpone considering this until a later section. The first reason that supports our rejection of Hare's theory is that Baudelaire's apathy and nihilism are based on a *correct* ordinary use of "arbitrary." It is a commonplace of ordinary language analysts that the same word is often used in different senses in different contexts and that we should "look and see" to determine its sense in a given usage, but this commonplace seems to have been forgotten by Hare in his remarks about "arbitrary."

If we are confronted with a series of ethical principles among which we are to choose, for example, *that constitutional democracy is the best system, that communism is the best system, and that fascism is the best system,* and we can give no reason for our choice (namely, that one of these principles is true and the others false), then our choice is in this sense "arbitrary." We may reserve the expression "arbitrary$_1$" for this sense of "arbitrary." It is not arbitrary in Hare's sense ("arbitrary$_2$"), for everything that could be used to justify the principles has already been taken into account. What Hare means is that all the *effects* of obeying the principle and all the other principles *implicated* by the chosen principle are taken into account in choosing the principle. If I choose fascism, my choice may be "justified$_2$" in Hare's sense in that I have taken into account all the effects of fascism (for example, suppression of freedom of speech) and all the implicated principles, but it still may be "unjustified," in the sense that none of the principles have a truth-value (that is, an absolute truth-value), and therefore that I cannot justify my choice by saying, "I choose this principle because it is the true one or because it is soundly derived from a more basic true principle."

A defender of Hare might object that it is built into the ordinary sense(s) of "arbitrary" that what is arbitrary must be missing a *possible* justification. If no justification is even possible, then it is senseless to call a choice arbitrary. Ultimate ethical principles, Hare claims, lack (absolute) truth-values, and it is not logically possible that they possess them; it is no more possible for an ethical principle to be true or false than it is for a command to be true or false.

Now it may be conceded that it belongs to some ordinary uses of "arbitrary" that an arbitrary choice lacks a justification it might have had. But these are not the only ordinary uses. Consider a person choosing a stamp from a page of identical stamps; it is indifferent which one she chooses in that there is no possible reason to choose one rather than the other. We ordinarily call her choice arbitrary.

It is noteworthy that this is an example Hare himself gives in his later book *Freedom and Reason.* There he mentions as "a quite arbitrary business . . . the choice of one postage stamp from the sheet rather than another."[38] But Hare's point is that this sense of arbitrary requires that the choice "not matter" and that since the choice among ethical principles does matter, it is not arbitrary in this sense. It "matters very much" what ultimate choices we make, since it will affect the entire course of our life and our relation to the world.

But I submit that even for unjustifiable choices that "matter" in Hare's sense there is an ordinary sense of "arbitrary." There are at least three ordinary senses of "arbitrary." In one sense, a choice is arbitrary if it is made for no reason and yet there is possible reason the person could have taken into account; in this sense, an "arbitrary choice" is roughly similar to a "careless choice" (the person did not take sufficient care to examine the possible reasons). (This is "arbitrary$_2$.") In another sense, there is no possible justification and the choice does not matter; in this sense, one may say, "It is indifferent which one she chooses." (This may be called "arbitrary$_3$.") In still another sense, there is no possible reason and yet it does matter (in the sense that it will affect the rest of the person's life); this is the sense that applies to ultimate ethical decisions and is something one might ordinarily put by saying, "It is ultimately unjustifiable." (This is "arbitrary$_1$.")

The reason I am pursuing this issue at some length is to show (contra Hare, Toulmin, and Nowell-Smith) that it is built into ordinary usage and common sense that human life is objectively ethically meaningless if ethical sentences have the relativity attributed to them by these philosophers. It is not the case that nihilism arises only as a consequence of "falling into nonsense" as a consequence of "misusing ordinary language." "Nihilistic alienation" is no less a part of common sense than "cheerful conformity." "She believed that human life is meaningless" is a perfectly ordinary explanation of why somebody committed suicide. Hare and the others seem to think that "happily going about one's daily business" is built into the framework of ordinary life but that "despair and alienation" are not, yet this limited understanding of the dimensions of ordinary life may reflect merely a temperamental limitation of these philosophers. It is perhaps not unfair to say that they do not live on the deepest end of the spectrum of superficiality-depth that is found in ordinary life. There is no doubt of their intellectual sharpness, but intellectual acuteness is independent of depth of experience of life.

There is a fundamental difference between the personality type of a Hare or an Austin and that of a person who lives at the deeper end of the ordinary spectrum. A character such as Harry Haller in Herman Hesse's novel *Steppenwolf* is somebody whom these analysts would find antipathetic and would want to dismiss as "muddled," but I think most people would recognize Harry Haller as one who is concerned with problems that are real and that affect most people to some degree or other and at some time or other. Haller may live at an extreme end of the depth-level of life and at an extreme alienation from the surface dimension of life, but he is recognizable by most as living in a dimension of which they have a comprehension. Haller is described as a person quite unlike the typical ordinary language analyst:

> He was not a sociable man, as a matter of fact, he was unsociable to a degree I
> had never before experienced in anybody. He really was a wolf of the steppes,
> as he called himself, a strange, wild, shy—very shy—being from another

world than mine. I certainly did not know how deep the loneliness was into which his life drifted because of his disposition and destiny and how consciously he accepted this loneliness as his destiny.

. . . By chance I was there at the very moment when the Steppenwolf entered our house for the first time and became my aunt's lodger. . . . Altogether he gave the impression of having come out of an alien world, from another continent perhaps. He found it all very charming and a little odd. I cannot deny that he was polite, even friendly. He agreed at once and without objection to the terms for the rent and breakfast and so forth . . . and yet he seemed at the same time to be outside it all, to find it funny, what he was doing, and to be unable to take himself seriously. It was as though it were a very odd and new experience for him, occupied as he was with quite other concerns, to be renting a room and talking to people in German.

[At a public lecture given by an academic professor] the Steppenwolf threw me a quick look, a look which criticized both the words and the entire personality of the speaker—an unforgettable and frightful look which spoke volumes! It was a look that did not simply criticize that lecturer . . . it was indeed utterly and hopelessly sad . . . the Steppenwolf's look pierced our whole epoch, its whole overwrought activity, the whole surge and strife, the whole vanity, the whole superficial play of a shallow, opinionated intellectuality. And alas! The look went still deeper, went far below the faults, defects, and hopelessness of our time, our intellect, our culture alone. It went right to the heart of all humanity, it bespoke eloquently in a single second the whole despair of a thinker, of one who perhaps knew the full worth and meaning of man's life. It said: "See what monkeys we are! Look, such is man!" and at once all renown, all intelligence, all the attainments of the spirit, all progress towards the sublime, the great and the enduring in man fell away and became a monkey's trick![39]

Hare, Toulmin, Austin, and others try to represent the depth-level of common sense as not part of common sense at all but as an expression of "metaphysical nonsense" that certain philosophers fell into as a result of muddled thinking. But I would suggest that it is Hare, Austin, and the like who are "nonordinary," for it is a typical part of ordinary life to be concerned about objective meaning, and only a few relatively shallow-minded people like Hare and Austin and their followers do not take these questions seriously. Whence the complaint commonly made by ordinary people against analytic philosophers: they have "abandoned the important questions of philosophy." So far from being ordinary, Hare, Austin, and the like are "extraordinarily" superficial, regardless of how "intellectually skillful at argument" they may be. Perhaps this is a bit too harsh, but it seems at least true that Hare and associates do not fall at the deeper end of the depth-shallow continuum of normal human beings. Although some ordinary language analysts—Wittgenstein, for one—evince depth, it seems true to say of most that they can be described as "cheerful conformists who are not disturbed by the profound questions of life." They are happy performing their social function as teachers of the young and supporting and caring for their families, and the real problems that lie beneath this surface of life remain foreign to them.

Part of the difficulty for analytic philosophers to appreciate the depth-dimension of human life is that virtually all philosophers today are professors at colleges and universities, and the desire to conform to and live an institutional life is more rare in the deeper elements of humanity than in the more superficial. Owing to the psychological necessities of defending their self-esteem, the more superficial people typically do not want to acknowledge that there are deeper persons but instead try to dismiss them as "muddled thinkers" or as "psychologically abnormal." Another problem is that the more superficial humans, by virtue of being superficial, are unable to conceive of the depth-dimension in the lives of deeper people and thus must try and fit this depth-dimension into their own categories. Depth-dimensions are typically characterized as either instances of muddled thinking or cases of psychological pathology. The superficial person is not able to distinguish between a genuinely deep person and a shallow but muddled thinker and is not able to distinguish deep people from people with psychological pathologies (depressive disorders, manic phases accompanied by religious delusions, and so on).

I do not want to say that nihilism is the only deep attitude, but that it is *a* deep attitude. Another deep attitude is the life of the genuine mystics or moral saints. If nihilism is false and mysticism or profound moral idealism are true attitudes, that does not show nihilism is not deep. The deep/shallow contrast is not logically dependent on the true/false contrast.

Hare, Toulmin, Austin, and the like want to deny that the attitude of a Steppenwolf fits into the framework of common sense, but ordinary usage counts against them and in favor of a depth-level in ordinary life.

(viii) "Nothing Matters"

No doubt the ordinary language analysts will want to accuse my last remarks of reflecting a "muddled thinking" that is due to the misuse of ordinary language. But my account of the depth-dimension and the potential nihilism of ordinary life can be defended against such charges. I have already distinguished a relevant sense of "arbitrary," but other and related features of ordinary usage can be specified as well. Consider Hare's discussion of the ordinary use of the phrase "nothing matters" in his well-known essay "Nothing Matters."

Hare recounts an incident in which a young friend of his had been reading

Camus's novel *The Stranger* and had become convinced that nothing matters and had begun to despair. Consistently with his philosophical method, Hare thought the "correct way to start my discussion was to ask what was the meaning or function of the word 'matters' in our language."[40] When we say something matters, Hare continues, we express concern about that something. Thus, when we say something matters, it is always somebody's concern that is being expressed. Thus the expression "Nothing matters" expresses somebody's unconcern for absolutely everything. Now if the character in Camus's novel expressed his own absolute unconcern for everything, why should that cause Hare's young friend to despair? Why should his friend share the same sentiments? "I therefore asked him whether it was really true that nothing mattered to him. And of course it was not true . . . he was concerned not about nothing, but about many things" (244–45).

The point underlying this story, according to Hare, is that "my friend had not understood that the function of the word 'matters' is to express concern; he had thought mattering was something (some activity or process) that things did. . . . If one thinks that, one may begin to wonder what this activity is, called mattering; and one may begin to observe the world closely . . . to see if one can catch anything doing something that could be called mattering; and when we can observe nothing going on which seems to correspond to this name, it is easy for the novelist to persuade us that after all *nothing matters*" (246). But, Hare alleges, this is just a misunderstanding of the ordinary rules of use of "matters"—it is not used to describe an activity that things do but to express concern and our being disposed to make certain choices (244).

Camus and Hare's young friend had been attempting to express the idea that nothing is intrinsically of value; nothing possesses any value-properties. Hare's response is to say that "nothing matters" is not correctly used in this way. According to Hare, values are inherently values-for-someone, and they depend upon people's choices to be "real." Now Hare would say that to state that "human life is meaningless" because values are not intrinsic properties of things is analogous to saying "Nothing matters" because values are not intrinsic to things. This is a misuse of "meaningless"; "meaning" is always meaning-for-someone, and if something is said to be meaningless, we may always ask, For whom is it meaningless? "Human life is meaningless," if it has a sense at all, means simply that human life is meaningless to somebody, to somebody, say, who is entirely unconcerned about human life. In short, Hare's allegation is that "matters" and "the meaning or meaninglessness of life" are ordinarily used only in the sense of subjective meaning or meaninglessness and that it is a piece of metaphysical nonsense to use these expressions in a purported objective sense.

Now one may respond to this line of thinking by showing that ordinary objective senses of the expressions "Nothing matters" and "Human life is meaningless" can be specified. Indeed, this is immediately obvious, inasmuch as the question "What is the meaning of human life" is a part of ordinary use, and the two possible answers, whether they be true or false, are also part of ordinary use: "Human life is meaningless" and "The meaning of human life is [to do God's will, to do what is good, and so on]."

This line of thought recalls an analogous argument developed by Austin, that it makes sense to ask, "What is the point of standing on your head?" but that it makes no sense at all to ask, "What is the point of doing anything?"[41] Only specific acts have points or fail to have them; it is senseless to ask about the point or pointlessness of activity in general. Austin's allegation is that specific questions about this or that phenomenon belong to ordinary usage, but that only the muddled metaphysician asks general questions, questions about everything in general. But Austin has his mind fixated on the surface dimensions of ordinary life. "What is the point of doing anything?" is a *deep* ordinary question, and it has two possible ordinary answers, "There is no point at all" and "The point is to . . . [do God's will, do what is good, and so forth]." What is *unordinary* is the rejection of these questions and answers as "senseless because they lack an ordinary use."

Returning to Hare's essay "Nothing Matters," I can indicate that the expression "Nothing matters" also has a well-established ordinary use. One of its uses, which Hare tries to deny, is to indicate that nothing has intrinsic value, that all values are subjective and projected by humans, who arbitrarily decide to regard this or that as valuable. The sense in which Camus and Hare's young friend had been using this phrase is the objective and intrinsic sense, in which "Nothing objectively and intrinsically matters" means "Nothing has intrinsic value." Hare's friend had an appropriate response to this statement until Hare confused him by misusing ordinary language and maintaining that "Nothing matters" has only one ordinary sense. The situation of Hare's young friend is in fact the situation Hare should have himself been in had he correctly understood the ordinary implications of his own ethics. Hare recounts that before his friend's discovery that nothing matters he was "a cheerful, vigorous, enthusiastic young man" but that upon his discovery he became depressed: "He surprised us one morning by asking for cigarettes—he had not smoked at all up till then—and retiring to his room, where he smoked them one after the other, coming down hurriedly to meals, during which he would say nothing at all" (241). I think this person, like Sartre's Baudelaire, has the appropriate response to life if life is ethically meaningless.

First of all, what is missing from the world if nothing intrinsically matters? If things have intrinsic value-properties, then they can be argued to provide a *justification* for acting, and, for a person who wants to live an ethical life, the true belief that certain things have intrinsic value-properties can arguably provide an *incentive or motivation* for action (see chapter 6). But if nothing has intrinsic value-properties, then there is arguably nothing in things that can ethically justify an action and enable a true belief to be an ethical motivation for acting. What I had normally taken to be objective ethical justifications to act were in reality arbitrary projections on my part. It had seemed to me that certain things objectively ought to be done, but I recognize now that this seeming was delusive, and so I slip into a nihilistic apathy.

It might be objected that many people believe values are relative and subjectively projected and yet live enthusiastic and seriously committed lives. Many philosophers today argue that they can happily pursue their subjectively valuable projects; for example, E. D. Klemke, among others, makes this claim in the volume he edited, *The Meaning of Life*. Indeed, if values are relative, is not enthusiasm no less a "relatively valid" response to "the lack of intrinsic mattering" as an apathetic despair?

I would respond that I am not saying that if values are relative, then one ought to be apathetic. That would be a merely relative value-judgment (or else the contradiction that "values are relative, therefore it is absolutely true that one ought to despair"). Rather, I am saying that for a person who wants to live an objectively meaningful ethical life, apathy and despair are the only honest and sincere responses to the relativity of values. The person who professes value-relativism and yet enthusiastically pursues certain moral ends, such as alleviating the suffering of the disadvantaged, is living a compartmentalized life. On the one hand, she has the "intellectual belief" that she expresses on the occasions of theoretical discussions about morals ("It is my belief that morals are relative"), and yet in her daily life she is continually making intuitive or perception-based value-judgments that it is (absolutely) true that such and such ought to be done. If she is a social welfare worker, she will be making such intuitive judgments as *parents ought not to be beating their young daughter with a bicycle chain.* If this person actually lived in accordance with her intellectual belief that "morals are relative," she would instead have to make judgments like *it is (absolutely) neither true nor false that the parents ought not to be beating their daughter with a bicycle chain; it is arbitrary whether I choose to live by and enforce this value-statement or to live by and accept the opposite one ("the parents ought to beat the girl"); there is no reason to decide one way or the other.* However, this is not how the person makes value-judgments; if it were, she would be in the situation of Sartre's Baudelaire and Hare's young friend. Rather, she acts with outrage, compassion, or deep concern precisely because she judges *that the parents ought not to be beating the girl,* and to judge this, without the qualifications of truth-valuelessness or arbitrariness, is to make an absolute value-claim, even if the person is not explicitly and intellectually aware that she is making such judgments.

The point can be put more precisely. In our first-level moral beliefs, we tacitly believe there are objective moral facts. Our first-level moral beliefs tacitly involve the notion of moral truth as correspondence to moral facts (and do not involve the notion of truth valuelessness or truth as coherence with our other moral beliefs); I have argued for this claim about our first-level moral beliefs in chapters 1, 2, and 3 and will present further arguments in chapter 6. Our first-level moral beliefs imply there is an objective ethical meaning to human life; they imply that moral facts obtain independently of whether or not we believe they obtain, and that a moral belief is true if and only if it corresponds to some of these moral facts. The desire for an objective ethical meaning is, in effect, a desire that the commitment to moral realism implicit in our first-level moral beliefs be true.

If morals are relative, this is consistent with a variety of moral antirealist positions, for the sentence "Morals are relative" may be analyzed in a way consistent with emotivism or prescriptivism or with constructivism (for example, Rawls's constructivism, in which moral truth is defined in terms of its coherence with certain moral beliefs). Morals may be said to be relative to an individual, a culture, or the human species, but in each of these cases, moral choices will be arbitrary in the sense that none of them will be based on moral beliefs that correspond to moral facts that obtain independently of whether or not we believe them to obtain.

Moral relativism entails moral antirealism. The sentence "Moral attitudes vary among actual or possible individuals, cultures, or species, and there are no objective moral facts to which any of these attitudes correspond" implies "There are no objective moral facts." And the sentence "The truth of moral beliefs is relative to what actual or possible individuals, societies, or species believe" implies "The truth of moral beliefs is not their correspondence to moral facts that obtain independently of whether they are believed to obtain."

Moral antirealism need not be taken to imply moral relativism, if moral relativism is defined as the view that beliefs have a relative truth-value (for emotivists are antirealists who deny that moral beliefs have any truth-value). Talk of logical relations between moral antirealism and moral relativism, however, is problematic because (as I argued in the section on the ordinary language philosophy of religion) the notion of "relative truth" is logically incoherent. Moral relativism is coherent if it is formulated as the position that (a) in our first-level moral beliefs, we believe there are objective moral facts, but (b) these first-level beliefs are all mistaken and (c) different actual or possible individuals, cultures, or species have some incompatible first-level beliefs about what the (alleged) moral facts are. As far as I know, only Jean-Paul Sartre and John Mackie have advocated a logically coherent form of moral relativism.

At the risk of being repetitious, let me make my point about honesty and despair in this way: People who have the verbally and intellectually articulated belief that moral relativism or moral antirealism is true and yet whose first-level moral behavior shows an enthusiastic commitment to moral projects are in the following situation: Their "official philosophical beliefs" about moral antirealism are both logically inconsistent with and psychologically isolated from their intuitive first-level moral realist beliefs. In this sense, they can live happily but only at the price of abnegating their self-honesty. Of course, most philosophers who are moral anti-realists will strongly resist this conclusion; but the burden of proof is on them to refute the various arguments presented in this book that our first-level moral beliefs (evinced in our behavior as well as in the way we ordinarily talk) are implicitly committed to moral realism. (This commitment to moral realism is further argued in section 12.3.)

For a person who wants to live an ethical life and yet who sincerely believes that moral antirealism is true, the only honest way to live is to live in despair that there is no ethical justification or motivation for acting. It is to live in apathetic indifference to everything, not caring whether things happen in this way or in that way. Samuel Beckett portrays such a character in his novel *Malone Dies.* To borrow a phrase from Colin Wilson, Malone "saw too deep and too much" to be able to go on playing the game of life with its arbitrary rules.[42] Beckett writes,

> It is a game, I am going to play. . . . People and things ask nothing better than to play, certain animals too. All went well at first, they all came to me, pleased that someone should want to play with them. . . . But it was not long before I found myself alone, in the dark. That is why I gave up trying to play and took to myself for ever shapelessness and speechlessness, incurable wondering, darkness, long with stumbling with outstretched arms, hiding. . . .
>
> A little darkness, in itself, at the time, is nothing. You think no more about it and you go on. But I know what darkness is, it accumulates, thickens, then suddenly bursts and drowns everything.[43]

12.3. The Commitment of Ordinary Usage to Objective Ethical Meaning

In this section I present some arguments additional to those in chapter 2 that first-level moral talk is committed to objective ethical meaning, even though (as I argued in the previous section) ordinary second-level talks allows as a genuine possibility that morals be relative and despair the honest attitude.

The ordinary language analysts claim that ultimate ethical sentences are neither true nor false. But this conflicts with ordinary usage because it is ordinarily accepted that it is either true or false, for example, that "communism is better than democracy," that "the Christian way of life is better than the Muslim way of life," and the life. Hare and Toulmin say that it all comes down to a personal decision in the end, and in a sense they are right, but the ordinary reason for this is not that the principles are neither true nor false but that *we do not know for sure if they are true or false,* and in the absence of such knowledge each of us must make his best guess.

Ordinarily, this "personal decision" is permitted for certain controversial ethical principles but not for ones that are uncontroversial. It violates ordinary usage to say, for example, "It all comes down to a personal decision in the end as to whether *it is wrong to torture children for the fun of it.*"

But the issue is more complicated than this. As I indicated, there is both first- and second-level ordinary talk about ethical matters. First-level talk (for example, "You ought not beat your dog") is committed to absolute values, as I shall argue shortly. But second-level ethical talk leaves open the question as to whether values are absolute. The second-level sentence "Values are relative" is built into ordinary usage (of late-twentieth-century Western culture), but it is also built into ordinary usage that the relativity or absoluteness of values is an open question and a matter for disagreement and debate. "John says that morals are relative, but David says they are not" is a perfectly good example of an ordinary sentence. Second-level ordinary moral talk, however, is too vague, ambiguous, and logically unrigorous to be able to *resolve* the issue about the relativity of morals. For example, many people confuse "Morals are relative" with "People hold different moral beliefs," and many others confuse "Morals are relative" with "There is no way to decide which are the absolutely true moral judgments." Or I should say that the ordinary sense of "Morals are relative" is ambiguous as among several different propositions, and the technical philosophical sense of this sentence (in which I use it) is only one of the senses it has in ordinary use. Another example of the inadequacy of this talk is that the invalid inference "Morals are relative, so we ought to respect the values of other people and cultures" is a more or less established part of ordinary second-level moral talk. It was the failure to appreciate that second-level moral talk and other vestiges of philosophical talk belong to ordinary language that led ordinary language philosophers to the false belief that philosophical perplexities arise only in technical philosophical theories and that ordinary language is "clear as it stands." If Wittgenstein is right that "ordinary language is alright as it is," then we must accept that the invalid inferences, fallacies of equivocation, and so on that belong to ordinary philosophical talk are also all right as they are.

But it is a different issue as to whether moral realism is built into first-level ordinary use. Although second-level ordinary moral discourse is too unrigorous to decide this issue, a technical philosophical investigation of first-level ordinary moral talk may contribute to resolving the issue. Of course, determining this fact about first-level ordinary usage cannot answer the question about whether *there is* an objective ethical meaning of life, as I shall indicate in the next section, but it does provide some evidence relevant to this question; moreover, it is an interesting issue in its own right, and for these reasons it is a project worth undertaking.

I shall contribute to the goal of showing that first-level ordinary moral talk is committed to objective ethical meaning by responding to Toulmin's and Hare's arguments against this thesis. Toulmin and Hare argue that ordinary language is not committed to objective ethical meaning by arguing that ordinary language is not committed to the view that things have intrinsic moral properties. If things have intrinsic moral properties, then all the moral sentences that correspond to these things-as-possessing-moral-properties (the moral facts) would be (absolutely) true moral sentences. If things do not possess value-properties, then there are no moral facts and therefore nothing to which some ethical sentences could correspond and nothing that could make any ethical sentence (absolutely) true.

Toulmin intends to "show, by comparing the ways in which we talk about properties and values, that in at least one important respect values differ from *all* such properties" (9). Toulmin alleges that there are three types of properties: simple qualities (for example, redness), complex qualities (for example, being 259-sided), and scientific qualities (for example, radiating such-and-such type of electromagnetic radiation). The simple and complex qualities are directly perceived (but the complex qualities are directly perceived only after going through a certain routine, for example, counting the 259 sides); the scientific qualities are not directly perceived. If goodness is a property, Toulmin contends, it must be of one of these three types. I shall content myself with showing that Toulmin fails to demonstrate that goodness is not a directly perceived simple quality.

Toulmin advances as one of his two strongest arguments that disagreements about simple qualities (for example, about whether a lemon we are both looking at is yellow or gray) must be due to (1) organic defect, (2) deliberate deception, or (3) linguistic differences (for example, one person uses "gray" to mean what the other person means by "yellow"), but that disagreements about values are often due to none of these three sources (17). It follows, according to Toulmin, that goodness is not a simple quality. But this does not follow. The three sources of disagreement mentioned are exhaustive only for readily apparent sensible qualities like yellowness. They do not pertain to nonsensible simple qualities. Specifically, an organic defect is hardly relevant to disagreement about moral matters. Rather, *defect of character* is relevant to grasping moral qualities. Ordinarily, one might say that the reason a certain person, for example, an extremely vicious person, systematically did cruel things is that his character or moral sensibility was impaired by bad experiences earlier in his life, for example, by persistent and severe child abuse or by being tortured for years on end when he was a prisoner of war. Ordinarily, defects of character may also be attributed to an indoctrinating education or a rigid religious upbringing; the reason a person cannot grasp certain moral values, we think, is that his moral sensibility or "moral sense" is distorted by his upbringing. For example, in the debate about abortion some may say that "pro-life advocates" have their moral sense impaired by a fundamentalist or Catholic religious upbringing, whereas others may say that "pro-choice advocates" have their moral sense impaired by their "falling away from God" or their "secular humanist education." This way of viewing things suggests that moral values are intrinsic to things but that the human moral sense is fragile and easily distorted by a bad education or bad experiences. The combination of the fragility of this moral sense with the diversity of educations and experiences explains why there is much more disagreement about moral values than about sensible qualities (physical sense organs are not nearly so fragile). Innate character traits, such as a natural sensitivity to the feelings of others or a naturally volatile temper that makes a person prone to angry outburst, are also said to be relevant to a person's ability to apprehend what ought or ought not be done. And it is sometimes said that the psychological category of a "sociopath" refers to a person who is "born without a conscience," which suggests that the sociopath is born without a moral sense somewhat as a congenitally blind person is born without a visual sense. Of course, my various remarks here are not conclusive, but they suggest that Toulmin's argument is not strong enough as it stands to rule out the "value-property and moral sense" theory.

Toulmin's second argument is even weaker because it is based on a transparent fallacy of equivocation upon "goodness" and a misrepresentation of ordinary usage. Toulmin considers a man who we agree is good and who consistently does good things—is kind, sober, modest, and so on. Ordinarily, we might say of this man, "If ever a man knew what goodness was, he does!" (23). And yet, Toulmin continues, if I "asked him whether, when, making up his mind what to do, he is conscious of observing any 'non-natural property', any 'fittingness', in the action he decides on, [he would say] that he isn't" (23).

The first problem with this argument is that "non-natural property" and "fittingness" are technical philosophical terms (of Moore and Broad, respectively) and are not ordinarily used to refer to the property of goodness. This fact by itself suffices to explain why the ordinary person says he is not conscious of any such property. Indeed, he probably has no real idea what "non-natural property" means.

Second, "conscious of observing" is ordinarily used to refer to our awareness of readily apparent physical properties, not nonphysical and nonsensible properties such as goodness would be if ethical nonnaturalism were true. Thus the fact that the person says he does not "observe" goodness does not show that he believes he is not comprehending goodness when choosing among different actions.

Third, the original sentence "If ever a man knew what goodness was, he does!" uses "goodness" in the sense of *the kinds of things that are good,* and the fact that an ordinary person may know this does not show that he has the philosophical acuteness to separate clearly the kinds of things that are good from the property they possess of being good. Thus, Toulmin is using an equivocation upon "goodness" in this argument.

Hare also presents two arguments for the thesis that first-level ordinary moral talk is not committed to value-properties. The first argument concerns indicatives and imperatives. If moral sentences ascribed value-properties, Hare maintains, they would be sentences describing what is the case, namely, that something possesses a value-property. They would be indicatives, statements of fact. But no indicative can entail an imperative. Thus, ethical sentences cannot ascribe value-properties because it is a rule of their use that they entail imperatives.

Hare offers the following definition of "entailment": "A sentence P entails a sentence Q if and only if the fact that a person assents to P but dissents from Q is a sufficient criterion for saying that he has misunderstood one or the other of the sentences."[44] Hare regards assent to an indicative as *believing* it and assent to an imperative as *doing or resolving to do* the action the imperative enjoins. Thus, Hare's argument is that assent to an ethical sentence implies assent to an imperative and that assent to the imperative consists in doing or resolving to do the action indicated by the ethical sentence. If ethical sentences were indicatives, assent to them would consist in believing them, not acting upon them, and this suffices to show they are not indicatives (because we do in fact act upon them).

The proponent of objective ethical meaning could respond that ordinary ethical sentences do not entail imperatives and therefore that Hare's argument fails to show that ethical sentences are not indicatives. For example, "God is perfectly good" does not entail an imperative and yet is an ethical evaluation. But it may be admitted that some ethical sentences do entail imperatives. Hare seems right that "You ought not to smoke in this compartment" entails "Do not smoke in this compartment."

But what supports Hare's contention that no ethical sentence would entail an imperative if it were an indicative? Hare notes that nothing can appear in the conclusion of a valid deductive inference that is not implicit in the conjunction of the premises; thus, if there is an imperative in the conclusion, there must be an imperative implicit in the premises.

But the proponent of objective ethical meaning could respond that an imperative *is* implicit in the relevant ethical indicative, for the ethical indicative *does* entail the imperative. It is a fact of ordinary usage, the proponent may say, that the indicative "It is true that you ought to give him the money back" entails the imperative "Give him the money back!" Hare would deny that this ethical sentence is an indicative *because it entails an imperative,* but what argument does he give for his dogma that "no imperative can be entailed by an indicative"?

The only argument Hare gives for his dogma is based on a fallacy of equivocation. Hare says a descriptive or factual statement (a typical indicative) has sense if "there is something that would be the case if it were true."[45] These are statements of fact. The theory of value-properties is committed to the thesis that ethical statements are statements of fact; they state that something is the case, namely, that something in fact possesses some property (some value-property). But no matter of fact can entail that something *be done.*

But Hare's argument equivocates upon "statement of fact." There are two senses of "statement of fact," one in which something is stated to *in fact* possess some property and a second sense in which something is stated to *in fact* possess some factual (descriptive) property. Now it may be granted that a statement of fact in the second sense never entails an imperative, since something's possession of a factual property does not entail anything about what is to be done. But this truth does not entail that statements of fact in the first sense never entail imperatives. It may be argued that some statement that something *in fact* possesses some value-property does entail an imperative. "The suffering of the child *in fact* possesses the property of *being a state that ought to be alleviated;* therefore, *alleviate it!*" I think this inference is valid. Of course, it may be objected that there are no value-properties and therefore that the first statement is senseless. But I would note that in the present context this objection is tantamount to begging the question because Hare is attempting to demonstrate that there are no value-properties on the basis of premises about indicatives and imperatives. He cannot nonfallaciously assume as an additional premise that there are no value-properties. Thus, Hare's animadversions on indicatives and imperatives are insufficient to show that ordinary moral talk does not ascribe value-properties.

Hare presents a further argument for the thesis that there is no property corresponding to "good" or "ought to be." Hare notes that the meaning (sense) of simple property-words such as "red" is explained ostensively, by pointing out various red objects and contrasting them with objects that are not red. "Red" refers to the quality that the various red objects have in common. But pointing to the various things to which we apply "good" gives us not the sense of the word (its evaluative sense) but merely criteria of its application. Hare argues that if "good" had an ostensively explainable sense and were similar to property-words like "red," then we could "find something that we can point to in any class of [good] objects whatever, and say 'There you are, that's what makes a thing good; when you've learnt to identify that elusive quality, you will know the meaning of the word.' "[46] But because there is nothing common to the various things that are good that makes them all good (for example, what makes a charitable deed good is not what makes aesthetic appreciation good), there is no common quality that is the referent of "good."

This argument, like Hare's first argument, is based on a fallacy of equivocation, in this case upon the phrase "what makes a thing good." His argument contains the premise that there is nothing in common to the various good things (charitable deeds, the pursuit of knowledge, aesthetic appreciation, paying back one's debts, and so forth) that makes them all good, where "what makes a thing good" refers to the nonnormative descriptive properties of the actions, emotions, and so on, that are the criteria for the application of the word "good." But Hare concludes from this that there is nothing that "makes them all good," where this phrase has the different sense of a value-property that supervenes upon the relevant descriptive properties of the things. This conclusion does not follow because the absence of a non-normative descriptive characteristic common to all good things does not entail that there is no common value-property of things that is the referent of "good." This absence is consistent with the claim that there is a property of goodness that super-venes upon different nonnormative, descriptive properties for different classes of actions or attitudes.

On the other hand, if Hare is using "what makes a thing good" only to refer to the supervenient value-property, then his premise that there is nothing common to all good things that "makes them good" is unsupported by his observation that no common property can be "pointed to." The idea that goodness is not "something we can point to and say 'There you are, that's what makes a thing good' " amounts to a refutation of the property-theory of goodness only if goodness is construed as some sensible property to which one can point. But the theory that goodness is an intrinsic property of things is not that goodness is a sensible property like round-ness; it is not something that can be pointed to or otherwise ostended. Rather, it is something we comprehend as supervening upon (at least in some cases) properties to which we can point.

Thus, I conclude that Hare has not given us any reason to think that first-level ordinary moral talk does not imply that goodness is an intrinsic property of things. Toulmin and Hare have failed to impugn the thesis that our ordinary first-level language carries an implicit commitment to the idea that human life has an ob-jective ethical meaning. But whether this commitment entails that human life *does* have an objective ethical meaning is a different matter altogether, as we will now see.

12.4. The Inadequacy of the Ordinary Language Method to Answer the Question about Life's Meaning

A central topic of this book is whether the linguistic method can provide an answer to the question Does human life have an objective meaning? Philosophy may be viewed in part as *the attempt to find and use some method to answer the question about the objective meaning of life,* and analytic philosophy may be viewed in part as *the attempt to find and use a linguistic method to answer this question.* If one adopts this perspective on analytic philosophy, one may say that the key idea of the ordinary language movement is that *describing the ordinary uses of religious and ethical sen-tences* is the method by which the question about life's meaning may be answered.

So far in this chapter I have not evaluated this method per se. My criticisms have been largely of the results of the analysts' employment of this method; I have argued that in many instances the analysts misdescribed ordinary usage. My aim in this section is to determine if the ordinary language method, *even if correctly employed*, can answer the question about life's meaning; I shall argue that it cannot (even though it can supply some evidence relevant to answering this question).

In the Preface, I defined a linguistic method as a procedure for deducing conclusions in the various philosophical disciplines from premises about the nature of linguistic sense. The ordinary language method is a procedure for deducing conclusions about minds, matter, God, the good, and so forth from premises describing the ordinary uses of such expressions as "minds," "matter," "God," and "the good." One problem with this method can be highlighted by discussing the implications this method has for descriptive sentences. The ordinary language method implies that if a descriptive expression has an ordinary use, then there must be, in reality, a fact or situation that it describes; this method implies, furthermore, that if a descriptive expression has no ordinary use or runs counter to ordinary use, then there are no states of affairs corresponding to it. This view is encapsulated in a standard argument-form of ordinary language philosophers:

1. It is correct ordinary language to use the descriptive sentence "Fx" in circumstances of the sort C.
2. There are circumstances of the sort C in which "Fx" is used,
3. Therefore, "Fx" is true in some circumstances.
4. Therefore, there obtains the state of affairs Fx.

An example of an employment of this argument-form is Austin's "refutation" of the theory that we are immediately aware of sense-data rather than material things. Austin notes that it is "quite natural and proper to say 'That patch of red there *is* the book'" and concludes from this that the red patch *is* the book. More generally, Austin argues from

5. "Coloured shapes, patches of colours, etc. can quite often and correctly be said to *be* the things we see"[47]

to

6. It is the case in many instances that colored shapes, patches of colors, and so on *are* the material things we see.

But this argument is invalid because "being ordinarily correct to say" does not entail "being true to say." Suppose at a Sunday school session a child says to another, "God damn you!" and an adult berates the child, "That is a blasphemy against God." Now

7. It is correct to say in these circumstances, "That is a blasphemy against God"

does not entail

8. There is a blasphemed God.

Somebody who argued from (7) to (8) commits the fallacy of equivocating upon "correct." If (7) is true, then "correct" means "appropriate" or "conventionally proper," but if (7) is to entail (8), "correct" must mean "true." The propriety of a saying is determined by the *beliefs* people typically hold in a certain context, and these beliefs need not be true. A Sunday school session is a context in which it is normally assumed by the participants that there is a God, and this assumption plays a major part in the determination of what it is proper or improper to say in the session. The context consists in part of the participants' having this belief, but it does not consist in this belief being true.

It will be of no avail to defend Austin from this charge by introducing his oft-quoted remark that "ordinary language is *not* the last word . . . it is the *first* word"[48] because in spite of this official pronouncement, Austin's practice was to treat ordinary language as the last word, at least in the sense that he (and other ordinary language philosophers) frequently employed the invalid argument-form (1)–(4).

But criticizing the ordinary language method is not so easy as this. For some defenders of this method claim that (1)–(4) is validly employed only in cases of ordinary language expressions that require ostension to be learned. Malcolm writes, "In the case of all expressions the meanings of which must be *shown* and cannot be explained, as can the meaning of 'ghost', it follows, from the fact that they are ordinary expressions in the language, that there have been *many* situations of the kind which they describe; otherwise so many people could not have learned the correct use of those expressions."[49] Malcolm gives as examples the expressions "material thing," "to the left of," and "earlier than." But his argument is unsound. All that is required to learn the correct use of such expressions is that there be situations which normally *seem* to be of the kind the expressions describe. In order to learn "material thing," it is necessary that there be situations in which there normally seem to be material things, but there need not be any material things. It is possible, for example, that in these situations there really are only sense-data, which deceptively appear to us to be material things or parts or properties of material things.

Another invalid argument-form is

8. The descriptive sentence "Fy" has no ordinary use or is contrary to ordinary use.
9. Therefore, "Fy" does not have the truth-value of true.
10. Therefore, there is no y that is F.

For example, it might be argued, if "Physical objects do not have color" runs contrary to ordinary use, then it cannot be true and there are no colorless physical objects. But this is invalid because being contrary to ordinary use implies merely being contrary to beliefs or what seems to be the case, not being contrary to truths or what is the case.

A related problem affects the attempt to derive normative conclusions, conclusions about what ought to be, from statements about correct ordinary usage. It is noteworthy that the ordinary language ethical philosophy, *by its very method*, is based on an invalid fact/value (is/ought) inference. Consider, for example, Toulmin's procedure. He says the aim of his ethical theory is to determine "which of the reasons [for ethical judgments] are good reasons" (3) and that we can determine which reasons are good if we discover the *function* of ethical judgments. The function of ethical judgments is found by examining ordinary usage, that is, by investigating "the occasions, on which we are in fact prepared to call judgements 'ethical' and decisions 'moral'" (160). As noted in an earlier section, Toulmin concludes that we call decisions "moral" (that is, "morally good") when they conform to accepted social practices or aim to prevent suffering. Toulmin's argument has this structure:

1. We ordinarily call a decision morally good when it conforms to an accepted social practice or aims to prevent suffering.

Therefore,

2. A decision is morally good if it conforms to an accepted social practice or aims to prevent suffering.

This argument is invalid for two reasons, one the already familiar one that "it is correct ordinary usage to call x 'an F'" does not entail "x is an F"; and the other that it is an inference of a value from a fact. If (1) entails (2), then the following inference is valid:

3. *It is the case that* conformist decisions are called "morally good."

Therefore

4. *It ought to be the case that* decisions are conformist.

But this is invalid because ought-statements are not entailed by is-statements. What follows from (1) or (3) is merely that conformist decisions ordinarily *seem* to be the sort of decisions that ought to be made. And this conclusion is consistent with the statement that this seeming is deceptive or delusive.

These considerations also show that my argument in the previous section that ordinary usage is committed to objective ethical meaning does not provide the conclusion that there is objective ethical meaning. It does, however, provide *some* evidence that is relevant to the argument that life is meaningful or meaningless. But further evidence or arguments are needed, as I shall endeavor to show in part II.

Part II
Linguistic Essentialism

4 The Essentialists' Method of Linguistic Analysis

13. Introduction

Linguistic essentialism emerged in the 1960s, reached full flower in the early 1970s, and remains one of the predominant philosophical movements in the 1990s. The emergence of linguistic essentialism differed from that of logical positivism and ordinary language analysis; each of these two movements originally emerged as critical responses to the prior philosophical movement. The decline of the ordinary language analysis movement was due to criticisms coming not from essentialism but from other movements that succeeded ordinary language analysis.

One of these successor movements is sometimes called the school of Scottish criticism. Consisting of E. Gellner, C. Mundle, P. Heath, L. G. Cohen, and others, it produced mostly critical studies of the ordinary language philosophers, with few positive theses of its own. A second source of criticisms came from such philosophers as the later Carnap, Ayer, Russell, and Moore (and younger philosophers influenced by them, such as Roderick Chisholm), who had contributed to the philosophical tendencies that ordinary language philosophers challenged or replaced.

The third and most influential source of criticisms came from the dominant philosophical movement in America and Australia during the 1950s and 1960s, which has no widely accepted name but which may be called postpositivist physicalism. This movement included W. V. O. Quine, Wilfred Sellars, Adolf Grünbaum, Carl Hempel, J. J. C. Smart, D. M. Armstrong, and many others and is continued today by a younger generation of physicalists, among them David Lewis,

Paul Churchland, Patricia Churchland, Paul Humphreys, William Lycan, Hartry Field, Michael Devitt, John Post, James Fetzer, Eliot Sober, Alvin Goldman, Daniel Dennet, Wesley Salmon, and many others. Although linguistic essentialism did not become a leading movement until the early 1970s, and in this sense began after the postpositivist physical movement, both movements still flourish today. Indeed, postpositivist physicalism and linguistic essentialism have been the two main movements in analytic philosophy in the 1970s, 1980s, and 1990s; no other analytic movement even compares with them in influence and acceptance. (For example, Michael Dummet's antirealism and Bas Van Fraassen's constructive empiricism are important new trends but are not nearly as influential as postpositivist physicalism or linguistic essentialism.)

The postpositivist physicalist movement began with the work of Quine and others, whose early philosophizing was a critique of the basic theses of both logical positivism and ordinary language analysis. Specifically, the main theoretical substance of early postpositive physicalism was a critique of the positivist physicalism of Otto Neurath and Rudolf Carnap. The new physicalists rejected the observation language / theoretical language distinction (the new claim was that all observation is theory laden); they rejected the positivists' distinction between empirical statements and analytic truths by convention (whether because of a rejection of analyticity or because of a rejection of the idea that analyticity was merely conventional); they rejected the idea that individual sentences had meaning or could be verified by themselves, as opposed to the entire theory to which they belonged (holism); and, most important, they held the belief that *physical reality is the microscopic or macroscopic referents of the theoretical sentences in the physical sciences,* rather than the ordinary and "directly observable" middle-sized physical objects to which an alleged observation language referred.

Of course, there are numerous other ideas associated with postpositivist physicalism, for example, the successive positions in the philosophy of mind: the Identity Theory of U. T. Place and Smart, the functionalism of Putnam and others, and the cognitive science movement of Churchland, Goldman, Fetzer, and others. I shall not concentrate on postpositivist physicalism in this book, however, despite the fact that it is at least as influential in contemporary analytic philosophy as linguistic essentialism. The reason is that postpositivist physicalism has less to say about the question of the ethical and religious meanings of human life than does linguistic essentialism (with some rare exceptions, such as the work of John Post, which I shall discuss in chapter 6 and the Conclusion).

The focus of part II of this book is linguistic essentialism, a movement originated by Ruth Barcan Marcus and others, such as Stig Kanger, Jaakko Hintikka, and Alvin Plantinga. In the present chapter, I shall explain the philosophy of language of this movement. In chapter 5, I shall discuss the philosophy of religion,

concentrating on the work of Alvin Plantinga in his *The Nature of Necessity.* In
chapter 6, I shall discuss the application of linguistic essentialism to metaethics and
normative ethics in the work of R. M. Adams, David Brink, and Thomas Hurka. I
shall modify and develop Hurka's perfectionism, so as to construct a viable theory
of the ethical meaning of human life, and (in the Conclusion) a pantheistic theory
of the religious meaning of human life. These theories of ethical and religious
meaning will be the positive result of the critical study of the various analytic
movements undertaken in chapters 1–6.

In the present chapter, my topic is the essentialists' philosophy of language.
During the 1970s, 1980s, and early 1990s, the prevalent view of the history of
linguistic essentialism was that the major ideas were originated in the work of Saul
Kripke, namely, in his articles on modal logic in 1959 and 1963 and especially in his
writings on the philosophy of language in 1971 ("Identity and Necessity") and
1972 ("Naming and Necessity"). Kripke is commonly thought to have originally
developed the theory that proper names are rigid designators, to have developed
the modal argument for direct reference, to have made the distinction between a
reference-fixing description and the semantic content of a name, the epistemic
argument for direct reference, to have developed the argument for a posteriori
necessities, to have presented the theses that identities between names are necessary if true and that variables are rigid designators, to have developed the semantics
for modal logic that allows for rigid designators and nontrivial essential attributions, the distinction between logical and metaphysical necessity, and other ideas. I
have argued in "Marcus, Kripke and the Origin of the New Theory of Reference,"
"Marcus and the New Theory of Reference," and "Rigid Designation and A
Posteriori Necessity: A History and Critique"[1] that Marcus originated most of
these ideas. This is now becoming a more accepted idea, primarily owing to the influential editorial work of James H. Fetzer and Paul W. Humphreys.[2] For example,
in the August, 1995 volume of *Synthese* on the New Theory of Reference, edited by
Fetzer and Humphreys, Hintikka and Gabriel Sandu write, "The originators of the
new theory are Ruth Marcus and Saul Kripke," and they credit such crucial
notions as rigid designation to Marcus, for example, when they write, "Ruth
Marcus advocated as early as in 1947 logical principles that embody the necessary
identity thesis. . . . This Marcus did years before she formed the rigid designation
idea in 1961."[3] David Kaplan, who in his 1970s writings referred to Kripke as the
leading figure in developing the New Theory of Reference, now acknowledges that
Marcus is the main figure and wrote in 1995, "Marcus is a brilliant, original,
learned, tenacious, and productive scholar, many of whose early out-of-fashion
ideas have now come into fashion and have largely swept the competition away. . . .
The topics to which Marcus has contributed are high on the agenda of philosophers throughout the world."[4]

As I briefly noted in "Rigid Designation and A Posteriori Necessity," Devitt was the first person to recognize (or at least publish) the idea that Marcus originated the concept of rigid designation; he stated this in 1989 in his article "Against Direct Reference."[5] Because Devitt has not received sufficient recognition for his role in correcting the inaccurate historical account of the origins of the New Theory of Reference that has prevailed from the 1970s until the mid-1990s, I will begin my discussion by explaining and evaluating how he implicitly derives the notion of rigid designation from Marcus's work (although I will argue that his way of deriving his notion is not fully adequate).

I have also argued in "Rigid Designation and A Posteriori Necessity" that Peter Geach originated the causal theory of reference for proper names,[6] contrary to the standard assumption that the theory was first stated by Kripke and Keith Donnellan. I shall not repeat in this chapter the comparisons between Marcus's, Kripke's, Geach's and Donnellan's work that I presented in my articles in Fetzer's and Humphrey's (eds.) *The New Theory of Reference* (Kluwer Academic Publishers, 1998) and I will not reproduce the material in these articles. Rather, I shall focus on formulating the basic ideas that constitute the linguistic method of the essentialists; most of these ideas originally appeared in the work of C. I. Lewis, Marcus, Carnap, Kanger, Hintikka, Geach, Plantinga, and others. The crucial idea is rigid designation, first developed in its "direct reference" version by Marcus (1961) and in its descriptivist version by Plantinga (1969 and 1970), and I shall present and contrast their theories of rigid designation, as well as give some background in modal logic that I did not present in my three earlier articles. My decision to omit from this chapter the material in my three articles on the relation between Marcus's and Kripke's ideas will not result in an incomplete history of linguistic essentialism; if the arguments in these three articles are sound, the basic ideas of linguistic essentialism are not originally found in the work of Kripke, and thus a historical account of the original sources need not concentrate on his work.

In chapter 5, I shall explain and critically examine the major philosophy of religion of the linguistic essentialist movement, Alvin Plantinga's. I shall explain his ontological argument and his "free will defence" against the problem of evil. Much of my effort in chapter 5 will be critical, and I shall conclude that there is a sound deductive argument from evil. This conclusion implies that there is no objective religious meaning of human life, at least if "religious" is understood to mean monotheistic.

In chapter 6, I begin by explaining Adams's and Brink's use of linguistic essentialism to argue for moral realism. I shall conclude that they made significant advances in the metaethical argument for moral realism, but that some of their specific arguments for moral realism do not succeed. But most of chapter 6 is devoted to establishing a certain normative ethics, perfectionism (the good is to develop a thing's essential nature). I examine Hurka's use of linguistic essentialism to establish a certain normative ethics, namely, a novel version of perfectionism. Apart from its connection to linguistic essentialism, Hurka's perfectionism seems important inasmuch as it is arguably the most important advance in perfectionist ethics since Aristotle's *Nicomachean Ethics.* Although the substance of Hurka's perfectionism is largely plausible, I shall criticize his nonnaturalist formulation of it. In the second half of chapter 6, I shall develop at length a new version of perfectionism that is based more extensively on the method of linguistic essentialism than is Hurka's theory; this new perfectionism will be called global, naturalist perfectionism. Although chapter 6 explores new territory in the *history* of philosophy (Essentialist Ethics has never been recognized, let alone discussed, as a historical movement in analytic philosophy), the main substance of the chapter will be the theory of an objective ethical meaning of human life I construct under the name of a moral realist "global, naturalist perfectionism."

The conclusions I reach about a perfectionist ethical meaning of human life lead naturally to the thesis of the Conclusion of this book, that there is an objective religious meaning of human life if "religious" is understood to mean pantheistic. In the Conclusion, I shall argue for a naturalistic pantheism, namely, that the natural universe is the rigid designatum of "the holy."

14. The Formal Basis of Linguistic Essentialism in Modal Logic

The extensional logic of Whitehead and Russell (earlier developed by Frege) constituted the formal backbone of both logical positivism and ordinary language analysis. But a certain intensional logic, specifically, modal logic, constituted the formal basis for linguistic essentialism. Modal logic is about the argument-forms that involve the notions of necessity and possibility. Modal logic shares the vocabulary of standard propositional or predicate logic and extends these logics by adding new terms (for example, "possibly," "necessarily," "strictly implies," and so on), new theorems, and new inference-forms involving the new terms.

The first crucial step occurred in 1918 with the first axiomatization of modal propositional logic, in C. I. Lewis's *Survey of Symbolic Logic* (1918); a more complete presentation appeared in Lewis's and Langford's book *Symbolic Logic* (1932).

There are various systems of modal propositional logic. In his 1918 work, Lewis presented system S3, and in the 1932 work systems S1, S2, S4, and S5 are presented. In 1937, R. Feys presented system T (later proved equivalent to G. H. Von Wright's system M of 1951). Although S5 is now widely taken as the standard system, Lewis relegated it (and S4) to an appendix of the 1932 work and rejected it as an unacceptable system of strict implication. In spite of its early neglect, S5 is the modal logic system that underlies most work in linguistic essentialism. The crucial feature of S5 is the thesis that the modal status of a proposition is a matter of necessity. Specifically, S5 states that if a proposition p is possibly true, then *it is necessarily true* that p is possibly true; if a proposition q is necessarily true, then *it is necessarily true* that q is necessarily true. Since S5 is widely assumed in the philosophy of language, metaphysics, philosophy of religion, and so on of linguistic essentialism (with some exceptions, for example, Nathan Salmon's article in the *Philosophical Review*, "The Logic of What Might Have Been" [1989] argues for system T), I shall show how S5 can be constructed by adding axioms to some weaker systems, namely, systems T and S4.

System T takes for its axioms all the truth-functional tautologies and the following two modal axioms (the box means "Necessarily" or "It is necessarily true that" and the diamond means "Possibly"):

1. $\Box A \supset A$.
2. $\Box (A \supset B) \supset (\Box A \supset \Box B)$.

Axiom (1) means (if translated somewhat awkwardly into ordinary language) "It is necessarily true that A" implies "It is true that A."

Axiom (2) means "Necessarily, A implies B" implies that "Necessarily A *implies* Necessarily B." (In other words, if "A implies B" is a necessary truth, then if A is a necessary truth, B must also be a necessary truth.)

System T also includes modus ponens and the rule of necessitation (if A is an axiom or theorem of T, then $\Box A$ is also an axiom or theorem of T).

A stronger system is S4, which contains T and the additional modal axiom

3. $\Box A \supset \Box \Box A$.

Axiom (3) means "It is necessarily true that A" implies "It is necessarily true that it is necessarily true that A."

The system S5 includes S4 and the additional modal axiom

4. $A \supset \Box \Diamond A$.

Axiom (4) means "A" implies that "It is necessarily true that it is possibly true that A."

Among the theorems of S5 are

5. $\Diamond A \equiv \Box \Diamond A$
6. $\Box A \equiv \Diamond \Box A$.

Theorem (5) means "*It is possibly true that A* is equivalent to *It is necessarily true that it is possibly true that A.*" Theorem (6) means "*It is necessarily true that A* is equivalent to *It is possibly true that it is necessarily true that A.*"

As we shall see in chapter 5, theorem (6) and axiom (1) are crucial premises in the essentialist philosophy of religion, specifically, in Plantinga's ontological argument for the existence of God. For example, in line with theorem (6), "It is necessarily true that *God exists*" is implied by "It is possibly true that it is necessarily true that *God exists.*" And according to axiom (1), "It is necessarily true that

God exists" implies "*God exists.*" Thus, if it is merely possible that God necessarily exists, we can infer, using the principles of S5, that God exists.

Theorems (5) and (6) allow us to take any formula prefaced by a string of two or more modal operators and replace it by the same formula prefaced by the last operator in the string. For example, $\Diamond \Box \Diamond \Box \Box$ p, can be replaced by $\Box$ p. (But here ordinary language translations do not increase clarity, for the translation is: "It is possibly true that it is necessarily true that it is possibly true that it is necessarily that it is necessarily true that p" can be replaced by "It is necessarily true that p".)

As I indicated, the first major step in the development of a modal logic framework for linguistic essentialism was made in 1918 with Lewis's first systematization of a modal propositional logic. The next major step was taken in 1946 when Marcus systematized modal predicate logic. Marcus's quantification of modal logic antedated Carnap's by two months; her article "A Functional Calculus of First Order Based on Strict Implication" was submitted to the *Journal of Symbolic Logic* in September 1945 and published in March 1946, and Carnap's article "Modality and Quantification" was submitted to this journal in November 1945 and published in June 1946.

Marcus's article was the first work to develop principles governing the interrelations between unrestricted quantification and modalities (see Terence Parsons's article "Ruth Barcan Marcus and the Barcan Formula"[7] for a good discussion of the difference between her work and the medievals' work on logic). Corresponding to different systems of propositional modal logic, such as T and S5, there are systems of quantified modal logic. A system of quantified modal logic includes all the theses of the relevant propositional modal logic, the theses of first-order predicate logic, and certain modal formulas involving quantifiers. One of the most well known modal formulas involving quantifiers is Marcus's "Barcan formula," which reads,

7. $\Diamond (\exists x) Fx \equiv (\exists x) \Diamond Fx$.

This translates as "*It is possibly true that there is some x, such that x has the property F is equivalent to There is some x, such that it is possible that x has the property F.*" "$\exists$" is the existential quantifier, meaning *some* or *there exists some*. In terms of the necessity operator and the universal quantifier, the Barcan formula reads,

8. $\Box (x) Fx \equiv (x) \Box Fx$.

This translates as "*It is necessarily true that everything has the property F is equivalent to Everything necessarily has the property F.*" Both (7) and (8) are valid if the domain of individuals is fixed across possible worlds. But if we assume, as Kanger first did in his *Provability in Logic* (1957),[8] that different possible worlds can contain different individuals, then (7) and (8) are not valid. (For a discussion of the significance of Kanger's work, see the works by Nino Cocchiarella in 1975 and

Hintikka in 1980 and 1982.)[9] On the varying domain assumption, there is some possible world in which nothing has the property of being a winged horse, but in which it is possible that there is something that has the property of being a winged horse. This is not equivalent to the assertion that there exists something that possibly has the property of being a winged horse. But this equivalence holds in Marcus's system, where the same individuals exist in all possible worlds.

Lewis and Marcus were the first to provide the *syntax* for some propositional and predicate modal logic systems. The third major step in the development of a logical framework for linguistic essentialism (after Lewis's systematization of a propositional modal logic and Marcus's quantification of modal logic) was the provision of a *semantics* for the modal logic systems. A semantics gives us models for the modal logic systems, or sets of objects we can take the syntactic formulae to be about. This was accomplished by Carnap in his article "Modalities and Quantification" (1946) and in his book *Meaning and Necessity* (1947). Carnap's key idea was that the semantics for "□ A" was based on the Leibnizian idea that necessary truth is truth in all possible worlds (what Carnap called "state descriptions"); thus "□ A" means A is true in all possible worlds (in all state descriptions). A state description is a maximally consistent set of atomic sentences. Specifically, it is a set W of sentences, such that for every atomic sentence S, either S is a member of the set W or the negation of S is a member of the set W. A sentence is necessarily true if and only if it is true in every state description, and a sentence is possibly true if and only if it is true in some state description.

Carnap's semantics, however, did not include a satisfactory semantical characterization of validity, for example, as was argued by Gustav Bergmann in "The Philosophical Significance of Modal Logic" (*Mind*, 1960). The important work that remedied this and other problems with Carnap's semantics and that enabled a viable semantics for modal logic to be developed was first accomplished in 1957, in Kanger's *Provability in Logic*. Kanger showed how the semantical interpretation of □ and ◇ could be applied to a diversity of modal systems, so that the box and diamond have a uniform meaning when used in different and nonequivalent systems of modal logic. During the late 1950s other authors also developed semantical interpretations of the necessity and possibility operators that enabled them to apply to diverse modal systems. Notably, Richard Montague was the first to present publicly a theory that used *models* rather than Carnap's *state descriptions* in a paper he read in May 1955 at the University of California ("Logical Necessity, Physical Necessity, Ethics, and Quantifiers," first published in 1960),[10] although the first publication using models was Kanger's above-mentioned book of 1957 (his doctoral dissertation). One main advantage of Montague's semantics was that it allowed two individual constants to name the same thing, whereas Carnap's did not, and the issues involving the modalities can be adequately treated only in semantical systems allowing coextensive individual constants. (Two of the most important other early semantical treatments of modal logic that avoided the problems with Carnap's state descriptions were developed by Kripke in his paper "A Completeness Theorem in Modal Logic" [1959] and by Hintikka in his paper "Modality and Quantification" [1961].)[11]

The fourth crucial step in modal logic was to introduce into modal logic systems the notion of *de re* modalities and the distinction between trivial or nontrivial *essential* properties and *logically necessary* properties. This step was made in Marcus's article "Modalities and Intensional Languages" (1961). (A slightly modified version is reprinted in her book *Modalities* [1993].) Marcus argued in this and later articles that standard systems of quantified modal logic, such as quantified T, quantified S4, or quantified S5, do not include any nontrivial essential attribution as a theorem. However, we can *add* to a system of quantified modal logic a definition of a nontrivial essence and thereby use that system to formalize our talk about nontrivial essences. In 1961, Marcus showed that we can add to quantified S4 a distinction between nontrivial essential attributes and logically necessary attributes. If we use "necessary" to include both essential attributes and logically necessary attributes, we can explain Marcus's definitions. In item (57) of her "Modalities and Intensional Languages," she presents the following definition:

D1. $x \in \Box\, r =\,_{df} \Box\, (x \in r)$.

This translates as "x exemplifies the necessary attribute r = $_{df}$ necessarily, x exemplifies the attribute r." This definition allows for nontrivial essential attributions as well as logically necessary attributions. For example, it allows "necessarily, Plato exemplifies *self-identity*" and "necessarily, Plato exemplifies *being a rational animal.*" Self-identity is a logically necessary attribute and being a rational animal is a nontrivial essence.

Definition (D1) contrasts with the second definition presented in Marcus's item (57), which corresponds only to logically necessary attributes:

D2. $\vdash \Box\, r =\,_{df} (x)\, (x \in \Box\, r)$.

This translates as "r is a logically necessary attribute r = $_{df}$ for every x, x exemplifies the necessary attribute r." No nontrivial essential attribute is exemplified by every x because the definition of a nontrivial essential attribute of an individual x implies that the exemplification of this attribute sorts individuals into kinds or distinguishes between individuals of the same kind. The sentence "For every x, x exemplifies the necessary attribute *self-identity*" is a true substitution instance of the defining formula in (D2), but the sentence "For every x, x exemplifies the necessary attribute *being a rational animal*" is not a true substitution instance of this formula.

The distinction between logically necessary attributes and essential attributes corresponds to Marcus's terminology; for instance, she observes that "the kind of uses to which *logical* modalities are put have nothing to do with essential properties in the old ontological sense. The introduction of physical modalities would bring us closer to this sort of essentialism" [Discussion, 141; see *Modalities*, 32]. Definition (D2) pertains only to logical modalities, whereas definition (D1) is designed to allow both logical modalities and "essential properties in the old ontological sense."

Marcus's definitions enable us to understand de re modalities, which is a central notion of linguistic essentialism. A necessary attribute is a case of de re necessity. An assertion of de re necessity ascribes a necessary attribute to a thing. An assertion of *de dicto* necessity, on the other hand, ascribes the property of necessary truth to a proposition or sentence. Marcus's definition (D1) allows us to explain de re necessity in terms of de dicto necessity. According to (D1), the de re assertion "x exemplifies the necessary attribute r" is defined in terms of the de dicto assertion "It is necessarily true that x exemplifies r."

A precise formulation of the distinction between logically necessary attributes, nontrivial essences, and trivial essences is crucial to linguistic essentialism, for many of the conclusions reached in metaphysics, the philosophy of religion, ethics, and other disciplines are theses about the nontrivial essences of things. Marcus makes the relevant distinctions in the 1961 paper I have discussed, in her paper in *Noûs*, "Essentialism in Modal Logic" (1967), and in her paper in the *Journal of Philosophy* "Essential Attributions" (1971).

In her 1967 paper, Marcus distinguishes between *weakly* and *strongly* essential properties. A property is weakly essential just in case it is necessary to some object but not necessary to all objects (such as the property of being identical with Plato). A property is strongly essential just in case it is necessary to some object but is contingently possessed by some other object; for example, *being born later than M* (where M refers to Socrates' mother) is necessary to Socrates but is only contingently possessed by Plato.

A different distinction is between trivial and nontrivial essences. Marcus explains trivial essences in terms of referential attributes. An attribute is referential with respect to an object *a* if it is expressed by a predicate that mentions *a; being identical with Nancy Cartwright* is a referential attribute of Cartwright because "being identical with Nancy Cartwright" mentions her. An attribute is nonreferential with respect to *a* if it is expressed by a predicate that does not mention *a;* the logically necessary attribute, *being self-identical,* is a nonreferential attribute of Cartwright. *Being identical with Nancy Cartwright* is trivially essential to Cartwright because it is essential to her and can be "analyzed away" in favor of a property that is not a trivial essence of Cartwright, namely, in favor of the nonreferential and logically necessary property of being self-identical.

Precisely put, this means that "Cartwright is identical with Cartwright" is strictly equivalent to "Cartwright is self-identical" and therefore that the latter sentence can be substituted for the former in quantified S5, such that any proof that Cartwright possesses *being identical with Cartwright* is paralleled by an equivalent proof that Cartwright possesses the nonreferential attribute *being self-identical*. Because no step in the parallel proof depends on its being that particular object (Cartwright) that has the attribute *being self-identical*, the proof in question may be repeated for any object whatever. In this sense, the provably essential attribute of *being identical with Nancy Cartwright* is "trivialized" in quantified S5.

But the most relevant of Marcus's categories where linguistic essentialism is concerned is that of nontrivial essences. She mentions them in her 1961–62 work, but her most extensive discussion appears in her article "Essential Attribution" (1971). One type of nontrivial essences is *Aristotelian essences:* sortal properties corresponding to natural kinds, such as a sample of mercury's property of being a metal. Another type is *individuating essences:* properties partially definitive of the special character of an individual and which distinguish the individual from some other objects of the same kind. Perhaps *being a philosopher* is an individuating essential property of Socrates, whereas *being snub-nosed* is an individuating inessential property of him.

If a property F is an Aristotelian essence, F is exemplified necessarily if exemplified at all; thus, Aristotelian essences are weakly essential properties—they are necessary to some objects but not to all.

But if a property G is an individuating essence of some individual x, the property G, although exemplified necessarily by x, may be exemplified contingently by some other individual y. If x's individuating essence G is contingently possessed by y, then G is a strongly essential property of x. For example, if God's individuating essence, *being always good*, is contingently possessed by some finite creature y, then being always good is strongly essential to God—it is necessary to some object (God) but is possessed contingently by some other object (the creature y).

The essentialists' philosophy of religion and essentialist ethics involve deriving conclusions about both individuating essences and Aristotelian essences, as will appear in chapters 5 and 6. (But I shall discuss a different sort of individual essence from Marcus's "individuating essences" when I discuss Plantinga's theory, namely, Plantinga's "individual essences," which are necessarily possessed by, and necessarily unique to, a given individual.)

But how are these various essences *known?* This question pertains to the linguistic method of the essentialists, first formulated in Marcus's 1961 article. The linguistic method pertains to the thesis that many locutions are rigid designators. A rigid designator can be directly referential (the notion first formulated by Marcus) or can refer by means of a rigid sense (a notion first fully developed by Plantinga). Marcus's and Plantinga's theories of rigid designation are the subject of the next several sections.

15. Marcus's Theory of Rigid Designation

The linguistic method of the essentialists involves the claim that many locutions are rigid designators. The origin of the rigid / nonrigid conceptual distinction is in Marcus's 1961 article. Devitt was the first to recognize this, and I shall begin by examining his interpretation of her rigid designation theory. I shall examine Devitt's 1989 theory; he presents a new and different theory and history of rigid designation in his forthcoming writings of the late 1990s.

Devitt argues that Marcus's discovery of this distinction is present in her theory of direct reference. Devitt writes,

> The Rigid Designation theory has much more claim to be considered "new" though it is, in effect, to be found in Ruth Barcan Marcus (1961). Kripke is famous for urging the theory (1971, 1980). When Kaplan says that names are "directly referential," Rigid Designation is part of what he means. The other part is Nondescription (1988a, 512–16, 521–26). Donnellan did not discuss the Rigid Designation theory in his early articles. However, his idea of a "referential use" of definite descriptions (1966, 1968) was suggestive of the idea, as Kaplan points out (1979a, 383–85). Donnellan did embrace the theory later (1979, 50).
>
> The main interest of the Rigid Designation theory was for logic and formal semantics; in particular, for intensional logic and possible-world semantics. The new wave are very interested in this theory.[12]

Devitt argues that the rigid designation theory can be derived from the direct reference theory or, more exactly, from what he calls the Fido–Fido theory, which is that a name is just a tag; the meaning of a name is its direct referent. (Devitt correctly points out that this theory can be traced as far back as Plato; what is new is the arguments for it.) Devitt finds that the theory of rigid designation is present in Marcus's 1961 article by virtue of her "tag" theory, her idea that names do not express a descriptive sense but directly refer to individuals. The rigid designation theory is derived by way of the nondescription theory, as Devitt calls it, which is that a name does not have a Fregean sense determining its reference; a name is nondescriptive. Devitt argues that the reference of a name can vary from world to world, that is, can be nonrigid, only if the name is descriptive. The reason is that some descriptions, such as "the author of *Waverley*," can be satisfied by different individuals in different possible worlds. But if a name is nondescriptive, it cannot be satisfied by different individuals in different possible worlds.

Devitt does not cite or quote any passages from Marcus's 1961 article that shows she possessed these ideas, but I shall quote some of them to show how she articulates these ideas.

It is true that Marcus held that names are mere tags and are nondescriptional;

for example, she writes, "But to give a thing a proper name is different from giving a unique description. . . . [An] identifying tag is a proper name of the thing. . . . This tag, a proper name, has no meaning. It simply tags. It is not strongly equatable with any of the singular descriptions of the thing."[13] It may be questioned, however, if Marcus's theory that names are mere tags and are nondescriptional implies the theory of rigid designation in the way Devitt suggests. Let us reconstruct the general argument for the rigid designation theory that is suggested by Devitt's paper:

   1. Names are mere tags; they are not descriptional.

   2. Only if names are descriptional can their reference vary from world to world.

Therefore,

   3. Names do not vary their reference from world to world.

   Therefore,

   4. The theory of rigid designation is true.

Marcus does hold all four of these theses; nonetheless, this presentation of her theory is incomplete and this argument is not valid; or rather, it is valid only if one makes explicit a series of suppressed premises. All of these suppressed premises are explicit in Marcus's 1961 article, but to show what they need to be, let me first introduce their negations in order to show how their omission can render Devitt's argument invalid.

   Suppose we add the premise that

   1a. There is no theory of possible worlds.

If we add (1a) to the argument, propositions (2), (3), and (4) are false. Thus, if Marcus has the theory of rigid designation, she must have a theory of possible worlds. In a later section, I shall show that she does.

   Other ideas are also needed in order to have a theory of rigid designation. For example, there is no such theory if we add the following premise to the argument:

   1b. Names are intersubstitutable salva veritatae with contingent descriptions in modal contexts.

Because Devitt's argument includes the premise that names are nondescriptional, we can take (1b) to mean that names, although not descriptional, nonetheless can be substituted with them, without loss of truth value, in modal contexts. Clearly, names, even if nondescriptional, can be intersubstituted with descriptions in extensional contexts; for example, "Scott is a human" has the same truth-value as "The author of *Waverley* is a human." But if (1b) is true, then "Scott" varies its reference from world to world because "Necessarily, the author of *Waverley* is male" is false. Since "the author of *Waverley*" designates a female in some possible world, "Scott" will also designate a female in some worlds. Given this, if (1b) is true, then premise (3) is false, where (3) reads,

3. Names do not vary their reference from world to world.

Further premises are needed, such as the necessity of identity. Suppose we add a premise about the contingency of identity:

1c. Identity statements involving coreferring names are contingently true.

This is the denial of Marcus's theory of the necessity of identity involving names. If (1c) is true, then the sentence "Scott is Walter" is contingently true because in some possible worlds Scott is not Walter. Given this, it is false that "Scott" and "Walter" have the same referent in every possible world. Propositions (2), (3), and (4) are false.

Accordingly, if Marcus has the theory of rigid designation, one must find in her work a theory of the necessity of identity between coreferring proper names, a theory of the nonintersubstitutability of names and contingent descriptions in modal contexts, and a theory of possible worlds. I will begin with the necessity of identity.

If proper names are rigid designators, then identity statements with coreferring proper names are necessarily true if true at all. How can this thesis about the necessity of identity be derived?

In her article "The Identity of Individuals in a Strict Functional Calculus of First Order" in the *Journal of Symbolic Logic* (1947), Marcus proved the necessity of identity for variables; she argued that

5. $(x)(y)[xIy \supset \Box xIy]$

is a theorem of quantified S4. Here "I" is the symbol for identity. Marcus's proof of (5) in her 1947 article represents one way to prove it, but a simpler way would be to derive it from the conjunction of

6. $\Box (xIx)$

and a law of substitutivity of identity for variables:

7. $(x)(y)[\{xIy \& Fx\} \supset Fy]$.

In order to reach the theory that proper names are rigid designators, this theorem needs to be related to a corresponding thesis about proper names, namely, the thesis

8. For any two ordinary proper names a and b: $aIb \supset \Box (aIb)$.

Marcus makes this application in her 1961 article. She writes,

> Consider the claim that
> 13. aIb
> is a true identity. Now if (13) is a true identity, then a and b are the same thing. It doesn't say that a and b are two things which happen, through some accident, to be one. True, we are using two different names for that same thing, but we must be careful about use and mention. If, then, (13) is true, it must say the same thing as
> 14. aIa.

But (14) is surely a tautology, and so (13) must surely be a tautology as well. This is precisely the import of my theorem (8). (308)

Marcus's theorem (8) is the theorem of the necessity of identity for variables, which she states as (xIy) ≡ □ (xIy), where the quadruple bar is the sign for strict equivalence. By "tautology" she does not mean what philosophers currently mean by a "tautology," namely, logical truth in propositional logic, and accordingly in her reprint of this article in *Modalities*, Marcus changed "But (14) is surely a tautology, and so (13) must surely be a tautology as well" to "But (14) is surely valid, and so (13) must surely be valid as well."[14] "Valid" means *provable in an interpretation of quantification theory*. Her point was that since identities are necessary, then if "aIa" is valid (is provable in an interpretation of quantification theory) and if "a" and "b" have the same object assignment (refer to the same thing), then "aIb" is also valid, that is, is also provable in that interpretation of quantification theory.

But the question may be asked why the necessity of identity between variables supports this claim about names. Marcus does not go into the details here, but the most plausible line of reasoning pertains to the intersubstitutivity of proper names and variables. The theorem about variables does not by itself entail proposition (8) about names ["For any two ordinary proper names a and b: aIb ⊃ □ (aIb)"]; we need an intermediary premise, that *names are constants that can replace variables in modal contexts.* This is a version of the broader thesis that proper names are the constant expressions which replace variables according to the laws of existential generalization and universal instantiation. In first-order predicate logic, there are two forms of inference, existential generalization and universal instantiation, which intersubstitute names with variables. In modal predicate logic, substitutions are made in the relevant modal contexts.

Proposition (8) about proper names implies that coreferring proper names are intersubstitutable in modal contexts. Consider some examples from Marcus's 1961 article (I use her numbering of the sentences):

10. The evening star eq the morning star.
15. Scott is the author of *Waverley*.

The symbol "eq" stands for an equivalence relation, which may be identity, indiscernability, congruence, strict equivalence, or material equivalence. Given the thesis (8) about the identity of necessity for names, one can determine if the noun phrases in (10) and (15) are being used as names or as contingent definite descriptions by examining their behavior in modal contexts. Marcus writes,

If we decide that "the evening star" and "the morning star" are names for the same thing, and that "Scott" and "the author of *Waverley*" are names for the same thing, then they must be intersubstitutable in every context. In fact it often happens, in a growing, changing language, that a descriptive phrase comes to be used as a proper name—an identifying tag—and the descriptive meaning is lost or ignored. (308–09)

Marcus writes,

Let us now return to (10) and (15). If they express a true identity, then "Scott" ought to be anywhere intersubstitutable for "the author of *Waverley*" and similarly for "the morning star" and "the evening star." If they are not so universally intersubstitutable—that is, if our decision is that they are not simply proper names for the same thing; that they express an equivalence which is possibly false, e.g. someone else might have written *Waverley*, the star first seen in the evening might have been different from the star first seen in the morning—then they do not express identities. (311)

Marcus's modal argument demonstrates the falsity of the "disguised contingent description" theory of proper names. Because (10) and (15) do not express identities, the expressions flanking "is" are not names for the same entity. Consider these modal contexts:

    9. It is necessarily true that Scott is Scott.
   10. It is necessarily true that Scott is the author of *Waverley*.
   11. It is necessarily true that Scott is Walter.

If "Scott" and "Walter" are proper names of the same thing, and "the author of *Waverley*" is instead a definite description that is contingently satisfied by Scott, then (9) and (11) are true and (10) is false. If "the author of *Waverley*" is intersubstituted for an occurrence of "Scott" in either (9) or (11), then the resulting sentence becomes false.

This account of Marcus's theory supplies most of the missing premises in the argument for rigid designation suggested in Devitt's article. We now have the following argument:

    1. Names are mere tags; they are not descriptional.
   1b'. Names are not everywhere intersubstitutable salva veritatae with contingent descriptions in modal contexts.
   1c'. Identity statements involving coreferring names are necessarily true.
   2. Only if names are descriptional can their reference vary from world to world.

Therefore,

    3. Names do not vary their reference from world to world.

Therefore,

    4. The theory of rigid designation is true.

But this is still not sufficient to give the theory of rigid designation, for I have not shown that Marcus's theory entails the falsity of

1a. There is no theory of possible worlds.

If (1a) is true, then propositions (2), (3), and (4) in the argument for the theory of rigid designation are not true. I turn next to the theory of possible worlds Marcus presented in her 1961 article.

Marcus presents a semantics that "corresponds to the Leibnizian distinction between true in a possible world and true in all possible worlds" (320).[15] She adopts the simplifying assumption that there is only one two-place predicate (R). Her semantics includes

a language (L), with truth functional connectives, a modal operator ($\Diamond$), a finite number of individual constants, an infinite number of individual variables, one two-place predicate (R), quantification and the usual criteria for being well-formed. A domain (D) of individuals is then considered which are named by the constants of L. A model of L is defined as a class of ordered couples (possibly empty) of D. The members of a model are exactly those pairs between which R holds. To say therefore that the atomic sentence $R(a_1a_2)$ of L holds or is true in M, is to say that the ordered couple (b_1,b_2) is a member of M, where a_1 and a_2 are the names in L of b_1 and b_2. If a sentence A of L is of the form ~B, A is true in M if and only if B is not true in M. If A is of the form $B_1 \cdot B_2$ then A is true in M if and only if both B_1 and B_2 are true in M. If A is of the form $(\exists x)B$, then A is true in M if and only if at least one substitution instance of B is true (holds) in M. If A is $\Diamond$B then A is true in M if and only if B is true in some model M_1.

We see that a true sentence of L is defined relative to a model and a domain of individuals. A logically true sentence is one which would be true in every model (319).

The models M, M_1, and so on are possible worlds, the individuals b_1, b_2, in the domain D exist in each of the worlds, and these individuals are referents of the individual constants a_1, a_2, and so on. The domain D includes all and only the individuals that exist in the actual world; "there are no specifically intensional objects. No new entity is spawned in a possible world that isn't already in the domain in terms of which the class of models is defined."[16] As Marcus says, "If one wishes to talk about [merely] possible things then of course such a construction is inadequate" (322). Marcus's possible worlds are coextensive, that is, the same set of individuals (the individuals in the domain D) is the domain of quantification for each world. In a later article, Marcus says of her 1961 semantics for modal logic that "the domains of individuals assigned to alternative worlds were coextensive. Given that one of the worlds is the actual world, no entities are spawned that are not in this world and no entities of this world are absent in others."[17]

Marcus uses the phrase "*members* of a model" to refer to *pairs of individuals between which the relation R holds.* The "empty model" she mentions is a model M_0 that contains the individuals in the domain D but has no members, that is, none of the individuals in M_0 are related by the relation R. Accordingly, the quantifiers are not world-bound but range over the domain D. If the quantifiers were world-bound, then the Barcan formula, $\Diamond (\exists x) Fx \equiv (\exists x) \Diamond Fx$, would not be true. Let us introduce a monadic and nontrivially essential property F to illustrate this. Suppose there is a model or world M_3 that contains just two individuals, b_3 and b_4. If quantifiers are world-bound and neither b_3 nor b_4 has the property F in the model M_3, then "it is possible that something is F" would be true in M_3 but would not imply "there exists something that is possibly F." In Marcus's semantics, however, the quantifiers in each model range over the domain D; thus, in the model M_3 it is true both that "it is possible that something is F" and that "there is something that is possibly F" because there is something in the domain D that has the property F in some other model M_4.

The worlds in Marcus's system have all and only the same individuals but differ by virtue of the relation R holding between different individuals in different worlds. For example, if R is the relation *( ) being an unrequited lover of ( )*, then b_1 may stand to b_2 in this relation in M, but in M_1, b_1 may not stand in this relation to b_2 but instead to b_3. The simplifying assumption about only one relation R obtaining corresponds to the more realistic idea that two different possible worlds, even if they contain all and only the same individuals, contain individuals that exemplify different monadic properties or stand in different relations to each other.

This theory features a rule of interpretation that connects a name *a* to an individual *b* in the domain D. Here an individual b_1 in the domain D is assigned to the name a_1, as a_1's direct referent, and thus a_1 is guaranteed to "tag" b_1 and nothing else vis-à-vis each model M, M_1, and so on. The rigidity of a_1 can be deduced from the thesis that the member b_1 in the domain D of actual individuals is assigned to a_1 as a_1's direct referent in the language L we are using (in this deduction, I am of course assuming the other premises previously discussed in this section). It follows from this assignment that the name a_1 in the sentence $R(a_1a_2)$ is guaranteed to tag the same individual, b_1, regardless of which world at which we evaluate this sentence.

Intuitively, when I utter, "Jane is an unrequited lover of Fred," I directly dip into the domain D, and the names "Jane" and "Fred" pick up direct referents logically prior to any counterfactual considerations about the relation of "Jane" and "Fred" to the individuals in M, M_1, and so on. Because Jane is assigned to "Jane" as its direct referent prior to any counterfactual considerations, the rigidity of "Jane" is guaranteed. Of course, we may also evaluate "Jane is an unrequited lover of Fred" at each world M, M₁ and find that "Jane" tags Jane in each world in which Jane exists and does not tag anything else in any world.

Accordingly, we have this definition of the rigidity of individual constants:

DR. An individual constant a is a rigid designator if and only if (i) the semantic rules of our language L determine that a names an individual b in the domain D, such that (ii) a tags b, (iii) b is tagged by a in the actual world M, and (iv) a tags b in each possible world M_1, M_2 and so on in which b exists.

Regarding condition (iv), I do not mean that the name a is used in each different world M_1, M_2, to tag b; rather, I mean that a, as used in the actual world M, tags b in each possible world in which b exists. This is similar to the definition of rigidity that David Kaplan later adopted. Kaplan's mimeograph "Demonstratives" (1977), published in 1989, formulates the direct-reference definition of rigidity as follows:

> I intend to use "directly referential" for an expression whose referent, once determined, is taken as fixed for all possible circumstances, i.e., is taken as being the propositional component.
>
> For me, the intuitive idea is not that of an expression which turns out to designate the same object in all possible circumstances, but an expression whose semantical *rules* provide *directly* that the referent in all possible circumstances is fixed by the actual referent.[18]

Kaplan's theory of rigid designation incorporated Marcus's distinction between a statement and "what is said" by a statement, a contrast that Kaplan also marked by distinguishing (for sentences with directly referential expressions) between the singular proposition expressed by a sentence used on a particular occasion and the sentence used. This distinction is important because it involves some of the consequences about the sentence / proposition distinction that belongs to the rigid designation theory. To quote again the passage from Marcus's article in which she makes this distinction,

> 13. aIb
>
> is a true identity. Now if (13) is a true identity, then a and b are the same thing. It doesn't say that a and b are two things which happen, through some accident, to be one. True, we are using two different names for that same thing, but we must be careful about use and mention. If, then, (13) is true, it must say the same thing as
>
> 14. aIa.

The statement aIb says the same thing as aIa. What is said by the statement "Venus is Venus" is also what is said by the statement "Hesperus is Venus," namely, that a certain thing, Venus, is identical with itself. Marcus's 1961 notion of "what is said" by a statement is partly similar to her later theory of "states of affairs," which can include concrete individuals as parts.[19] Kaplan takes up this "statement/what is said" distinction in "Demonstratives." He suggests that we "think of the vehicles of evaluation—the-what-is-said in a given context—as propositions. . . . in the case of a singular term which is directly referential, the constituent of the proposition is just the object itself" (494). Kaplan is thus able to explain "designates the same object in all circumstances": "We should be aware of a certain confusion in interpreting the phrase 'designates the same object in all circumstances.' We do not mean that the expression *could not have been used* to designate a different object. We mean rather that given a use of the expression, we may ask of what has been said whether it would have been true or false in various counterfactual circumstances, and in such counterfactual circumstances, which are the individuals relevant to determining truth-value" (493-94). There is a certain problem, however, with Kaplan's definition of rigid designation that does not appear in Marcus. Kaplan argues that a directly referential rigid designator designates an object x even in worlds in which x does not exist. This would amount to a vacuous condition if we used Marcus's 1961 fixed domain semantics, which imply that if an object exists in the actual world, it exists in all possible worlds. Kaplan, however, is using a varying domain semantics. If we use varying domain semantics, then we should follow Marcus's suggestion in her 1971 article that we add the condition that a rigid designator of x does not designate x at worlds where x does not exist. The reason for this is that Kaplan's contrary position results in a logical contradiction. Consider one of the examples that Kaplan offers: "Suppose I say 'I do not exist.' Under what circumstances would what I said be true? It would be true in circumstances in which I did not exist" (495). Kaplan's use of "I do not exist" expresses the singular proposition *David Kaplan does not exist*. This proposition includes David Kaplan as a constituent. Now in order for this proposition to possess the property of being true in a circumstance in which Kaplan does not exist, this proposition must exist in that circumstance, for something can possess a property (such as being true) only if it exists. However, this singular proposition exists in a circumstance only if its constituents exist in that circumstance, for a whole composed of x, y, and z exists only if x, y, and z exist. Because David Kaplan is a constituent of this singular proposition, David Kaplan exists in each circumstance in which the proposition exists. It follows that David Kaplan exists in the circumstance in which this proposition possesses the property of being true. But this entails the contradiction that David Kaplan both exists and does not exist in that circumstance, for in that circumstance the singular proposition *David Kaplan does not exist* has the truth-value of true.

This shows why Kaplan's idea that a rigid designator designates an object even in worlds where the object does not exist is unacceptable. A definition of the rigidity of individual constants that allows for a varying-domain conception of possible worlds must instead include the condition that Marcus introduced in her 1971 article, which appears as the fifth condition in this definition of the rigidity of an individual constant:

> D2. A constant a is a rigid designator if and only if (i) the semantic rules of our language L determine that a names an individual b in the domain D, such that (ii) a tags (directly refers to) b, (iii) b is tagged by a in the actual world M, (iv) a tags b in each possible world M_1, M_2. etc., in which b exists. (v) a does not refer to anything in the worlds M_3, M_4, etc., in which b does not exist.

The distinction between the rigidity of proper names and the nonrigidity of definite descriptions such as "the author of *Waverley*" also appears in Plantinga's theory, but without the direct reference apparatus of Marcus's philosophy of language. Plantinga had a theory of rigid designation in his 1969 and 1970 articles, as I shall discuss in the next section, but these articles do not represent the second published account of the rigid/nonrigid distinction (after Marcus's 1961 theory). The second published theory of rigid designation appears in Hintikka's article "The Modes of Modality" (1963), even though this fact is not widely known. I quote at length his formulation:

> Why do some terms fail in modal contexts to have the kind of unique reference which is a prerequisite for being a substitution-value of a bound variable? An answer is implicit in our method of dealing with modal logic. Why does the term "the number of planets" in (i) ["the number of planets is nine but it is possible that it should be larger than ten"] fail to specify a well-defined individual? Obviously, because in the different states of affairs which we consider possible when we assert (i) it will refer to different numbers. (In the actual state of affairs it refers to 9, but we are also implicitly considering other states of affairs in which it refers to larger numbers.) This at once suggests an answer to the question as to when a singular term (say a) really specifies a well-defined individual and therefore qualifies as an admissible substitution-value of the bound variables. It does so if and only if it refers to one and the same individual not only in the actual world (or, more generally, in whatever possible world we are considering) but also in all the alternative worlds which could have been realized instead of it; in other words, if and only if there is an individual to which it refers in all the alternative worlds as well.[20]

16. Plantinga's Theory of Rigid Designation

Marcus's 1961 theory of rigid designation was formulated only in terms of a theory of directly referential proper names. Of course, Marcus did not equate rigid designators with proper names. Indeed, she has resisted using the terminology "rigid designates" because it can obscure the different semantic roles of names and rigid definite descriptions. She wrote in the preface to *Modalities* that in her theory "proper names are not assimilated to what later came to be called 'rigid designators' by Saul Kripke, although they share some features with rigid descriptions." Marcus's point is that if we indiscriminately classify proper names along with attributive rigid descriptions as "rigid designators," then we lose sight of the different semantic features of proper names (they "tag") and attributive rigid descriptions (they "describe").

The first fully developed descriptivist theory of rigidity was presented by Plantinga in his article "De Re et De Dicto" (1969) and especially in his article "World and Essence" (1970). The descriptivist theory of rigidity is not to be confused with the fact that some definite descriptions can be used referentially (to directly refer to something) rather than attributively (to designate whatever uniquely possesses a certain property). Donnellan made this distinction between referential and attributive uses of definite descriptions in his article "Reference and Definite Descriptions" (1966), although he is erroneously regarded as the "originator" of this referential/attributive distinction between uses of definite descriptions in the "standard history" of the new theory of reference or linguistic essentialism. This distinction was first made by Marcus in her 1961 article, as I argued in the volume edited by Fetzer and Humphreys, *The New Theory of Reference.* Donnellan merely argued that some definite descriptions, such as "the person in the corner drinking a martini," can on some occasions be used to refer directly to a certain person the speaker has in mind, regardless of whether or not that person satisfies the description. Kripke made a plausible case that Donnellan's distinction is merely pragmatic and does not show there is a semantic distinction.[21] Marcus's referential/attributive distinction, however, is explicitly semantic. For example, she argues that "the evening star" may have first been used attributively but later have become used referentially, like a proper name that directly refers to Venus. Donnellan did not have the modal semantics to support the theory that his "referential uses" of definite descriptions were rigid, but Marcus had this semantics in her 1961 paper, and her referentially used definite descriptions were rigid designators.

But this is not the sort of descriptivist theory of rigidity developed by Plantinga; Marcus's referentially used definite descriptions are rigid because they are used as "tags," as directly referential expressions, and not by virtue of containing rigid descriptive conditions. Plantinga's theory also does not consist merely in pointing out the "obvious" cases of attributively used definite descriptions, such as "the number that immediately succeeds the number two," which refers to the number three in each possible world. Rather, Plantinga developed a theory of rigid descriptions that he argued could account for all cases of rigidity, even proper names, so that an appeal to direct reference is not needed at all. I will not decide here whether the Marcus-based "direct reference" account of rigidity is preferable to the Plantinga-based "descriptivist" account of rigidity, but I will mention the points of contrast between them. The "linguistic method of the essentialists" requires a theory of rigidity, but this rigidity can be of the Marcus-based sort or the Plantinga-based sort.

Plantinga's 1969 article makes a distinction between definite descriptions that are used de re or de dicto. Plantinga considers the definite description (I use his numbering)

32. It is possible that the number of apostles should have been prime.

Plantinga writes, "Now (32) can be read de dicto, in which case we may put it more explicitly as

32a. The proposition, the number of apostles is prime is possible;

It may also be read de re, that is, as

32b. The number that numbers the apostles (that is, the number that as
        things in fact stand numbers the apostles) could have been prime."[22]

The first thing to note is that Plantinga's de dicto and de re "readings" of the definite description "the number of apostles" do not correspond to Marcus's distinction between referential and attributes uses of definite descriptions. The similarity is that Plantinga's "de re reading" and Marcus's "referential uses" (or to use her terminology, the use of definite descriptions as mere tags) both imply that the definite description refers rigidly. The difference is that Plantinga's "de re reading" of the description involves the description referring rigidly by virtue of its descriptive conditions, whereas Marcus's "tag reading" of the description involves the description referring directly and not by virtue of its descriptive conditions. Plantinga uses the phrase "as things in fact stand" to express a rigid descriptive condition that belongs to the "de re reading" of the description "the number of apostles." This descriptive condition is that "the number of apostles" refers to whatever number is the number of the apostles in the actual world. In other words, the descriptive condition is a world-indexed condition, a condition that picks out a certain possible world. This is analogous (although Plantinga does not say so) to two different temporal readings of "The sun is shining." On one reading, it can be read as temporally indexed, that is, as meaning "The sun is now shining," where "now" refers to the date of the utterance (for example, noon, April 8, 1996). But it can also be read (more naturally) as not temporally indexed, as meaning "The sun's shining has presentness, rather than pastness or futurity" without a reference to the date being a part of the semantic content of the sentence.

One year later, Plantinga is in full and explicit possession of this descriptivist theory of rigidity. In his article "World and Essence" (1970), the relatively vague talk about how "things in fact stand" is replaced by a precise theory of the property of *being actual* and world-indexed properties that belong to the semantic content of the description.[23]

Plantinga defines possible worlds as abstract objects, states of affairs, or propositions. In his 1974 book, Plantinga says that states of affairs and propositions may be identical (two names for the same abstract objects, with "The state of affairs p does not obtain" meaning "The proposition p is not true"), but I shall follow Plantinga's terminology and talk about "states of affairs."[24] Plantinga's states of affairs contain only abstract objects as parts and thus differ from what Marcus calls "states of affairs" in her writings in the 1980s and 1990s, which contain concrete objects.

Plantinga writes in 1970, "A possible world is a state of affairs of some kind—one which could have obtained if it does not. . . . Furthermore, a possible world must be what we may call a fully determinate state of affairs. . . . A fully determinate state of affairs S, let us say, is one such that for any state of affairs S', either S includes S' (that is, could not have obtained unless S' had also obtained) or S precludes S' (that is, could not have obtained if S' had obtained)" (463).

A merely possible individual—say a unicorn—is (reductively analyzable as) a state of affairs T that includes the state of affairs U, *something's being a unicorn*, such that for any state of affairs U' that is compatible with the state of affairs U, T includes U' or T precludes U'. Thus merely possible individuals are reductively analyzable as a kind of actually existent abstract object, a state of affairs (or, if you prefer, a proposition).

How do we achieve rigid designation of a merely possible individual? Plantinga does not elaborate, but his theory implies an explanation. The designation is achieved by means of a world-indexed definite description. Suppose, for example, that Lucifer does not actually exist but possibly exists. There is a class of fully determinate states of affairs, $W_1, \ldots W_n$, that do not obtain but are such that, if they were to obtain, Lucifer would exist. One can then rigidly refer to Lucifer by means of a world-indexed definite description, such as "the most powerful evil angel in world W_1." This description designates the same individual, Lucifer, in each world in which Lucifer exists and designates nothing else in any world. Because Lucifer does not actually exist, there is no concrete individual that satisfies this description. But the individual essence expressed by this description would be satisfied by one and only one individual, Lucifer, if any of the worlds $W_1, \ldots W_n$ had been actual. Talk of "rigidly designating a merely possible individual" can be made precise by means of the ontological and semantic apparatus set forth in Plantinga's 1970 article.

The important difference between Marcus's "direct reference" theory of rigid designation and Plantinga's descriptivist theory lies in their respective treatments of proper names and a posteriori necessities. Both Marcus and Plantinga (in his later writings of the 1970s) show that the "traditional analytic theory of proper names," that proper names express contingent descriptive senses or are disguised contingent descriptions (associated in its various versions mainly with Frege, Russell, and Searle), cannot be true. But they refute this traditional theory with different versions of "the modal argument against the traditional theory of names."

The modal argument, originally presented by Marcus in 1961, is that proper names cannot be intersubstituted salva veritate with contingent descriptions in all modal contexts. Marcus's "direct reference" version of this argument was explained in the last section; Plantinga's version of the argument involves the hypothesis that proper names express necessary descriptive senses, mainly world-indexed descriptive senses. Plantinga's theory, presented in its mature form in his article "The Boethian Compromise" (1978), implies that "the actual author of *Waverley*" is intersubstitutable with "Scott" in any modal context, such as the first occurrence of "Scott" in "Necessarily, Scott is Scott." Because no contingent description can be substituted for "Scott," "Scott" does not express a contingent descriptive sense.

One crucial difference between the "direct reference" theory of rigid names and the descriptivist theory of rigid names is the role that definite descriptions play. According to the descriptivist theory, the same definite description is (1) the semantic content of a proper name, (2) what fixes the reference of the name, and (3) the cognitive significance of the name. Although "reference-fixing descriptions" and "cognitive significance" are phrases first used by Kripke and Kaplan, respectively, these notions have their origin in earlier writings. They are clearly implicit in Marcus's 1961 article and are first given a fully explicit articulation in articles by Peter Geach and H. P. Grice in 1969 (especially Geach's article).

Geach presented an account of reference-fixing descriptions and cognitive significance in association with his causal theory of reference (a theory standardly and mistakenly thought to have been originated by Kripke and Donnellan). According to the "direct reference" theory, a reference-fixing description is a definite description that is used to fix the reference of a locution, for example, a name, but is not the semantic content of that locution. Geach makes the point that the use of a definite description to fix the reference of a name does not imply that the name is semantically equivalent to that description: "I introduced the use of the proper name 'Pauline' by way of the definite description 'the one and only girl Geach dreamed of on N–Night'; this might give rise to the idea that the name is an abbreviation for the description. This would be wrong."[25] H. P. Grice discussed his notion of a reference-fixing description:

A name α may be introduced *either* so as to be inflexibly tied, as regards the truth-value of utterances containing it, to a given definite description δ, *or* so as to be not so tied (δ being univocally employed); so the difference between the two ways of introducing α may reasonably be regarded as involving a difference of sense or meaning for α; a sense in which α may be said to be equivalent to a definite description and a sense in which it may not.[26]

On the descriptivist theory of Plantinga, a rigid descriptive sense is both the semantic content of the name and fixes its referent. But on the direct reference theory, a description (usually nonrigid) serves to fix the reference, *if* the reference is not fixed by ostension in an original act of "baptism."

The direct reference theory also includes the notion that definite descriptions serve as the cognitive significance of directly referential locutions. "Cognitive significance" refers to what the speaker has in mind when she uses a term. If I use a directly referential proper name, I may have in mind, in connection with my use of the name, some descriptive sense that is satisfied by the direct referent of the name. If a certain definite description fixes the direct reference of a name, it may also continue to be associated with the name as its cognitive significance (at least for some users of the name). But a definite description may function *only* as the cognitive significance of the name. For example, it is possible that the reference of "Venus" is fixed, not by a description, but by an original act of baptism, for example, pointing at Venus and saying, "Let us name that 'Venus.' " Consistently with this, the cognitive significance of "Venus" for some language-users may be a descriptive sense, such as *the second planet from the sun.*

On the descriptivist theory of rigidity, the rigid descriptive sense not only is the semantic content of (a given use of) the name, but also fixes its reference and is its cognitive significance for the user of the name. These various distinctions between a reference-fixing description, cognitive significance, and semantic content will become especially relevant in the chapter on essentialist ethics, where I shall construct a normative ethics that is based on the distinctions among the direct referent (semantic content) of "good," its cognitive significance, and reference-fixing description.

In my earlier articles on Marcus's theory in *The New Theory of Reference,* I claimed that her direct reference theory was superior to Plantinga's descriptivist theory because it provided "an epistemic argument for direct reference." It seems to me now, however, that the descriptivist theory articulated in Plantinga's "The Boethian Compromise" can provide a reasonable response to the epistemic argument.

What is the epistemic argument? Marcus points out that somebody may be surprised to learn that, as a matter of empirical fact, her use of "Venus" referred to the first heavenly body to be visible in the evening. One could not learn this information if "Venus" expressed the contingent descriptive sense *the first heavenly body to be visible in the evening,* for it would be an a priori truth that "Venus is the first heavenly body to be visible in the evening." The same argument could be repeated for any contingent descriptive sense that "Venus" allegedly expresses. I claimed that Plantinga's descriptivist theory faced difficulties with this "epistemic argument for direct reference."

In truth, however, Plantinga's theory can handle this argument by virtue of his 1978 theory of *epistemically inequivalent* rigid descriptive senses. Plantinga's basic idea is that "proper names express essences, and different proper names of the same object (or the same name on different occasions of use) can express different and epistemically inequivalent [but logically equivalent] essences."[27] Thus, I may use "Venus" to express *being the second planet from the sun in the actual world* and may be surprised to learn a posteriori that Venus in addition has the essential property of *being the first heavenly body visible in the evening in the actual world.*

One implication of this view is that for some essence expressible by a name, it will be an a priori truth for a given person that the name has that essence. For example, for me it may be an a priori truth that "Venus is the second planet from the sun in the actual world," but an a posteriori truth that "Venus is the first heavenly body visible in the evening in the actual world." This result is parallel to a situation with the direct reference theory, for on the occasions of fixing the direct referent of a proper name by means of a description, it will be an a priori truth for the person fixing the reference that the named object satisfies the description. This need not be an a priori truth for subsequent users of the name, for the reference may subsequently be determined by a Geach-type historical chain.

17. Metaphysical Necessity

The descriptivist theory of rigidity also leads to a different theory of a posteriori necessary truths than does the "direct reference" theory. I will contrast Marcus's "direct reference" theory of a posteriori necessities with Plantinga's descriptivist theory of a posteriori necessities.

Some a posteriori necessities are identifications. If a and b are two proper names for the same thing, then aIb (a is identical with b) states the same thing as aIa. What is said by the statement aIa is an identity proposition and is known a priori. For example, what is said by "Hesperus is Phospherus" is the singular proposition *Venus is Venus*, and *Venus is Venus* is an a priori truth. It is also a logically necessary truth, being a theorem of quantified S5. The a posteriori feature pertains to the metalevel, that is, to the metalevel proposition that *"Hesperus is Phospherus" states the singular proposition Venus is Venus, rather than some other singular proposition.* We may learn by empirical investigation that the reference-fixing description of "Hesperus" (the description used to fix its reference), which may be the contingent description, *the first heavenly body to be visible in the evening,* is satisfied by the same object that satisfies the reference-fixing description of "Phospherus," the description, *the last heavenly body to be visible in the morning.*

The second sort of a posteriori necessities pertain to propositions that ascribe nontrivial essences to individuals or natural kinds. In her 1971 article, Marcus gives as examples "Socrates is a man" and "A sample of mercury is a metal." These sentences state metaphysically or ontologically necessary propositions, as distinct from logically necessary propositions, and these propositions are known a posteriori. We may say that something is logically necessary if it is a theorem of quantified S5 (of course, there are many sorts of logic, so this is in effect a stipulative definition of "logical necessity" I am using for purposes of discussion). But as Marcus and Parsons have shown, no nontrivial essential truth is a theorem of quantified S5 or any other standard modal logic system. The sort of necessity of nontrivial essences is an ontological or metaphysical necessity. In the 1962 Discussion following her paper, Marcus notes that "the kind of uses to which *logical* modalities are put have nothing to do with essential properties in the old ontological sense. The introduction of physical modalities would bring us closer to this sort of essentialism."[28] As discussed at the beginning of this chapter, Marcus distinguished two sorts of nontrivial essences, Aristotelian essences (such as being a metal) and individuating essences (such as being a philosopher). *What is said* by statements that ascribe an Aristotelian or individuating essence to something has the property of *being metaphysically necessary and a posteriori.*

Can we define metaphysical necessity? On Marcus's theory, "Hesperus is Phospherus" states the singular proposition *Venus is Venus,* which is a theorem of the modal logic system S5 (and indeed of first-order predicate logic with identity). But if proper names express world-indexed essences, then this sentence will state not a logical truth but a metaphysical truth, such as:

P. The first heavenly body to be visible in the evening in the actual world is identical with the last heavenly body to be visible in the morning in the actual world.

Proposition (P) is not a theorem in first-order logic with identity or in modal logic S5. Nonetheless, it is a necessary truth, a truth in all possible worlds. What sort of necessity is this?

Plantinga distinguishes between narrowly logical necessity and broadly logical necessity. Narrow logical necessities are truths of propositional logic and first-order quantification theory. Broadly logical necessities are "necessary" in a wider sense, but in a narrower sense than causal or natural necessities. "Broadly logical possibility" is what Plantinga calls "metaphysical possibility" in "World and Essence" (475). In *The Nature of Necessity* (2), he gives as examples of broadly logical necessities, "No one is taller than himself," "Red is a color," "If a thing is red, then it is colored," "No numbers are human beings," and "No prime minister is a prime number."

Most if not all of these examples, however, have often been argued to be analytic truths, which are reducible to narrowly logical truths by substitution of synonyms for synonyms. It is arguable, for example, that "red" expresses the same concept as "the color red," in which case "Red is a color" is reducible to the narrowly logical truth "The color red is a color."

Plantinga's examples suggest that he has not clearly captured the sort of necessity that is expressed in (P). (P) is a synthetic truth that is known a posteriori, and it is necessary in a narrower sense than physical necessity but in a wider sense than the truths in propositional logic or first-order quantification theory. Again: What sort of necessity is metaphysical necessity?

I suggest defining metaphysical necessity in terms of nontrivial essences. First are the "logically possible worlds," where "logically" is used in the sense of quantified S5. (Some other modal logic system may be used, but I agree with Plantinga that S5 seems the most appropriate in capturing our modal logical notions.) The metaphysically possible worlds are all and only the logically possible worlds that include nontrivially essential truths and no proposition that is inconsistent with these truths. A proposition is metaphysically possible just in case it is logically consistent with the conjunction of all true propositions that ascribe a nontrivial essence to something. A property is a metaphysically necessary property if and only if it is a nontrivial essence (for example, being human), a trivial essence (for example, being identical with Socrates), or a logically necessary property (for example, being self-identical).

The class of metaphysically possible worlds is a part of the class of logically possible worlds; all metaphysically possible worlds are logically possible worlds, but not all logically possible worlds are metaphysically possible. (Possible worlds cannot be defined as "sets" but can be defined as "proper classes," for reasons relating to set-theoretic paradoxes.)[29] Physically possible worlds—those in which the actual laws of nature obtain—are a part of the class of metaphysically possible worlds; all physically possible worlds are metaphysically possible, but not all metaphysically possible worlds are physically possible.

An additional characteristic of metaphysical modalities is that they are the modalities of existence. In the expressions "can exist," "cannot exist," and "must exist," the words "can," "cannot," and "must" have the sense of metaphysical possibility, impossibility, and necessity. A sentence of the form "x must exist" can express a true proposition if "must" is taken in the sense of physical necessity. However, the significance of the thesis that the metaphysical modalities are modes of existence is to identify the class of all metaphysically possible worlds as the *most inclusive* class of worlds of which it is true to say of *any one* of its members W that "world W can exist." (Technically, we should say "be actual" rather than "exist.") All physically possible worlds are included in the class of all metaphysically possible worlds. But some logically possible worlds and some epistemically possible worlds are not included in the class of metaphysically possible worlds, and it is not true to say of any of these excluded worlds "W can exist." For example, there is a logically possible world in which Socrates is a triangle, but it is not true to say of this world, "It can exist."

The "direct reference" theory of rigid designation allows for two senses of "a posteriori necessities," identifications and nontrivially essential truths. Metaphysical necessity pertains to nontrivial essences and logical necessity to identifications. Is there a parallel distinction in the descriptivist theory of rigid designation?

In *The Nature of Necessity* Plantinga gives an account of a posteriori necessary identifications in terms of a descriptivist theory. He writes, "The Babylonian astronomers were ignorant of the fact that (20) *Hesperus is identical with Phospherus* and (20′) *Phospherus is identical with Phospherus* express the same proposition." (85). Plantinga is supposing that "Hesperus" and "Phospherus" both express the same essence, call it E. Thus, both (20) and (20′) express the same logically necessary proposition, namely, *whatever has E is identical with whatever has E.* This de dicto proposition is no less an identity proposition than is Marcus's de re or singular proposition *Venus I Venus.* On Plantinga's theory, the a posteriori feature is also a metalevel fact, namely, that "Hesperus" and "Phospherus" name the same object: the Babylonians "did not realize that (20) expresses the proposition that Hesperus is identical with Hesperus; and they were not apprised of this fact because they did not know that Hesperus bore the name 'Phospherus' as well as the name 'Hesperus.' (87)"

Plantinga's descriptivist theory of rigidity also features a theory of a posteriori necessities in the second, or metaphysical, sense. I argued in Fetzer's and Humphreys' *The New Theory of Reference* that the doctrine of a posteriori necessary identifications was originally stated in 1961 by Marcus, not in 1971 and 1972 by Kripke, as the "standard history" has it. But the "standard history" is in error in another respect; the doctrine of a posteriori metaphysical necessities was explicitly stated by Plantinga in "World and Essence" in October 1970 and did not first appear in print in 1971 or 1972 with Kripke's essays. Plantinga states a descriptivist version of this doctrine, based on his notion of a world-indexed property. Where "Kronos" is the name Plantinga gives to the actual world, he writes,

> The argument here implicit [that all a posteriori truths are contingently true] takes for granted that the discovery of necessary truth is not the proper business of the historian and astronomer. But this is at best dubious. I discover that Ephialtes was a traitor; I know that it is Kronos that is actual; accordingly, I also discover that Kronos includes the state of affairs consisting in Ephialtes' being a traitor. This last, of course, is necessarily true; but couldn't a historian (*qua*, as they say, *historian*) discover it, too? It is hard to

believe that historians and astronomers are subject to a general prohibition against the discovery of necessary truth. Their views, if properly come by, are a posteriori; that they are also contingent does not follow. (481)

Here Plantinga's a posteriori necessities, although de dicto propositions, are analogous to Marcus's propositions about nontrivial essences. For just as it is a nontrivial essence of Socrates that he is a man, so it is a nontrivial essence of Ephialtes that he is a traitor in the actual world Kronos.

How do we know nontrivial essences? World-indexed essences are relatively unproblematic, but what of the nontrivial essences Marcus distinguishes, her Aristotelian essences and individuating essences? Marcus says in her 1971 article that a sample of mercury is nontrivially essentially a metal. How do we know such nontrivial essences? Clearly, we observe the universe to see if a sample of mercury in fact possesses the property of being a metal. But how do we know it is essentially a metal? Do we know this by an occult faculty of metaphysical intuition, as critics of linguistic essentialism might charge?

18. Justifying the Method of Linguistic Essentialism

Marcus provides the key to the response to such a charge; she writes in her 1971 article:

> A sorting of attributes (or properties) as essential or inessential to an object or objects is not wholly a fabrication of metaphysicians. The distinction is frequently used by philosophers and nonphilosophers alike without untoward perplexity. Given their vocation, philosophers have also elaborated such use in prolix ways. Accordingly, to proclaim that any such classification of properties is "senseless" and "indefensible" and leads into a "metaphysical jungle of Aristotelian essentialism" is impetuous. It supposes that cases of use that appear coherent can be shown not to be so or, alternatively, that there is an analysis that dispels the distinction and does not rely on equally odious notions.[30]

This suggests that we are justified in accepting ordinary and philosophical insights or intuitions about nontrivial essences unless talk of such essences can be shown to be incoherent or reductively analyzable. Marcus and others have made a good case that attacks on their coherence and attempts to reductively analyze them by Quine and others are unsuccessful.

This defense of a posteriori nontrivial essential attributions can be formally presented as follows:

1. Philosophers and nonphilosophers normally make nontrivial essential attributions without untoward perplexity and believe these attributions are true.

2. There is no a priori or a posteriori reason to believe that their nontrivial essential attributions are always or normally incoherent, false, or reductively analyzable.

Therefore,

3. Philosophers and nonphilosophers normally have reason to believe their nontrivial essential attributions are true.

4. Philosophers and nonphilosophers have no reason to believe that the conjunction of (1) and (2) is a defective reason to believe their nontrivial essential attributions normally are true.

Therefore,

5. Philosophers and nonphilosophers normally are indefeasibly justified in believing that some of their nontrivial essential attributions are true.

One way this argument may be attacked is to question the validity of the inference of (3) from the conjunction of (1) and (2). Imagine a skeptic who claims (1) and (2) do not entail (3). The skeptic might ask, Why should what seems to be the case to us in our normal or commonsense attitudes have any evidential force at all? If there is no compelling argument for nontrivial essentialism, and no compelling argument that such essentialism is false, should we not remain agnostic on this issue, rather than abide by "what seems to be the case" to common sense or by what philosophers and nonphilosophers normally believe?

This skeptical argument is based on this skeptical principle:

S. If p (for example, nontrivial essential attributions) seem to be true, then, even in the absence of empirical and a priori reasons to disbelieve p, p's seeming to be true does not justify a belief in p.

Now what could justify a belief in the skeptical principle (S)? The skeptic cannot appeal to the fact that (S) seems to be true to her to justify her belief in (S). For (S) rules out the epistemic legitimacy of this very appeal.

The skeptic might then introduce some reason R and claim R is a reason to believe (S). If so, then it seems to the skeptic that R is true and that R justifies (S). But by (S), *this* is no reason for believing (S) or that R justifies (S). The skeptic cannot trust her own beliefs and thus cannot trust any of her beliefs about the justification of (S).

This shows that the argument (1)–(3) cannot be shown to be invalid. But can we also show that we are justified in believing the argument-form instantiated by (1)–(3) is valid? Yes, for this argument-form is self-justifying. The argument seems to be valid, there are no a priori or empirical reasons to believe it is invalid, and therefore it is justified to believe it is valid. This is tantamount to saying that (4) is true, that is, that there is no reason to believe that the conjunction of (1) and (2) is a defective reason to believe that p or our nontrivial essential attributions normally are true. Proposition (4) is a version of the principle of *no undermining defeaters for justified beliefs*, and the truth of (4) follows from the above-mentioned argument that (3) validly follows from the conjunction of (1) and (2).

This defense of a crucial tenet of the method of linguistic essentialism avoids the fallacy inherent in the method of ordinary language philosophers. Mohan Matten writes of linguistic essentialism that "to argue from facts about our use of language to a kind of Aristotelianism has reminded scientifically-minded philosophers such as Paul and Patricia Churchland of the worst excesses of Oxford in the fifties and sixties."[31] However, if we take (1) as meaning that ordinary language embodies talk of nontrivial essences, then the argument to (5) will still not commit the fallacy of ordinary language analysis. The method of the ordinary language analysts implied that "The declarative sentence Fx is sometimes used in a correct ordinary way" entails "The sentence Fx is sometimes true". But this is invalid, as I argued in chapter 3. The argument (1)–(4) instead implies that if a modal declarative sentence Fx is sometimes used in a correct ordinary way, and there are no a priori or a posteriori reasons to think Fx is incoherent, false, or reductively analyzable, then there is a defeasible reason to think that Fx is sometimes true. Further, if there is no undermining defeater of this reason, that is, no reason to think that the combined facts of *correct ordinary use* and *the absence of successful arguments that this use is faulty* are a defective reason to believe that Fx is sometimes true, then belief that Fx is sometimes true is indefeasibly justified. Because (4) is true, as I have argued, this argument provides a viable method of linguistic analysis, and for this reason I shall use it in chapters 5 and 6 and the Conclusion to construct a theory of the ethical and religious meaning of human life.

The argument (1)–(5) can also be stated in terms of modal intuitions, which concern not merely nontrivial essences but counterfactuals, the rigidity of names, indexicals, natural kind terms, and all other phenomena involved in linguistic essentialist arguments. Stated in this broader form, the argument goes,

    1a. Humans have modal intuitions.

    2a. There is no a priori or a posteriori reason to believe that their modal intuitions are not normally true.

Therefore,

    3a. There is reason to believe that humans' modal intuitions are normally true.

    4a. There is no reason to believe that the conjunction of (1a) and (2a) is a defective reason to believe humans' modal intuitions are normally true.

Therefore,

    5a. The belief that humans' modal intuitions are normally true is indefeasibly justified.

Having stated this justification of the essentialist method of linguistic analysis, I can turn to an examination of essentialist philosophy of religion and ethics.

5　Essentialist Philosophy of Religion

19. Introduction

A considerable degree of uniformity could be ascribed to the respective philosophies of religion of the logical realists, logical positivists, and ordinary language philosophers. For example, all the logical positivists adopted the same position in the philosophy of religion: theism and atheism both are cognitively senseless. No such uniformity can be ascribed to the essentialists. Some are theists (Plantinga, William Craig, Robert Adams, Thomas Morris, Brian Leftow), others are either atheists (Nathan Salmon) or agonistics, and still others have not published any opinion (Marcus, Kripke, Putnam, Kaplan). The essentialists who have not published defenses of theism have said virtually nothing on the topic, apart from Richard Gale's important book *On the Nature and Existence of God,* and so I shall concentrate on the theistic essentialists in this chapter. Such a focus will provide an informative contrast to my previous discussions of the philosophy of religion, for in the case of the logical realists, positivists, and ordinary language philosophers my discussion amounted to an evaluation of arguments for the religious meaninglessness of human life. Here I shall evaluate arguments for the claim that human life has a religious meaning.

The four phases of analytic philosophy I am discussing in this book may be summarized as follows in regard to their position on religious meaning: the logical realists claimed that "God exists" *has a sense and is false;* the logical positivists claimed that "God exists" *has no sense;* the ordinary language philosophers claimed that "God exists" *has a sense but is neither true nor false;* the theistic essentialists, however, claimed that "God exists" *has a sense and is true.*

The philosopher commonly recognized as being the leading exponent of essentialist theism is Alvin Plantinga; indeed, it may be said without too much exaggeration that all subsequent essentialist theistic writings are but "footnotes to Plantinga." One cannot imagine such books as Thomas Morris's *Anselmian Explorations* without Plantinga's *The Nature of Necessity* and related writings. Accordingly, I shall concentrate almost exclusively on Plantinga's philosophy of religion, particularly as it is espoused in his main work on the essentialist philosophy of religion, *The Nature of Necessity.* Plantinga developed two main arguments I shall discuss, the ontological argument for God's existence and the free will defense of theism against the atheistic argument from evil.

20. Plantinga's Ontological Argument

(i) A Linguistic Version of Plantinga's Ontological Argument

The ontological argument states in part that *God possibly exists* and therefore *God exists.* The conclusion is effected via the additional premise, "If God possibly exists, then God necessarily exists." Given the truth of this additional premise, the crucial question becomes Does God possibly exist?

Plantinga's version of this argument is framed in terms of possible worlds and in terms of a property definitive of God, *maximal excellence.* To say that God is maximally excellent is to say God has the highest possible degree of metaphysical worth; God has the maximally metaphysically excellent conjunction of mutually compatible great-making properties, namely, the conjunction *being omniscient and omnipotent and morally perfect.*

Plantinga's ontological argument is not formulated as an argument from certain premises in the philosophy of language, and in this respect it differs from many other essentialist arguments. Plantinga's theory is logically dependent, however, on the theory of rigid designation and the associated notion of an individual existing in many possible worlds, and his theory is logically equivalent to an argument stated in terms of rigid designators.

The argument Plantinga actually states is

1. The property *has maximal greatness* entails the property *has maximal excellence in every possible world.*
2. *Maximal excellence* entails *omniscience, omnipotence,* and *moral perfection.*
3. *Maximal greatness* is possibly exemplified.

Therefore

4. There exists a being that has maximal excellence in every world.

Because (4) entails that there exist a being that has maximal excellence in the actual world, it follows that God actually exists.

Naturally, the crucial premise is (3). I shall examine shortly the question of whether (3) is true, but first I want to indicate how a linguistic version of Plantinga's ontological argument can be formulated in terms of the essentialists' philosophy of language and Kripke's distinction between strong and weak rigid designators.

   5. "God" is a strong rigid designator.
   6. For any expression E, if E is a strong rigid designator, then E's designatum exists in every possible world.

Therefore,

   7. The designatum of "God" exists in every possible world.

Plantinga does not share the view of Marcus, Geach, Kripke, Kaplan, Wettstein, Salmon, and others that proper names are directly referential but instead holds that they express properties. "God" expresses the property specified in (1), namely, the property *being whoever is maximally great.* It is by virtue of expressing this property that "God" refers descriptively to a being that exists in every possible world. A direct reference theorist might rephrase this and say that "God" refers directly to a being that exists in every possible world by virtue of obeying the rule of use or reference-fixing description that *"God" refers directly to whoever is maximally great.*

   Given that "God" is used to express the property of *being whoever is maximally great,* Plantinga's crucial premise,

   3. *Maximal greatness* is possibly exemplified,

is logically equivalent to the linguistic premise,

   5. "God" is a strong rigid designator.

Thus, if we find that there is reason to believe (5) false, that would suffice to show that (3) is also false.

   The issue regarding the truth or falsity of (5) may be explained in terms of the issue of whether "God" is a strong or weak rigid designator. If weak, "God" refers to a being that exists in some but not all possible worlds, and from this fact one cannot infer that God actually exists. If "God" is a weak rigid designator, then it expresses not the property *being whoever is maximally great* but instead property *being whoever is maximally excellent.* The difference is that maximal greatness entails *being maximally excellent in every possible world* and maximal excellence does not entail this property. Maximal excellence merely entails *being omniscient, omnipotent, and perfectly good,* and this latter property does not entail *exists in the actual world.* Given a descriptional theory of reference, it is possible to hold that a proper name is a weak rigid designator of something that does not actually exist; if God does not actually exist, "God" may nonetheless be a weak rigid designator of God in the sense that "God" expresses the property *being whoever is maximally excellent.* Given the descriptional theory of proper names, expressing this property is a necessary and sufficient condition of "God" being a weak rigid designator.

Accordingly, the linguistic version of the ontological argument comes down to this: Is "God" a strong or weak rigid designator?

(ii) Plantinga's Theory that It Is Rationally Acceptable to Believe "God" Is a Strong Rigid Designator

Although Plantinga believes

5. "God" is a strong rigid designator,

he admits that a rational person may disbelieve (5). Calling his ontological argument "Argument A," Plantinga writes,

> It must be conceded, however, that Argument A is not a successful piece of natural theology. For the latter typically draws its premises from the stock of propositions accepted by nearly every sane man, or perhaps nearly every rational man. . . . And ["*Maximal greatness* is possibly exemplified"], the central premise of Argument A, is not of this sort; a sane and rational man who thought it through and understood it might none the less reject it, remaining agnostic or even accepting instead the possibility of no-maximality. . . .
>
> Hence our verdict on these reformulated versions of St. Anselm's argument [such as the version A]) must be as follows. They cannot, perhaps, be said to *prove* or *establish* their conclusion. But since it is rational to accept their central premise they do show that it is rational to *accept* that conclusion.[1]

Plantinga says the premise *that maximal greatness is possibly exemplified* is similar in its rational acceptability or rejectability to Leibniz's Law:

For any objects x and y and property P, if x = y, then x has P if and only if y has P.

Some rational people accept Leibniz's Law and some rational people reject it, and a person who accepts it (or rejects it) is within his epistemic rights. Plantinga continues, "So if we carefully ponder Leibniz's Law and the alleged objections, if we consider its connections with other propositions we accept or reject and still find it compelling, we are within our rights in accepting it—and this whether or not we can convince others. But then the same goes for [the proposition *that maximal greatness is possibly exemplified*]" (221).

But this analogy is ill-advised because Leibniz's Law is a tautology, and *that maximal greatness is possibly exemplified* is not a tautology. A tautology is a theorem of logic and Leibniz's Law is a theorem of first-order predicate calculus with identity. Leibniz's Law as stated by Plantinga is a free English translation of the symbolic formula:

$(x)(y)(z)(x = y \supset (Hxz \equiv Hyz))$

where "Hxz" means z is a property and x has z, and "Hyz" means z is a property and y has z, and "$\supset$" means materially implies. This was first pointed out by Peter

Van Inwagen in his article "Ontological Arguments" in *Noûs* (1977).[2] Now, whatever else may belong to a definition of a rational person, accepting the theorems of standard logic belongs to it. I think Plantinga is not clearly distinguishing Leibniz's Law from some other thesis or theses, for example, some metaphysical thesis that belongs to the dispute about whether properties are universals or particulars, or whether all properties are exemplifiable by more than one individual or some properties are exemplifiable by only one individual.

Whereas Leibniz's Law is a tautology, "maximal greatness is possibly exemplified" is not. Neither is it analytic; if it were analytic, it would be reducible to a tautology by substitution of synonyms for synonyms, which it is not. Thus, it must be a synthetic statement. Because it is not determined to be true or false by observation or induction, it must be a priori. Although Plantinga does not say so, it seems undeniable that "maximal greatness is possibly exemplified" expresses a synthetic a priori truth if it is true at all.

Can we say the same about the crucial premise in the linguistic version of the ontological argument, the premise

5. "God" is a strong rigid designator?

We can, *if* we are assuming that "God" is used to express the property of *being whoever is maximally great*. Premise (5) taken without this qualification is contingent and a posteriori because it is an empirical fact that "God" is used to express this property or is used as a designator at all. To avoid any unclarity on this point, I shall henceforth include this qualification within (5), so that (5) becomes

5A. If "God" is used to express the property of *being whoever is maximally great*, then "God" is a strong rigid designator.

Premise (5A), but not (5) taken by itself, is a synthetic a priori truth if true at all. If "God" expresses this property but this property is unexemplified, then "God" is not a strong rigid designator. It is not weak either, for if "God" expresses this property and designates at all, it designates strongly. If this property is unexemplified, then "God" is a strong rigid nondesignator, that is, "God" designates nothing at all with respect to any possible world but is such that, if *per impossible*, it were to designate, it would designate the same being with respect to every possible world. The linguistic version of the ontological argument is unsound if "God" is either a weak designator or a strong rigid nondesignator.

Plantinga's implicit claim about the strong rigidity of "God" is quite different from the usual claims made by essentialists. Essentialists want to argue that *all* rational persons should find it modally intuitive that "two" is a strong rigid designator and that "water" or "Descartes" is a weak rigid designator. But Plantinga is proposing a novel twist to the typical essentialist argument, the novelty being his claim that some but not all rational persons may find it modally intuitive that "God" is a strong rigid designator.

This point deserves some elaboration. First, the use of modal intuitions as evidence is part and parcel of the essentialists' method of linguistic analysis. For example, Kripke remarks that "we have a direct intuition of the rigidity of names, exhibited in our understanding of the truth conditions of particular sentences."[3] Accordingly, we might say that whether "God" is strongly rigid is a matter about which some rational people have some intuitions and other rational people have different intuitions. Regarding Kripke's association of modal intuitions with the assignment of truth conditions to sentences, Plantinga's position suggests that some rational persons would assign to "God exists" the truth conditions, *"God exists" is true if and only if maximal excellence is exemplified in every possible world,* whereas others would assign the truth conditions, *"God exists" is true if and only if maximal excellence is exemplified in the actual world and some (but not all) merely possible worlds.*

By way of illuminating this method, I compare it with the logical positivists' method. It perhaps goes without saying that the logical positivists would regard the issue of the modal intuitions associated with "God exists" as senseless. They would object that there is no possible means of verifying which of these seeming modal intuitions is the correct one; the sentences articulating these intuitions do not refer to any possible sense-data and therefore are senseless. Modal intuitions are a species of metaphysical intuition and as such are to be rejected.

But the most interesting point here is that the positivists themselves were implicitly committed to modal intuitions of possibilities and impossibilities in the very formulation of their verificationist method. For they defined a sentence with sense as one that is verifiable by *possible* sense-data. Thus, in order to comprehend a sentence's sense, it is not necessary to experience a sense-datum. Indeed, in most cases this is out of the question because most sentences I understand are not about my actual sense-data. Rather, in most cases it is sufficient to have the modal intuition that the described sense-data or sensory experiences *are possible.* This intuition is not one of sense-data or any other sort of a posteriori mode of observation. Rather, it is by consulting my modal intuitions about what is and is not possible that I determine whether a sentence has sense or not.

The positivists, accordingly, left open a door to metaphysical knowledge, a door they themselves used (without explicitly reflecting upon it), namely, the *intuition of possibilities or impossibilities.* It is this method of obtaining metaphysical knowledge that lies at the basis of essentialism, for determinations of what is a strong or weak designator, what is possible, impossible, or necessary, are one and all based on the modal intuitions that belong to the "linguistic intuitions" that accompany the use of the relevant expressions. It is precisely these modal intuitions that Plantinga relies on in reaching his conclusions in the philosophy of religion.

Plantinga's implicit thesis that some but not all rational people will find it modally intuitive that "God" is a strong rigid designator entails that the rules of use of words, their "character" in Kaplan's terminology, are ambiguous across different people. Some people understand the rule of use of "God" to be a rule dictating its strong rigidity and others do not. These rules of use, however, are not the ultimate court of appeal. For the ordinary language philosopher, these rules *are* the last court of appeal, the bedrock of evidence upon which philosophical theories are based. But for the essentialists, the rules themselves are justified by and dependent upon our intuitions, principally our modal intuitions. We cannot ask which modal intuition about "God" is the correct one by appealing to rules of use of this name, but instead determine which rule is the correct one by appealing to our modal intuitions.

(iii) An Argument for the Rational Unacceptability of the Belief that "God" Is a Strong Rigid Designator

Is Plantinga correct that it is rationally acceptable to believe that "God" is strongly rigid and also rationally acceptable to believe it is not strongly rigid? I think not, for it is the case that *if it is equally rational to believe as to disbelieve some proposition p, then it is more rational to remain agnostic about p.* If this is the case, then it is not rationally acceptable to believe Plantinga's ontological argument. Neither is it rationally acceptable to disbelieve it. Rather, it is rationally acceptable to suspend judgment about it.

Richard Purtill suggests a similar point in his article "Plantinga, Necessity, and God," when he writes of Plantinga's ontological argument, "If theism and atheism are *equally* rational, it requires further argument (perhaps of a William Jamesian kind?) to show that agnosticism is not more rational than either theism or non-theism on the principle 'suspend judgement if contrary views are equally rational.'"[4] Plantinga responds to Purtill as follows: "Purtill's Principle 'suspend judgement if contrary views are equally rational' seems to me very bad advice. This principle seems to imply, for example, that a person has no right to believe in other minds, say, unless he knows or has good reason to believe that the epistemological problem of other minds has been solved."[5] But Plantinga goes wrong here, for the agnostic principle ("suspend judgement if contrary views are equally rational") does not imply a person has no epistemic right to believe in other minds unless she knows the epistemological problem of other minds is solved. Rather, it implies merely that the person has no right to believe in other minds if belief in other minds is equally rational as disbelief in them. Now it is both true and obvious to nearly every sane person that it is more rational to believe in other minds than to disbelieve in them *even if* the epistemological problem of other minds has not been solved. This follows from any plausible definition of a rational person. Plantinga uses but does not define "rational person" in his discussion of the ontological argument, which produces vagueness or ambiguity in his theory and contributes to the implausibility of his response to Purtill. A plausible definition is this:

Df. A person is rational if and only if her beliefs (1) do not violate any of the principles of deductive or inductive logic, (2) are not correctable in the light of currently accepted scientific theory, and (3) are not correctable in the light of the obvious facts of common sense.

Because it is unlikely that anybody's total set of beliefs meets all of these conditions, this notion of rationality should be understood as relativized to a proposition p or argument A. A person's beliefs about a proposition p or argument A are rational if and only if they meet the above three conditions. Consider the proposition *that other minds exist*. Now if anything at all is an obvious fact of common sense, it is that other minds exist. This is an obvious fact even if philosophers have not yet worked out to the satisfaction of all a complex argument for the existence of other minds. It is part of the notion of rationality to know when to believe something even if one does not have an argument for it and to know when to suspend belief unless one has an argument for it, and the case of other minds is a paradigmatic instance of the former.

I think, however, there is a good argument for other minds implicit in people's belief systems. The argument has the two premises (a) there are bodies that behave in ways relevantly similar to my bodily ways of expressing my mental states, and (b) the best explanation of this fact is that the behavior of these other bodies also expresses mental states. The conclusion is that it is probable that other minds exist.

In his reply to Purtill, Plantinga goes on to make the unsubstantiated claim that "few if any interesting philosophical theses or claims can be shown to follow from premises one cannot rationally reject via argument-forms with the same property" (71). This is a rather bold statement to make without any accompanying argument, for the statement seems very difficult to believe. If the statement were true, there would be no point (or hardly any point) in doing philosophy because for any (or virtually any) interesting philosophical thesis p, it would be just as rational to believe p as to disbelieve p, regardless of how complex and powerful the argument one developed for or against it. Plantinga's claim is in fact a principle of skepticism which he has given us no reason to believe and which goes against standard principles about rationality that nearly all philosophers find self-evident or plausible. If his claim has any plausibility it is a specious plausibility derived from conflating it with the true empirical observation *that philosophers throughout history have disagreed about most or all interesting philosophical theses.* This observation, however, is consistent with the plausible and nonskeptical principle, For any pair of interesting philosophical theses {p, ~p}, either p or ~p is rationally acceptable, but not both, even though philosophers may have a difficult time in determining which member of the pair is rationally acceptable.

Plantinga, then, has failed to rebut or even impugn the agnostic principle (if contrary beliefs are equally rational, it is more rational to suspend judgment), and because this principle is either a self-evident or plausible principle of rational belief-formation, we should endorse it. Accordingly, Plantinga has not shown that it is rationally acceptable to believe his ontological argument.

It might be objected to this account that I have not discussed Plantinga's writings on basic beliefs, published during the late 1970s, 1980s, and 1990s, in which he asserts that belief in God is a basic belief, not needing any justification. But my interest in this section on the essentialist philosophy of religion is not in Plantinga's writing as a whole but in his writings during his essentialist period, which centers on *The Nature of Necessity, God, Freedom and Evil,* and a number of associated articles. I am not discussing his pre-essentialist period, exemplified by his book *God and Other Minds* (1967), or his "epistemological period" (I do not call it postessentialist because he still holds essentialist theses but these are no longer at the forefront of his concerns), which in terms of published writings dates from his article "Is Belief in God Rational?" (1979). Plantinga's theory that belief in God is properly basic has been subjected to extensive criticism, and I refer the reader to these writings.[6]

(v) Van Inwagen and Morris on the Rationality of Plantinga's Modal Intuitions

Both Van Inwagen and Morris have argued against Plantinga's claim that belief and disbelief in *that maximal greatness is possibly exemplified* are rational acceptable. A discussion of their arguments will further clarify the issue.

In his article "Ontological Arguments," Van Inwagen makes a point somewhat similar to the one I have defended, namely, that the most rational attitude to *that maximal greatness is possibly exemplified* is neither belief nor disbelief but agnosticism. But Van Inwagen's justification for his claim is untenable. To begin with, he concurs with Plantinga that it is possible that there is some proposition that it is rationally acceptable to believe and also rationally acceptable to disbelieve (390–91); but if the principle of agnosticism is true, as I think it is, this is not possible. Van Inwagen, however, denies that the proposition, *that maximal greatness is possibly exemplified,* is one of these propositions. His reason is the alleged fact that the proposition is not relevantly dissimilar to the mathematical proposition

M. Possibly, some real number R both has a decimal expansion including
    7777 and measures the circumference of a circle whose diameter
    measures 1.

Van Inwagen correctly notes that nobody has any idea whatsoever if (M) is true or false and that (M) "is obviously such that no philosopher has a 'right to his opinion' about its truth-value" (391). That is, the most rational attitude is (M) is to suspend judgment about it. But Van Inwagen then incorrectly criticizes Plantinga for not implying any relevant difference between (M) and the proposition *that maximal greatness is possibly exemplified:* "Since Plantinga has not pointed out any epistemically interesting feature that [the proposition *that maximal greatness is possibly exemplified* does] not share with [M], his argument for the rationality of belief in God is, as it stands, no better than the argument involving [M] . . . ; that is to say, it fails" (392). Van Inwagen is mistaken here, in spite of the fact that Plantinga later responded sympathetically to Van Inwagen's criticism.[7] The difference is this: the reason we do not know whether (M) is true or false is that the proof of (M) or its negation is too complex for humans to have as yet discovered (or to discover at all). But Plantinga explicitly says that there is no proof (or disproof) of his premise *that maximal greatness is possibly exemplified:* "There seems to be no compelling argument for [this premise] that does not at some point invoke that very principle."[8] By contrast, there is a compelling argument for or against (M); it is just that it is too complex for humans to have discovered it.

Accordingly, the reason we should suspend judgment about *that maximal greatness is possibly exemplified* is not that it is relevantly similar to (M) (it is not); rather, the reason is that there is no proof or disproof of this proposition, and this allows for the claim that belief and disbelief in the proposition are equally rational, which in turn entails (by virtue of the principle of agnosticism) that it is more rational to suspend judgment.

This raises the question, Is Plantinga right that there is no compelling proof or disproof *that maximal greatness is possibly exemplified?* Morris constructed an argument that it is more rational to believe this proposition than to disbelieve it. He proposes to resolve the conflict of modal intuitions about *that maximal greatness is possibly exemplified* by showing that the Plantingians have a *justified* modal intuition, whereas the skeptics, or at least the atheists, do not. (The skeptics in the present context include atheists, agnostics, and some theists, such as Richard Swinburne and John Hick, who claim that God actually exists but does not exist in every possible world.) Morris claims that an intuition is justified if it can be traced to a reliable belief-forming mechanism. He argues that the Plantingian or Anselmian (the theist who believes God exists in every possible world) can explain his intuition by saying that God planted the intuition in him. Morris's criterion of justification is that if an intuition, on the assumption that it is true, provides the person who has the intuition with a means of explaining it as a result of a reliable belief-forming mechanism, then the intuition is more warranted than any incompatible intuition that does not provide such an explanation of itself. According to Morris, this criterion is met by the Anselmian modal intuition: "If an Anselmian God exists and creates rational beings whose end is to know him, it makes good sense that they should be able to come to know something of his existence and attributes. Such a being could, in his creation of us, render us at least capable under the right conditions of having reliable intuitions such as those which yield the Anselmian conception of God."[9] Insofar as the Anselmian has a plausible explanatory account of his intuitions and his opponents do not have such an account of their contrary intuitions, "the Anselmian's natural preference of his own intuitions is epistemically enhanced and has a higher epistemic status than the contrary preferences of his opponent" (190–91).[10] This epistemic criterion, however, is inadequate, for it is met by many conflicting intuitions. Suppose, for example, there exists a god (such as the god of Hick and Swinburne) who does not exist in every possible world; this god also would be likely to implant in his creatures the modal intuition (shared by Swinburne, Hick, and others) that he actually exists but does not necessarily exist. Both intuitions would be equally justified by this criterion, and the principle of agnosticism would again dictate suspension of judgment.

The fact is that Morris's criterion merely divides a subset of conflicting modal intuitions from the broader set of all conflicting modal intuitions and shows that other things being equal, this subset is epistemically enhanced relative to the members not in this subset. The subset in question contains all and only those that can be explained in terms of a reliable belief-forming mechanism, on the assumption they are true. But providing such a division is not sufficient to enable Morris's criterion to be epistemically adequate (to show that an intuition is justified) because this criterion is satisfied by all the conflicting intuitions in the privileged subset.

Does this mean we are left in the last analysis with undecidable modal intuitions regarding whether or not maximal greatness is possibly exemplified or whether "God" is strongly rigid? I believe some considerations suggest that we are not left in this agnostic position.

One pertains to an argument that Richard Gale has offered in *On the Nature and Existence of God* (1991), which ranks with Plantinga's *The Nature of Necessity* as one of the two most important books in the essentialists' philosophy of religion. Gale has offered the interesting argument that the modal intuition *that maximal greatness is possibly exemplified* has less epistemic weight than the modal intuition that there is at least one possible world in which there is gratuitous evil. Gale points out that if there is one merely possible world in which there is one gratuitous evil, then God does not exist in that world and therefore does not necessarily exist.[11] Gale's case may be strengthened by pointing out that the modal intuition that there is one merely possible world that contains galaxies, stars, planets, and animals but no God has greater epistemic weight than the modal intuition that maximal greatness is possibly exemplified. In response to theists who deny this, we may borrow Gale's argument: the concept of a maximally great being is very complex and problematic, whereas the notion of a gratuitous evil or a world with only matter and organisms as its concreta is relatively simple and unproblematic and thus has greater intuitive credibility.[12]

I believe an even stronger argument is possible, namely, that the logical argument from evil is sound and that God does not actually exist. I present a new version of this argument in the following section, in the context of an evaluation of Plantinga's free will defense.

21. Plantinga's Free Will Defense

(i) The Logical Problem of Evil

Essentialism may be understood as based in part on a theory about the meaning of two words, "necessarily" and "possibly." Corresponding to these two words are Plantinga's two main theses in the philosophy of religion, that *necessarily, God exists* and that *possibly, evil is consistent with God's existence.* The first theory is Plantinga's ontological argument and the second is his free will defense.

The free will defense is the focus in this section. To understand the need for a free will defense in the context of a theory that human life has an objective religious meaning is to understand the problem that evil poses; the main difficulty with the claim that there is a metaphysically perfect being that is meant by human religious attitudes is that such a being appears inconsistent with the moral imperfection of the world. To put the issue in a strong light, how can a person consistently believe that there is a wholly good, all-powerful, and all-knowing Creator if she is in a boxcar on the way to an extermination camp in Auschwitz? The logical argument from evil claims that a person cannot consistently believe this. The logical argument is that the proposition

G. God exists and is wholly good, omnipotent, and omniscient

is inconsistent with

E. There is evil.

The logical argument from evil should be understood as an argument that the beliefs of a theist are inconsistent, that she believes both (G) and (E). The logical argument does not aim to show that God does not exist, for that would require settling the empirical question of whether there is evil. But the logical argument— that if there is evil, there is no God—clearly has compelling force because the typical theist believes there is evil. I argued in the chapter on logical positivism that there probably is not only evil but also gratuitous evil, which is a *probabilist argument from evil;* I shall not assume here these results but shall independently discuss the *logical argument from evil.*

The free will defense against the logical argument is the argument that (G) and (E) are consistent. The defense proceeds by arguing that there is some proposition (p) whose conjunction with (G) is consistent and entails (E). If *that (G) and (p)* is consistent and entails *that (E)*, it follows that (G) and (E) are consistent, which would refute the logical argument from evil.

The free will defense aims to establish that it is possible that God could not have created a world with free creatures who always choose what is right. Plantinga wants to argue that the proposition (p) (or at least one candidate for the proposition [p]) is

p. For any possible world W that both contains moral good and is creatable by God, W also contains moral evil; and God creates a world containing moral good.

Plantinga does not need to show that (p) is true, merely that it is possibly true, for possible truth, not truth, is all that is needed to show (a) that (p) is *consistent* with (G) and (b) that *(p) and (G)* entail *(E)*.

Plantinga is widely regarded as having succeeded in his enterprise, that is, as having successfully mounted a free will defense against the logical problem of evil. As Plantinga notes in his article "Tooley and Evil: A Reply" (1981), "Now, as opposed to twenty or twenty-five years ago, most atheologians have conceded that in fact there isn't any inconsistency between the existence of an omnipotent, omniscient and wholly good God and the existence of the evil the world contains."[13] This concession is due almost exclusively to the impact of Plantinga's free will defense. I shall argue in this section, however, that Plantinga's free will defense does not succeed and that (G) is inconsistent with (E). Insofar as the results of the section on the ontological argument are to be taken as our guide about objective religious meaning, we may say that the only rationally acceptable attitude is *agnosticism*. But in this section, I shall argue that if there is evil the only rationally acceptable attitude vis-à-vis monotheism is *atheism*.

I shall first outline Plantinga's argument, then trace its ultimate presuppositions back to the basic doctrines of essentialism, and finally offer my criticisms of his argument.

(ii) Plantinga's Argument

Counterfactuals are propositions that state if a certain antecedent condition X obtained, then a certain consequent Y would obtain ("If it were the case that X, then it would be the case that Y"). The properties of counterfactuals in general will be explored at greater length in section (iii) below, but here I shall discuss one species of counterfactuals, the so-called counterfactuals of freedom, which state what a person would freely do or decide if she were in a certain situation. Consider these two counterfactuals about a possible bribe offer to Curley:

CA. If Curley had been offered $20,000, he would have accepted the bribe.

CR. If Curley had been offered $20,000, he would have rejected the bribe.

Plantinga states that either (CA) is true or (CR) is true. Suppose (CA) is true. Then if God actualized the state of affairs C, *Curley's being offered the bribe,* then Curley would have accepted the bribe. It follows that the possible world W consisting of C and Curley's rejecting the bribe could not have been actualized by God. In order to actualize W, God must actualize C, but if God actualizes C, then (because [CA] is true and [CR] false) Curley accepts the bribe.

Before proceeding any further, I must discuss the idea that God actualizes a certain state of affairs pertinent to the free decision of a creature. Plantinga's theory here will need emendation before his doctrine can be given an adequate formulation because he erroneously talks of God "strongly actualizing" the state of affairs C consisting of Curley being offered the bribe. By strong actualization Plantinga means causation; God strongly actualizes a state of affairs, such as *the earth's orbiting the sun,* if and only if he causes it to be actual. But God cannot cause a state of affairs consisting of a free decision to be actual, because if he caused the free decision, the decision would be not free but causally determined. According to Plantinga, states of affairs consisting of free decisions are instead weakly actualized by God; in these cases, God (1) strongly actualizes a state of affairs consisting of somebody's being free with respect to a given action and (2) God knows what free decision the person would make if she were free with respect to a given action. Plantinga writes in *The Nature of Necessity,*

> Not even God can cause it to be the case that I freely refrain from [action] A. Even so, he *can* cause me to be free with respect to A, and to be in some set S of circumstances including appropriate laws and antecedent conditions. He may also know, furthermore, that *if* he creates me and causes me to be free in these circumstances, I will refrain from A. If so, there is a state of affairs he can actualize, cause to be actual, such that if he does so, then I will freely refrain from A. In a broader sense of "bring about" [the sense of weak actualization], therefore, he *can* bring it about that I freely refrain from A.[14]

Plantinga then proceeds to talk of God strongly actualizing or causing the state of affairs consisting of Curley's being offered the bribe and thereby being in a circumstance in which he is free to accept or reject the bribe. Plantinga continues, "There is a possible world W where God strongly actualizes a totality T of states of affairs including Curley's being free with respect to taking the bribe, and where Curley takes the bribe."[15] But this is a mistake. If human beings are free, as Plantinga assumes in his argument, then God does not strongly actualize (cause) a person to offer Curley the bribe. Surely, if any human action is free, actions such as offering a bribe are free; certainly, they are free if accepting and rejecting bribes are free acts. Plantinga cannot be right when he states in "Tooley and Evil: A Reply" that "clearly there are possible worlds in which God strongly actualizes (among others) the state of affairs consisting in Curley's being offered a bribe of $20,000."[16] Perhaps this is possible if a robot offers Curley the bribe, but it is not possible if a human offers the bribe and Plantinga is correct that humans are essentially free in a libertarian sense (that is, their free acts are uncaused). This shows that Plantinga's definition of weak actualization (the "broader sense of 'bring about'") is defective because in only some cases in which a person is in a circumstance in which he is faced with a free choice, is it the case that the circumstance is caused by God. In many cases, the circumstance is itself a free action of another person or persons, in which case it is not caused by God. So we need a new category of actualization besides strong and weak, namely, *minimal actualization*. A state of affairs consisting of a free action A is minimally actualized by God if the circumstance in which the person is faced with the free choice to do A or not-A is itself a free action A′ of a creature. The state of affairs consisting of A′ will itself be either minimally actualized by God or weakly actualized by God.

Accordingly, by "actualized by God" I shall henceforth mean "strongly, weakly, or minimally actualized by God." Keeping in mind this modification to Plantinga's theory, we may proceed with the exposition. Plantinga wants to argue that it is possible that each free creature suffers from *transworld depravity*. A creature x has this condition if it is true of x that he freely does at least one thing morally wrong in each relevant possible world. This can be put more exactly as follows. Consider each world W in which x exists and is free with respect to at least one morally significant action. x is depraved if it is true that *if God had actualized W, then x would have freely chosen to do something wrong.*

If each free creature has transworld depravity, then God could not have actualized a world in which free creatures do only what is right. Of course, there will be possible worlds in which free creatures do only what is right, but they will not be actualizable by God. For in each such world, there will be at least one circumstance such that, if God were to actualize that circumstance, a free creature would freely chose to do something wrong. Consider the counterfactual,

CA. If Curley had been offered $20,000, he would have accepted the bribe,

which we presume to be true. Sentence (CA) is a would-counterfactual, and (CA)'s truth is consistent with the truth of the might-counterfactual

M. If Curley had been offered $20,000, he might have rejected the bribe.

Proposition (M) is true because there is some possible world in which Curley is offered the bribe and rejects it. But this world cannot be actualized by God because it is true that if Curley had been offered the bribe, he *would* have accepted it. The fact that Curley would have accepted the bribe is consistent with the fact that he might have rejected it.

This shows that John Mackie goes wrong in his discussion of Plantinga's theory when he claims that Plantinga's theory is that "Curley Smith suffers from what Plantinga calls 'transworld depravity'; in whatever world he exists, if he is significantly free he commits some wrong actions."[17] But this is a misunderstanding, as Plantinga notes in his article "Is Theism Really a Miracle?" (1986): "But to say that I suffer from transworld depravity is not to say that there is no possible world *at all* in which I am significantly free and always do only what is right; it is only to say that none of the worlds God could have weakly actualized is one in which I am significantly free and always do only what is right."[18] Thus, transworld depravity is not an essential property of anybody who possesses it; it is an accidental property, a property the person possesses in some possible worlds and not in others. If a world in which Curley does only what is right had been actual, then Curley would not have been depraved. As things stand, however, he is depraved. (Or at least this is possibly the case, Plantinga contends.)

Plantinga believes this gives us the proposition (p) that is needed to solve the logical problem of evil. The logical problem is that

G. God exists and is wholly good, omnipotent, and omniscient

is allegedly inconsistent with

E. There is evil.

The free will defense proceeds by arguing that there is some proposition (p) whose conjunction with (G) is consistent and entails (E). I earlier represented the proposition (p) as

p. For any possible world W that both contains moral good and is creatable by God, W also contains moral evil; and God creates a world containing moral good.

Now we can state (p) more informatively as the proposition

p'. Every possible free creature suffers from transworld depravity, and God creates a world containing moral good.

We need not suppose (p') is true in order to show that it is consistent with (G) and that (G) and (p') jointly entail (E). We need only suppose that it is possible that (p') is true.

Plantinga proceeds to argue that it is also possible that (owing to transworld depravity) there is no world creatable by God that contains a better mixture of good and evil than the actual world. He also argues that it is possible that (i) all natural evil (suffering due to earthquakes, disease, and the like) is due to the free activity of nonhuman rational creatures (angels), that (ii) there is a balance of good over evil with respect to the actions of these angels, and (iii) that there is no world creatable by God which contains a better balance of good over evil with respect to the angels it contains.

I shall evaluate Plantinga's free will defense in two stages. In section (iii) I discuss its basis in the essentialist philosophy of language and argue that in one respect it is inconsistent with the essentialist theory of counterfactual sentences and that because of this inconsistency the defense is untenable. In section (iv) I present a more direct argument against the defense and claim that even if its theory of counterfactuals is true, the defense fails to meet another condition of success.

(iii) Essentialism and Plantinga's Theory of Counterfactuals

Plantinga's free will defense hinges upon essentialism in at least three ways. It requires (a) the theory of rigid designators, (b) the theory of individual essences, and (c) the possible worlds theory of counterfactuals. The real difficulty with Plantinga's theory pertains to (c), but before I address this issue I shall set the background by discussing rigid designators and individual essences.

(a) Rigid Designation

Plantinga's free will defense succeeds only if the essentialist theory of rigid designation is true. Consider our familiar counterfactual,

CA. If Curley had been offered $20,000, he would have accepted the bribe,

which I shall now take as a sentence rather than as the proposition expressed by the sentence. Plantinga supposes it is possible that (CA) and a large number of similar counterfactuals are true. But this supposition cannot be maintained if "Curley" and other relevant expressions are not rigid designators. Suppose the theory of proper names accepted by most positivists and ordinary language philosophers were true, that these names express (nonrigid) descriptive senses, such as *the mayor of Boston*. If "Curley" expressed this descriptive sense, it would refer to different people in different possible worlds because different people in different worlds satisfy the description *the mayor of Boston*. For some of these people, (CA) would be true, and for others false. Thus, if "Curley" were nonrigid, it would not be possible that (CA) is true rather than false, and Plantinga's free will defense would be undermined. The problem in this case would be not that the sentence is ambiguous (expresses more than one proposition) but that the one proposition it expresses has conflicting truth-values, by virtue of the fact that the descriptive concept *being the mayor of Boston* that belongs to it is satisfied by different people in different worlds.

Counterfactual (CA) is true (and not false) only if "Curley" designates, in respect of other possible worlds, the same person that it designates in the actual world. There is a familiar explanation given by Kripke of how this is possible. He suggests that we take some actual individual and then stipulate that the possible worlds to which we are referring are the ones that include that person. But this method will not work for possible but unactual individuals, such as a possible daughter of Adolf Hitler. Merely possible individuals enter the free will defense because we need to consider the possibility that unactual persons do not suffer from transworld depravity. Plantinga writes, "Suppose all the people that exist in [the actual world A] suffer from transworld depravity; it does not follow that God could not have created a world containing moral good without creating one containing moral evil. God could have created *other people*."[19] Thus, Plantinga needs to show that it is possible that the relevant counterfactuals about "other people," that is, about merely possible persons, are true. Consider this counterfactual:

R. If Romulus were to be offered $20,000, he would accept the bribe,

where "Romulus" is the name of a merely possible individual. Because there is no such individual, "Romulus" has no extension; we cannot say that "Romulus" refers to *that person* (somebody we could point to) and that (R) says of a certain possible world in which *that person* exists that he accepts the bribe. A theory of individual essences is required.

(b) Individual Essences

The counterfactual sentence (R) can be given a sense and a truth-value if we suppose "Romulus" has an intension, namely, some individual essence. Given this supposition, (R) may be interpreted as saying, in effect, that if this individual essence were instantiated in the relevant circumstance in which the instantiation of this essence were offered a bribe, the instantiation of this essence would accept the bribe. Because this counterfactual makes sense (according to this theory) we can reasonably suppose that it is possible that it is true. The possibility that all relevantly similar sorts of counterfactuals are true would allow Plantinga to hold that it is possible that all merely possible free creatures, and not just the actually existing ones, suffer from transworld depravity.

But what is an individual essence? As discussed in chapter 5, the theory of essences formed an integral part of the essentialist movement, which is defined in terms of belief in de re necessity, that is, that there are some properties things possess essentially, which is to say, in each world in which they exist. One of the earliest comprehensive theories of essences is Marcus's, but her "individual essences" were not designed for the purposes needed by Plantinga's free will defense. Marcus's individual essences (such as *being philosophical*) are properties which are possessed necessarily by some but not all individuals and are partially definitive of the special character of the individual, distinguishing it from some other objects of the same kind. But what the free will defense requires is a property that is wholly definitive of the unique character of an individual and that distinguishes that individual from all other actual and possible individuals. An individual essence in Plantinga's sense is thus a property exemplified by an individual x in each possible world in which x exists and not exemplified in any possible world by anything other than x. He gives two sorts of examples of individual essences, properties such as *being identical with Socrates* and a certain species of world-indexed properties. World-indexed properties are normal properties as relativized to the world in which they are possessed; an example of a world-indexed property is Socrates' property of *being snub-nosed-in-A*, where A is the actual world. But this is not an individual essence of Socrates because other persons also possess it. Plantinga offers as examples of world-indexed properties that are individual essences of Socrates, *being married-to-Xantippe-in-A* and *being the shortest-Greek-philosopher-in-A*.

Plantinga argued in "The Boethian Compromise" (1978) that (contra the direct reference theory) proper names express individual essences. By virtue of this theory, we can explain how proper names of nonactual persons can be weak rigid designators. "Romulus" designates the same person in every world in which he exists, even though none are actual. This is achieved through "Romulus" picking out all and only the merely possible worlds in which the individual essence it expresses is instantiated.

As in the case of Romulus, we can give merely possible individuals proper names but this is not necessary in order to designate them; we can instead refer to them by means of rigid definite descriptions, such as "whoever is the shortest person in $W2$," where $W2$ is some merely possible world. We need not suppose, however, that for each *propositional* counterfactual of freedom about a merely possible individual, there is some proper name or definite description in English or any other language that designates the individual in question. The free will defense requires merely that there be counterfactual propositions about these possible individuals that are true and known by God logically prior to creation and God need not have articulated these propositions in some language.

This brings us to the next issue, whether Plantinga's theory that counterfactuals of freedom are true logically prior to creation is consistent with the standard essentialist theory of counterfactuals and if it is not, whether it is at all plausible.

(c) Can Counterfactuals of Freedom be True Logically Prior to Creation?

An element common to the essentialist theory of rigid designation, individual essences, and counterfactuals is that they all are based on the notion of possible worlds. The essentialist theory of counterfactuals concerns the rules of use of the locution "If it were to be the case that ———, then it would be the case that ———." These rules require only minimal assumptions about possible worlds, assumptions already implicit in the theory of rigid designation. The basic assumption is *that there are many merely possible worlds that are similar in some respects and dissimilar in others to the actual world.* This assumption entails that for any merely possible condition X, either (i) there is a possible world containing X more similar to the actual world than any other world including X, or (ii) there are several X-worlds tied for the X-world most similar to the actual world, or (iii) for any X-world similar to the actual world, there is another X-world that is even more similar to the actual world. This entailment provides the material for formulating the rules of use of the counterfactual locution "If it were the case that X, then it would be the case that Y," a formulation undertaken, first, by Robert Stalnaker in 1968 and then by David Lewis in 1973.[20] Stalnaker argued that the rule of use of counterfactuals is that they are used to state that in the most similar X-world, Y is the case. Lewis argued that counterfactuals are used to state that some world in which X and Y are the case is more similar to the actual world than any world in which X and not-Y hold. If we apply Stalnaker's rule to Plantinga's counterfactual of freedom (CA),

CA. If Curley had been offered $20,000, he would have accepted the bribe,

we may say that (CA) is used to state that in the possible world most similar to the actual world in which Curley is offered the bribe, Curley accepts the bribe.

It is obvious that the possible worlds theory of counterfactuals is crucial to Plantinga's free will defense. If we adopt some nonessentialist theory of counter-factuals, such as the theory adopted by many of the logical positivists, then the free will defense collapses. The positivists tended to regard counterfactuals as obeying the rules of use of material conditionals, in which case they are false if and only if their antecedent is true and consequent false. They are true if and only if either (a) their antecedent is false or (b) the antecedent and consequent are both true. But now consider Plantinga's two counterfactuals:

CA. If Curley had been offered $20,000, he would have accepted the bribe.

CR. If Curley had been offered $20,000, he would have rejected the bribe.

Because in fact Curley is not offered the bribe, both (CA) and (CR) are true (assuming they are to be analyzed as material conditionals). Because the same holds for every other relevantly similar pair of contradictory counterfactuals of freedom (whose antecedent is false), it cannot be argued that it is possible that of many such pairs, only the counterfactual describing the morally evil choice is true. The free will defense cannot get off the ground. Plantinga thus needs to resort to the essentialist theory of counterfactuals and the notions of rigidity, possible worlds, and similarity.

One reason the positivists interpreted counterfactuals as material conditionals is that they presupposed an extensional logic, which allowed only references to the actual world. But with the development of a semantics for modal logic by Carnap, Kanger, Marcus, Hintikka, Kripke, and others, a possible worlds theory became viable. Quantified modal logic introduced the operators $\Box$ ("necessarily") and $\Diamond$ ("possibly"), which were interpreted as referring to merely possible worlds as well as to the actual world. The logic of the conditional developed by Stalnaker and Lewis adds to modal logic a certain apparatus (for example, Stalnaker's "selection function" and "conditional connective") that enabled modal logic to be applied to counterfactuals.

Although Plantinga's free will defense requires the essentialist theory of coun-terfactuals, in another respect his defense is inconsistent with this theory, which points to a problem in the defense. Considering again (CA) and (CR), note that there are two possible worlds W_1 and W_2 that are exactly similar up to the time t at which Curley is offered the bribe; in W_1 Curley accepts the bribe, and in W_2 he rejects it. Both W_1 and W_2, however, are equally similar to the actual world. Given

Stalnaker's and Lewis's theories, both (CA) and (CR) are false, for a counterfactual whose antecedent is not impossible is true only if there is a world W in which the antecedent and consequent of one of the counterfactuals are both true, such that W is more similar to the actual world than another world W′ in which the antecedent is true and the consequent false.

Plantinga attempts to handle this problem by supposing that (CA) is actually true and therefore that W1 is more similar to the actual world, because W1 but not W2 shares with the actual world the truth of (CA). But this putative solution poses a serious problem, for it entails that we must presuppose the truth of (CA) in order to determine which world is most similar to the actual world. This conflicts with the Stalnaker-Lewis theory that the truth of a counterfactual is logically *conse-quential* upon which world is most similar to the actual world. Plantinga says of this situation,

> One measure of similarity between worlds involves the question of whether they share their counterfactuals.
>
> We should be unduly hasty, I think, if we drew the conclusion that the possible worlds explanation of counterfactuals is viciously circular or of no theoretical interest or importance. But it does follow that we cannot as a rule *discover* the truth value of a counterfactual by asking whether its consequent holds in those worlds most similar to the actual in which its antecedent holds. For one feature determining the similarity of worlds is whether they share their counterfactuals.[21]

This raises the question of how we can discover the truth-values of counterfactuals. Indeed, this passage suggests that they cannot be discovered, that they are unverifiable in principle, which conflicts with the ordinary and scientific rules of use of counterfactuals.

To appreciate the dimensions of this problem, we need to consider that Plantinga is supposing in *The Nature of Necessity* that counterfactuals of freedom have a truth-value logically prior to God's creation of the actual world. He is supposing that it is possible that God based his decision to create our world upon his knowledge of the truth-value of all counterfactuals of freedom and that he chose to create our world because it contained the best balance of good over evil choices made by creatures. The problem is this: Logically prior to creation, there is no actual world, so how can any counterfactual of freedom be true? A counterfactual of freedom is true only if its antecedent and consequent are true in some world that is *more similar to the actual world* than any world in which the antecedent is true and the consequent false. But if there is no actual world, how then can any counterfactual of freedom be true at all?

Robert M. Adams and Anthony Kenny originally suggested a problem of this sort (subsequently developed by William Hasker), and William Lane Craig has responded to this objection by noting that the actual world is *partly* actualized logically prior to creation.[22] Prior to creation, there actually is a deity and all necessary states of affairs.

But is this partial actuality enough to make (CA) true and (CR) false? It seems not because a world W1 in which the antecedent and consequent of (CA) are both true is equally similar to God-plus-all-necessary-states-of-affairs as a world W2 in which the antecedent and consequent of (CR) are true.

The response of Plantinga and Craig is, of course, that the relevant similarity relations do obtain prior to creation because prior to creation *counterfactuals of freedom are true*. Craig asserts that these counterfactual propositions correspond to counterfactual states of affairs; and Plantinga tersely comments in his "Reply to Adams," "What grounds the truth of the counterfactual, we may say, is just that in fact Curley is such that if he had been offered a $35,000 bribe, he would have freely taken it."[23]

Does this response beg the question? It does if in answer to the objection that "counterfactuals of freedom cannot be true logically prior to creation because there are no similarity relations among worlds that make them true," Plantinga and Craig retorted, "There are sufficient similarity relations prior to creation because counterfactuals of freedom are true prior to creation, and that provides the needed similarity relations among worlds." But in reality Plantinga and Craig are not offering this response because they are rejecting the standard Stalnaker-Lewis theory that counterfactuals are made true by similarity relations between the actual world and merely possible worlds. Instead, Plantinga and Craig suggest, they are made true by primitive *counterfactual states of affairs*, such as the fact that Curley is such that he would have taken the bribe. Craig writes that "a counterfactual is true in virtue of the fact that its corresponding counterfactual state of affairs obtains."[24]

But such a statement poses some difficulties, for it appears to render counterfactuals unverifiable in principle. In order to discover the truth-value of a counterfactual, I apparently must inspect reality to see if there is a corresponding counterfactual state of affairs. But this seems impossible. Obviously, I cannot observe (through inner or outer sense) any such state of affairs and for any counterfactual proposition, I can equally well conceive of a corresponding state of affairs as conceive that there is none. And there is no procedure I can follow (such as asking about the most similar world) that can give me any clue here. So there appears to be no means at all to determine the truth-value of counterfactuals. They are unverifiable in principle. This is inconsistent with the fact that some scientific and ordinary counterfactuals *are* verifiable.

On the Stalnaker-Lewis theory, on the other hand, we can discover counterfactuals' truth-values, by asking if their consequent holds in those worlds most similar to the actual world in which their antecedent holds. In this case, the similarity relations obtain logically prior to the truth or falsity of the counterfactual. But this similarity theory precludes counterfactuals of freedom from being true logically prior to creation, for there are then no similarity relations to *make* them true. As we have seen, the actuality of God and all necessary states of affairs cannot ground the truth-values of counterfactuals of freedom. Stalnaker writes, "It is, of course, the structure of inductive relations and causal connections [not counterfactual states of affairs] which make counterfactuals and semifactuals true or false, but they do this by determining the [similarity] relationships among possible worlds, which in turn determine the truth values of conditionals."[25]

If we ask whether the Stalnaker-Lewis or Plantinga-Craig theory of counterfactuals is true, we will find that the rules of use of counterfactuals reflect the Stalnaker-Lewis theory because these rules imply that counterfactuals are verifiable and that they are verified by determining which worlds are most similar in the relevant respects to the actual world. The rules do not imply that the truth-values of counterfactuals are determinable, if at all, by inspecting reality to see if there is a corresponding counterfactual state of affairs. Humans possess no such faculty of inspection.

In view of the amount of literature that has been published on the subject and Craig's lengthy defense of his theory in *Divine Foreknowledge and Human Freedom*, it may well be thought that my dismissal of the Plantinga-Craig theory is all too quick. Perhaps a rigorous refutation would require examining one by one the arguments offered by Craig. But this is a task best undertaken elsewhere.[26] A demonstration of the falsity of the Plantinga-Craig theory of counterfactuals is not necessary to arrive at an evaluation of the cogency of Plantinga's free will defense because there is a further argument that shows his defense to be untenable irrespective of whether the Plantinga-Craig theory of counterfactuals is true.

(iv) A Sound Logical Argument from Evil
The logical argument from evil aims to show that the following two propositions are implicitly self-contradictory:
    G. God exists and is omnipotent, omniscient, and wholly good.
    E. There is evil.
The argument for a contradiction is similar to the argument for consistency between (G) and (E) in that both aim to produce some third proposition (p). The free will defense and any other argument for consistency aims to produce a third proposition (p) that is consistent with (G) and whose conjunction with (G) entails (E), but the logical argument from evil aims to produce a third proposition (p) that

is both a necessary truth and whose conjunction with (G) produces an explicit contradiction. An explicit contradiction is a conjunction of propositions one of which is the negation of the other.

I believe that an explicit contradiction can be produced and that the necessary truth (p′) we need can be discovered by way of a criticism of Plantinga's free will defense. The problem with Plantinga's defense is located in the implicit assumptions he makes. The relevant assumptions are about freedom. Consider the following passage (in which by "significantly free" Plantinga means freedom with respect to a moral action): "Now God can create free creatures, but he cannot *cause* or *determine* them to do what is right. For if he does so, then they are not significantly free after all; they do not do what is right *freely*. To create creatures capable of *moral good,* therefore, he must create creatures capable of moral evil."[27] This suggests that by "free" Plantinga is referring (at least) to what I shall call *external freedom.* A person is externally free with respect to an action A if and only if nothing other than (external to) herself determines either that she perform A or refrain from performing A.

But Plantinga suggests in other passages that by "free" he also means *internal freedom:* "And a person is free with respect to an action A at a time t only if no causal laws and antecedent conditions determine either that he performs A at t or that he refrains from so doing" (170–71). A person is internally free with respect to an action A if and only if it is false that his past physical and psychological states, in conjunction with causal laws, determine either that he perform A or refrain from performing A.

Still later, Plantinga implies that he means *logical freedom* as well. This is implied by his claim that it is possible that each free creature chooses to do something wrong in at least one of the possible worlds in which the creature exists. A person is logically free with respect to an action A if and only if there is some possible world in which he performs A and there is another possible world in which he does not perform A. A person is logically free with respect to a wholly good life (a life in which every morally relevant action performed by the person is a good action) if and only if there is some possible world in which he lives this life and another possible world in which he does not.

It is possible to be internally-externally free but logically determined with respect to being morally good. This is the case with God, who is both internally and externally free but who does only good actions in each possible world in which he exists. God's logical determination with respect to moral goodness is entailed by his individual essence, for God's individual essence is *being maximally great,* which entails *being maximally excellent in every possible world.* Maximal excellence, as I noted above, includes the property of being wholly good.

Plantinga's failure to discuss these three senses of "freedom" *explicitly* has led to confusion among his commentators. Wesley Morrison, for example, conflates logical determinism with internal determinism. He puts forth this criticism of Plantinga:

> As Plantinga defines it, then, significant freedom [freedom with regard to morally relevant actions] is not compatible with determinism. The reason for insisting on this point in the context of a free will defense should be clear. If a compatibilist analysis of freedom and responsibility were acceptable, it would be open to an opponent of the free will defense to argue that God does not have to permit moral evil in order to create significantly free creatures who are capable of moral goodness. For example, He could instill in each of His creatures an irresistible impulse to do what is right and to refrain from doing evil, without thereby diminishing their freedom and responsibility. . . . [According to Plantinga] God's nature is such that it is logically impossible for Him to perform a wrong action. He is determined—in the strongest possible sense of "determined"—not to perform any wrong actions. Thus it seems to me that, on Plantinga's analysis of significant freedom, God is not significantly free. And since *moral* goodness presupposes significant freedom, it also follows that God is not morally good [which contradicts Plantinga's definition of God as maximally great].[28]

But Morrison's argument is based on a fallacy of equivocation with respect to "determined." According to the compatibilist theory of free will, humans are externally free but internally determined; nothing external to the agent causes her actions, but her past psychological or physical states cause her actions. If humans were internally determined, then God could make them so they always do what is right in this sense: he could make them with an "irresistible impulse to do what is right" that causally determines all their morally relevant actions. But, *pace* Morrison, this is not the sense in which God is determined to do only what is right. God is perfectly free and is not subject to any impulses, cravings, passions, urges, and so forth that causally determine his actions. God is internally free but *logically* determined to do what is right. In each possible world in which he exists, he is externally and internally free to choose what is wrong, but he chooses to do only what is right.

Morrison writes that "God has the power to perform wrong actions—in which case there will be possible worlds in which he does so" (262). This is false because the possession of a power to do something does not entail that one exercises it in some possible world. It is possible that one has the power to do A (that is, is externally-internally free to do A) but chooses not to exercise that power in each possible world in which one exists.

The distinction among these three senses of "determinism" enables us to reject Morrison's conclusion that God is not morally good. A necessary condition of being morally good, a libertarian may say, is that a person not be externally or internally determined with respect to morally relevant actions. Yet it is not a necessary condition of being morally good that a person not be logically determined with respect to morally relevant actions; a person is morally good if he freely (in the external-internal sense) chooses to do what is right in each possible world in which he exists.

With the distinction among external, internal, and logical freedom in hand, I can begin my evaluation of Plantinga's free will defense. Consider the assumption Plantinga makes at the outset: "A world containing creatures who are sometimes significantly free (and freely perform more good than evil actions) is more valuable, all else being equal, than a world containing no free creatures at all."[29]

Now what does "free" mean in this quotation? Presumably, it means external + internal + logical freedom. But one must ask, Does a person who has only external and internal freedom have less metaphysical worth than a person who is free in these two respects and also has logical freedom? The answer implied by Plantinga's own premises must be no, for God has internal-external freedom but not logical freedom, and God has the greatest possible degree of metaphysical worth. God does not have logical freedom because God has the property of maximal greatness, which includes the property of being wholly good in each world in which he exists. Thus, there is a proof that being internally-externally free but logically determined has greater metaphysical worth than being free in all three respects, the proof being

1. God possesses the maximally valuable consistent conjunction of great-making properties.
2. If it were intrinsically better to be logically free with respect to a morally good life than logically determined, and this logical freedom were consistent with God's omnipotence and omniscience, then God would possess this logical freedom.
3. Logical freedom with respect to a morally good life is consistent with omnipotence and omniscience.
4. God is logically determined with respect to a morally good life.

Therefore

5. It is false that it is intrinsically better to be logically free with respect to a morally good life than logically determined.

Premise (3) is true because "x knows all truths" does not entail "It is not logically possible for x to perform a morally wrong action," and "x is all-powerful" does not entail "It is not logically possible for x to perform a morally wrong action." Nor does the conjunction of omniscience and omnipotence entail this.

It follows that a possible world W1 containing N number of persons who always do what is right and who are logically determined with respect to moral goodness is (all other things being equal) a more metaphysically valuable world than a world W2 containing N number of persons who are logically free with respect to a morally good way of life. And this suggests that God, if he existed, would have created W1 rather than W2.

Although Plantinga does not address this issue, an unspoken assumption of his argument is that there are no possible creatures who are internally-externally free with respect to a morally good life but logically determined. This assumption is false, for "x is an internally-externally free creature with respect to a morally good life" does not entail "x is logically free with respect to a morally good life." If it did, there would have to be some relevant difference between God and creatures that ensured the entailment goes through in the case of creatures but not God. But what could this difference be? As I have suggested, none of the divine attributes (other than necessary goodness) entails necessary goodness. Nor does a conjunction of two or more of these divine attributes entail it. Further, the relevant nondivine attributes do not entail logical freedom with respect to a morally good life. For example, "x knows many but not all truths" does not entail "x freely chooses to do something wrong in at least one possible world in which x exists." Nor is this entailed by "x has the power to do many but not all things."

Very little by way of argument has been given in the literature for the claim that only God is necessarily good. Morris attempts to deduce this thesis from the thesis that the divine attributes are necessarily coextensive, that is, that the attributes of omnipotence, omniscience, perfect goodness, and so forth are exemplified by God and only God in each possible world. But then the question reverts to whether there is any reason to believe the thesis of necessary coextensivity. Morris offers the justification that he has an "intuition" of this necessary coextensivity and that this intuition is justified because it can be traced to a reliable belief-forming mechanism, namely, that if there were a god of this sort, he would have implanted this intuition in us. But we have already seen that this sort of argument fails because the same sort of argument can be used to justify the intuition that there is a god whose attributes are not necessarily coextensive.

Swinburne presents a different sort of argument in *The Coherence of Theism*, namely, that the conjunction of omniscience and perfect freedom entails necessary goodness. This argument, however, even if sound, does nothing to show that if any being is not both omniscient and perfectly free, it is not necessarily good. Swinburne argues that a perfectly free person "cannot do what he does not regard as in some way a good thing"[30] because the only constraint upon doing what one believes is right is a causal influence upon one's choices, and a perfectly free person is causally uninfluenced (as well as causally undetermined). A person other than God can be perfectly free in Swinburne's sense because there can be a finite disembodied mind, for example, an angel, who is not causally influenced by its prior psychological states or anything else. Further, a nonomniscient person can have only true moral beliefs, if only for the reason that it is possible to know all moral truths and not know all mathematical truths. Such a person would be necessarily morally good, given Swinburne's own premises. Indeed, using Swinburne's premises one can prove the possibility of necessarily good persons other than God:

6. It is possible that there is a nonomniscient mind x such that: for each possible world W in which x exists, and for each circumstance in which x is faced with a moral choice, x knows all the factual and moral truths he needs to know to make a correct choice.

7. This mind x is neither causally determined nor causally influenced by any external or internal factors.

8. Necessarily, if a perfectly free mind knows all the moral and factual truths needed to make the morally correct choice in any morally significant circumstance in which he finds himself, then this mind will make the correct choice.

If such persons are possible, worlds containing only such persons and God and no nature (a physical realm) are possible; in these worlds, there is no moral or natural evil. The counterfactual argument that it is possible that if God created these persons in certain circumstances, they *would* do something wrong, fails because these persons are necessarily good. Accordingly, Plantinga's free will defense cannot be used to show that a world containing these persons is not creatable.

The idea that there are possible creatures who are necessarily good and that God could have created a world containing only them does not depend on the truth of Plantinga's theory of counterfactuals of freedom. At first glance, it might appear there is a dependency because presumably God, if he existed, would have known logically prior to creation counterfactuals about these creatures and made his decision to create a world with them on the basis of this knowledge. For example, God would know prior to creation

9. If the individual essences of some necessarily good creatures were to be instantiated, the instantiations of these essences would always do what is right.

Proposition (9) is true logically prior to creation even if Plantinga's theory is false, for (9) is analytically true and thereby does not require similarity relations among worlds to make it true. Proposition (9) is true because the antecedent entails the consequent. Accordingly, if the Stalnaker-Lewis theory of counterfactuals is true, there are no *logically contingent* counterfactuals of freedom that are true logically prior to creation, but there are logically necessary counterfactuals of freedom that are true logically prior to creation, and the latter are all that God needs to know which world to create.

The fact that necessarily good creatures are possible supplies the missing proposition (p′) that will enable the conjunction of (G), (E), and (p′) to form an explicit contradiction. Statements (G) and (E) we recall, are

G. God exists and is wholly good, omnipotent, and omniscient.

E. There is evil.

There are several ways to formulate (p′), one being based on a proposition in Plantinga's first discussion of the free will defense in his article "The Free Will Defence" (1965). It reads as follows:

10. If God is all-good and the proposition *God creates free humans and the free humans He creates always do what is right* is consistent, then any free humans created by God always do what is right.

If the negation of (E) is to be deduced from (10) and (G), then (10) needs to be a necessary truth. But we need further premises. One is

11. It is consistent that God creates free humans and the free humans he creates always do what is right.

Another is

12. It is possible that: free humans who always do what is right exist without there being any natural evil, and if God creates these humans, he will not create natural evil.

If (10), (11), and (12) are all necessary truths, then the proposition (p′) is the conjunction of (10), (11), and (12) because the conjunction of these three propositions with (G) entails

-E. There is no evil.

This would give a sound logical argument from evil, for it would show that the theist is committed to a proposition two of whose conjunctions are *there is evil* and *there is no evil*.

In "The Free Will Defence" Plantinga attacks (10). He writes, "There seems to be no reason for supposing that (10) is true at all, let alone necessarily true. Whether the free men created by God would always do what is right would presumably be up to them; for all we know they might sometimes exercise their freedom to do what is wrong."[31]

In one sense Plantinga is right, for humans are logically free with respect to a morally good life and *being logically free* and *being logically determined* are plausibly thought to be essential properties. There is no possible world in which humans are logically determined with respect to a morally good life. But Plantinga overlooks the possibility that there are possible rational creatures who are internally-externally free but logically determined, and if we take "humans" in (10) in a broad sense as referring to any rational creature, then Plantinga's purported refutation of (10) fails. Thus, the logical argument from evil goes through unscathed by Plantinga's criticism.

The soundness of the logical argument from evil can be seen more clearly if we consider a relevant proposition from Plantinga's *God, Freedom and Evil*, a proposition that he concedes "for purposes of argument" is a necessary truth (although he subsequently makes no attempt to show it is not a necessary truth). The proposition is

13. An omniscient and omnipotent [and wholly] good being eliminates
every evil that it can properly eliminate.

A being *properly eliminates* an evil state of affairs if it eliminates that evil without either eliminating an outweighing good or bringing about a greater evil. A good state of affairs g outweighs an evil state of affairs e if the conjunctive state of affairs *g and e* is a good state of affairs. Given these definitions, it is plausible to think that (13) is a necessary truth. If a state of affairs is eliminated by its actualization being prevented, and if a possible world is a state of affairs (a maximal state of affairs), then (13) entails

14. God prevents from being actual any world W1 that contains evil if there
is another creatable world W2 containing at least as much good as W1
and no evil.

There is no world containing evil that contains more good than a creatable world W2 that contains no evil and that consists of God and an infinite number of necessarily good and internally-externally free rational creatures who perform an infinite number of good acts. This is true by virtue of the mathematics of infinity, for the addition of more creatures or acts to a world containing an infinite number of them does not increase the amount of good, for infinity plus N for any finite number N equals infinity. Thus we cannot say that there is a possible world containing evil and infinity-plus-N good acts and that this world contains more good than a world containing an infinite number of good acts and no evil. Of course, we can get *more* good acts if we add to a world with aleph-zero good acts an additional aleph-one acts, where aleph-zero is the number of all finite integers and aleph-one is (by the continuum hypothesis) the number of all real numbers. But this sort of argument can be blocked by supporting there is another world with no evil but with aleph-one good acts. The same holds for any other transfinite cardinal greater than aleph-zero.

The above arguments about necessarily good free rational creatures show that

15. There is some possible creatable world W2 containing only God and an
infinite number of necessarily good free rational creatures who perform
an infinite number of good acts.

This gives us our explicit contradiction, namely, the conjunction of the following propositions:

G. God exists and is wholly good, omnipotent, and omniscient.

E. There is evil.

14. God prevents from being actual any world W1 that contains evil if there is another creatable world W2 containing at least as much good as W1 and no evil.

15. For any possible creatable world W1 containing evil and an infinite number of free rational creatures who perform an infinite number of good acts, there is another possible creatable world W2 containing no evil and an infinite number of necessarily good free rational creatures who perform an infinite number of good acts.

-E. There is no evil (from G, [14], and [15]).

The logical argument from evil, then, appears to succeed, or at least Plantinga and nobody else known to me has given a good reason to think it does not. Accordingly, we must relinquish at least for the present the claim that human life has an objective, monotheistic religious meaning. It seems reasonable to believe on the basis of the considerations adduced in this chapter that the presence of evil makes human life religiously meaningless in the monotheistic sense.

Note that this logical argument from evil is not John Mackie's argument, which Plantinga is commonly credited with refuting. Mackie's argument is, "If God has made men such that in their free choices they sometimes prefer what is good and sometimes what is evil, why could he not have made men such that they always freely choose the good? If there is no logical impossibility in a man's freely choosing the good on one, or on several occasions, there cannot be a logical impossibility in his freely choosing the good on every occasion."[32]

In a possible worlds formulation, this may be construed as the claim that there is a logically possible world in which humans always choose what is right. But Plantinga counters this by noting that the existence of such a possible world does not mean that God could have actualized it, for it is possible that if God had created the people in this world and placed them in the relevant circumstances, they would have made wrong choices. In short, Mackie's argument fails because he supposes the logically possible world in which free creatures always do what is right contains *humans* who are *logically free* with respect to living a good life. Mackie's contention is that there is a possible world in which human beings are created by God and always do what is right; he does not argue for the stronger claim that there is a different sort of creature, rational persons who are internally-externally free but logically determined to do what is right, and that there is a possible world containing only them and God. This stronger claim is needed to withstand Plantinga's criticism that it is possible that if God created the persons in question, they would choose to do some wrong acts, even though they might not have.

A number of different arguments against Plantinga's free will defense are offered by Gale. He does not make a distinction among external / internal / logical freedom and tacitly assumes with Plantinga that finite rational creatures are logically free.

Gale's basic argument is that humans do not in fact have (external and internal) free will if they are created by God. He appeals to a principle about humans, namely, that if a person A's actions and choices result from psychological conditions that are intentionally determined by another person B, then A's actions and choices are not free. Gale supports this principle with the example of a cyberneticist operating on his wife's brain and replacing it with a preprogrammed computer analogue, which inculcates in his wife the desired psychological makeup, comprising desires, dispositions, and the like. This psychological makeup may incline toward or render probable certain choices by his wife, but these choices are not free because his wife does not have a mind of her own. Gale notes that, according to Plantinga, God intentionally causes a created person to have all of her freedom-neutral properties, which include her psychological makeup. This implies, according to Gale, that this created "person is rendered nonfree due to her not having a mind of her own."[33]

Gale points out that his argument is not conclusive because it "applies the same freedom-cancelling principles that apply to man-man cases to the God-man case,"[34] and the analogies may not be sufficiently strong. Nonetheless, Gale thinks his argument has some force against Plantinga's free will defense. But does it? I believe the disanalogies of the God-human case outweigh the analogies. Specifically, the human-human cases involve the husband altering the original, natural, psychological makeup of his wife and replacing it with a new, artificial one. But in the God-human case, God does not alter the person's original psychological makeup; rather, the person's original psychological makeup is precisely what is created by God. What is denoted by "a mind of her own" is precisely what is originally created by God. Thus, I think Plantinga's free will defense can survive this attack.

Gale has much more to say about the problems with Plantinga's free will defense, none of which he thinks conclusively refutes the defense. I believe that the distinction I made among external/internal/logical freedoms and the argument I based on this do conclusively refute Plantinga's free will defense, and thus we need not rely on Gale's many arguments to see that the defense does not succeed. But Gale's critique of the free will defense extends to versions other than Plantinga's, for example, Adams's, and Gale makes several plausible points in his extensive discussion of the various versions of the defense.

6 Essentialist Ethics

In chapter 5, I argued that a version of the deductive argument from evil is sound and that God does not exist. This argument implies that human life lacks an objective religious meaning, or at least a monotheistic religious meaning, where such a meaning is understood in terms of an all-knowing, all-powerful, perfectly good being that created the universe.

I argued in the three chapters of part I that our first-order ethical beliefs imply that ethical sentences have truth-value and sometimes correspond to moral facts that obtain independently of our beliefs about whether they obtain, that is, that human life appears in our first-order moral behavior to have an objective ethical meaning. There seem to be problems, however, with maintaining that our first-order moral beliefs are correct. One problem is "the problem of moral disagreement." I focused on this in chapter 1 in connection with the logical realists' ethical theory. I argued that Moore's theory runs afoul of the fact that one and the same ethical proposition seems self-evidently true to some people and self-evidently false to others, and that this fact raises the question about how we could ever know ethical truths, even assuming there are objective ethical truths. Other difficulties in the way of maintaining moral realism include the apparent "queerness" of moral facts. These ethical issues, as well as the issue of which normative ethics is correct (utilitarianism, perfectionism, and so forth), shall be addressed in this chapter.

Linguistic essentialism has dominated analytic philosophy of religion since the early 1970s; however, it has had much less of an impact on analytic ethics. Indeed, most of the major ethical theorists since the 1970s—John Rawls, Robert Nozick, Alan Gewirth, David Gauthier, Panayot Butchvarov, Gilbert Harman, John Mackie, Richard Brandt, Joseph Ellin, Judith Thompson, Samuel Scheffler, Michael Pritchard, Shelly Kagan, and the like—do not belong to the essentialist tradition of Marcus, Kripke, Plantinga, and others.

Consequently, an examination of essentialist ethics will in effect amount to an examination of a relatively minor movement in ethics, even though it appears to be increasingly influential in the late 1980s and early 1990s, with major books in this tradition published by Fred Feldman, David Brink, and Thomas Hurka.[1] The first work in essentialist ethics appeared in 1979 with Robert Adams's article "Divine Command Metaethics Modified Again."[2] This contrasts with the movements of logical realism, positivism, and ordinary language analysis, in which linguistic methods were the primary influence on the major ethical thinkers of their times.

Adams and Brink use the essentialist method of linguistic analysis to argue for moral realism, that is, the metaethical theory that human life has an objective ethical meaning. I shall examine Adams's and Brink's arguments in part A of this chapter, "Metaethics." I shall conclude that their arguments for moral realism are unsuccessful, even though both writers introduce important ideas that I shall use to formulate what I take to be a plausible version of moral realism. Following this metaethical discussion, I turn to normative ethics, the issue of which moral theory is true. In part B of this chapter, "Normative Ethics," I begin by examining Thomas Hurka's employment of the essentialist linguistic method to establish perfectionism (sometimes also called self-realization ethics). I shall conclude that Hurka's normative ethics, although it includes many plausible ideas, is not in fact a genuine perfectionist ethics and needs to be replaced by a different but related normative ethics, which I shall call global, naturalist perfectionism. The conclusion of this chapter will be that there is reason to think that an objective ethical meaning of human life exists and that this meaning is stated by the theory of global, naturalist perfectionism. This conclusion about ethical meaning will enable me to derive, in the Conclusion to this book, a theory about an objective religious meaning of human life that differs from monotheism, specifically, a naturalist pantheism. This will complete my search through the history of analytic philosophy, from Moore to Plantinga and Hurka, for materials to formulate a more adequate theory about the ethical and religious meanings of human life. We shall have seen how linguistic analysis has been used in this century to address the questions of ethical and religious meanings, and shall in addition have used a method of linguistic analysis, the essentialist method, to derive theories that contribute to answering these ethical and religious questions. If my arguments are sound, we shall have glimpsed a route from language to ethical and religious meanings.

Metaethics

22. Adams's Divine Command Ethics

As noted above, Adams inaugurated essentialist ethics in 1979 with his article on divine command ethics, which uses the essentialist method to argue for a certain type of moral realism. He applies the essentialist linguistic method to ethical terms, specifically, to the word "wrongness," to arrive at a divine command ethics. He wants to argue that it is an a posteriori and metaphysically necessary truth that wrongness is contrariety to the commands of a loving God. His conclusion is that it is necessary that the property of wrongness be identical with the property of *contrariety to the commands of a loving God,* but that this identity is known only a posteriori. Although I shall criticize Adams's conclusion, I shall endorse his method of ethical knowledge and shall later use it myself because I believe it is superior to the method of reflective equilibrium and other methods of ethical knowledge that have been practiced in the 1970s, 1980s, and 1990s.

Adams plausibly argues that every competent user of "wrong" need not know the nature of wrongness; indeed, people have different views about the nature of wrongness, and some have no views at all. This fact must be distinguished from views about *what actions* possess the property of wrongness. You and I could agree that stealing has the property of wrongness but disagree about the nature of the property designated by "wrongness" or even be ignorant of this nature. Every competent language-user, however, does know that wrongness is a property of actions and that people are generally opposed to actions they regard as wrong and generally count wrongness as a reason for opposing an action.

These commonly understood aspects of wrongness belong to what Adams calls the concept or understanding with which the word "wrong" is used. Using the distinctions previously made in my account of the essentialist philosophy of language, I may say that what Adams calls the concept of wrongness is both (a) the *cognitive significance* of "wrong" and (b) the *reference-fixing description* that governs the use of "wrong." The concept of wrongness is both (a) what speakers have in mind when they say something is wrong and (b) determines which property is the direct referent of the word "wrong." The semantic content or direct referent of the predicate "wrong" is the property *contrariety to the commands of a loving God.*

As I suggested in chapter 4, the cognitive significance of a locution may diverge from its reference-fixing description. For example, some items may be referents of proper names and the names may not have their reference fixed by any description; the reference of "John Doe" may be fixed by ostension (*that baby*), not a definite description, and yet the (or *a*) cognitive significance of "John Doe" may be the definite description *the president of University U in 1996.* What speakers "have in mind" when they think of John Doe is not *that baby* but the definite description *the president of University U in 1996* (or *the husband of Jane,* and so forth). Although Adams does not make this distinction, it is both plausible and consistent with what he does say, namely, that "wrong" has a reference-fixing description and that this is also its cognitive significance.

The property designated by "wrong" is the property that best fills the role assigned to wrongness by the *concept* (set of descriptive conditions). Adams lists several descriptive conditions for this role, some of which I have already briefly mentioned:

i. Wrongness is a property that actions possess independently of whether we think they do. (This is a moral realist criterion and conforms to the arguments I presented in chapter 1, 2, and 3 that our first-level ordinary moral beliefs are realistic. I argued that this pertains to both our particular attitudes to particular actions and to our general attitudes to basic types of actions.)

ii. Wrongness is exemplified by an important central group of those actions that are generally thought to be wrong, for example, stealing, torturing children for fun, murder.

iii. The property of wrongness plays a causal role in the relevant actions coming to be regarded as wrong.

iv. Understanding the *nature* of wrongness (that is, the referent of "wrongness") should give us one more, rather than one less, reason to oppose wrong actions.

v. Adams's fifth condition is a general condition that the theory about wrongness satisfy other intuitions about wrongness as far as possible.

Adams allows that many different theories about the nature of wrongness meet his five criteria but notes that "given typical Christian beliefs about God, it seems to me most plausible to identify wrongness with the property of being contrary to the commands of a loving God." Adams continues, "Ethical wrongness *is* (i.e. is identical with) the property of being contrary to the commands of a loving God. I regard this as a metaphysically necessary, but not an analytic or a priori truth. . . . It purports to be the correct theory of the nature of ethical wrongness that *everybody* (or almost everybody) is talking about" (115).

It is clear from this passage that Adams is relying on linguistic essentialism for his ethical conclusions. Although Adams does not go into detail, one may construct the following argument about wrongness. I shall assume as a suppressed premise, as Adams means to assume, that typical Christian beliefs are true. The argument goes

1. The reference-fixing description of "wrong" is that this word directly and rigidly designates whatever property (a) is exemplified by some actions, (b) gives us a reason to oppose those actions, (c) is an objective (moral

realist) property, (d) is exemplified by certain paradigmatic actions, such as stealing, murder, rape, torturing children for fun, and so on, and (e) plays a causal role in our coming to regard the relevant action, and so on as wrong.

2. The property that best fulfills the reference-fixing rule of use of "wrong" is *contrariety to the commands of a loving God.*

Therefore,

3. "Wrongness" rigidly designates *contrariety to the commands of a loving God.*

Therefore,

4. What is said by the statement "Wrongness is identical with contrariety to the commands of a loving God" is the same thing (proposition) that is said by the statement "Contrariety to the commands of a loving God is identical with contrariety to the commands of a loving God."

Although Adams does not make these distinctions, we may say that this is a case of a posteriori necessary identifications, such as "Hesperus is Phosphorus" and "Water is H$_2$O." The object-level fact is an identity proposition and thus a priori. The metalevel fact, namely, that *the statement "Wrongness is identical with contrariety to the commands of a loving God" states this identity proposition, rather than some other proposition,* is a posteriori and contingent.

In his article, Adams makes the comment that it is a metaphysically necessary a posteriori truth that wrongness is contrariety to the commands of a loving God. This does not seem to be correct, given the argument implicit in the article. Correctly formulated, one should say that *what is said* by the statement "Wrongness is contrariety to the commands of a loving God" is not an a posteriori truth but an identity proposition that is known a priori.

Second, this is a logical necessity in the sense of first-order predicate calculus with identity and does not involve the modality of *metaphysical* necessity any more than any other logical tautology.

Third, the a posteriori feature belongs to the metalevel proposition that *the sentence states this proposition rather than some other proposition.* The reference-fixing rule of use of "wrong" allows that this word refers to different properties in different possible worlds. Adams says, "There may be other possible worlds in which other properties best fill the role by which contrariety to a loving God's commands is linked in the actual world to our concept of wrongness" (118). Adams gives the example that in some possible worlds, "wrong" refers to the property of *failing to maximize human happiness.* In these worlds, the sentence "Wrongness is contrariety to the commands of a loving God" expresses the logically false proposition, *Failing to maximize human happiness is (identically one and the same property as) contrariety to the commands of a loving God.* Thus, the sentence "Wrongness is contrariety to the commands of a loving God" is a contingent a posteriori truth, even though it states a logically necessary proposition.

Apart from this restructuring of Adams's argument, I must reject at least one of the elements that Adams believes to belong to the concept of wrong, namely, that the property of wrongness plays a causal role in our coming to regard certain actions as wrong. This seems to be a doubtful condition, even though endorsed by Putnam ("I would apply a generally causal account of reference also to moral terms").[3] Adams offers no argument for this condition or even an explanation of what it could mean. Suppose I observe a woman beating her child, and I come to believe that her action is wrong. Light rays reflect from the woman and child, hit my retina, institute a brain process, and this results in my visual perception of her beating the child. If we suppose this action also possesses the property of being contrary to a divine commandment, how is this moral property supposed to play a causal role in my coming to believe that the beating is wrong? There is no physical causal process that extends from the beating's *being contrary to a divine commandment,* no physical information that is carried by light particles, air waves, or some other physical means and reaches my sense organs. For the wrongness of the beating to be causally effective, it must be identical with a certain sort of physical property that can causally interact with my sense organs. But Adams's divine command property cannot causally affect me in this way. (And God cannot directly intervene and cause my moral belief because that is inconsistent with the libertarian free will that Adams ascribes to people.)

Moreover, it seems that this causal condition is *not* a part of every competent language-user's concept of wrongness. For example, I believe right now that some wrong actions are being performed in China, and yet I also believe, quite correctly, that there is no causal process emanating from China (faster than the speed of light) to my current belief state.

As I have mentioned, Adams does not argue that his divine command ethics is true, but merely that a certain conditional statement is true, namely, "Given typical Christian beliefs about God, it seems to me most plausible to identify wrongness with the property of being contrary to the commands of a loving God" (115). I argued in my chapter on essentialist philosophy of religion that God does not exist. Thus, even if Adams's conditional is true, the falsity of the antecedent leaves us with no reason to assume that wrongness is identical with the divine property Adams mentions. If one wants to establish moral realism, one cannot do so in a supernaturalistic context. Nonetheless, the linguistic essentialist method that Adams uses, properly reconstructed, can be abstracted from a supernaturalist context and used to establish a different ethical theory, as I shall argue later in this chapter. But first in the order of things is to examine Brink's interesting attempt to establish a naturalistic moral realism.

23. Brink's Naturalist Moral Realism

In chapters 1, 2, and 3, I argued that ordinary language and our first-level moral beliefs imply moral realism. Since the decline of ordinary language analysis, with its antirealist account of ordinary ethical discourse, several philosophers have realized that ordinary moral talk is in fact realist. Even some moral antirealists, such as Mackie, concede this point.[4] John Post, a moral realist, plausibly notes that "the presumption should be that there are objective values. For this is what ordinary usage of moral terms overwhelmingly presupposes, as does most of our actual moral reasoning." Post observes that "Mackie is far more candid than most subjectivists in acknowledging that the burden of proof is on those who advance any such thesis [that is, moral antirealism]."[5]

Brink likewise adopts this stance: "We begin as (tacit) cognitivists and realists about ethics. . . . We are led to some form of antirealism (if we are) only because we come to regard the moral realist's commitments as untenable, say because of the apparent occult nature of moral facts."[6] The defense of moral realism, accordingly, amounts to responding to arguments against moral realism brought by antirealists. This is a project Brink undertakes in his book *Moral Realism and the Foundation of Ethics,* using in part the methodology of linguistic essentialism. There are several other recent defenses of moral realism, most importantly Butchvarov's *Skepticism in Ethics* and some articles by Geoffrey Sayre-McCord, Nicholas Sturgeon, Richard Boyd, and others.[7] Only Brink's defense, however, explicitly uses the method of linguistic essentialism, and for this reason I concentrate on his theory.

The two most familiar contemporary arguments against moral realism are the argument from queerness and the argument from moral disagreement. In the following sections, I shall critically discuss Brink's response to these arguments and his naturalist version of moral realism, and I shall formulate what I believe to be plausible responses to these arguments.

23.1. Brink's Compositional Naturalism

The argument from queerness, developed by Mackie, was primarily directed against nonnaturalist versions of moral realism, such as were espoused by Moore, Prichard, and other logical realists. Mackie's argument, in part, is that moral properties are so unusual that there is no good reason to postulate them. They are very unlike natural properties. A *nonnatural* property is queer. Further, the *relation* between moral properties and nonnatural properties is queer. Nonnatural properties do not entail moral properties or have any other sort of familiar relation to moral properties.

Brink's theory meets these two charges of queerness by implying that moral properties are natural properties and are related to other natural properties by being constituted or composed by them. Since "being natural" and "being composed of natural properties" are familiar or nonqueer predicates, moral realism is not metaphysically queer.

Brink argues for the naturalistic thesis that moral properties are constituted by natural properties, where the "is" in "The moral property F *is* the natural property G" is the "is" of constitution. Brink writes,

> A table is constituted by, but not identical with, a particular arrangement of microphysical particles, since the table could survive certain changes in its particles or their arrangement. Similarly, moral properties are constituted by, but not identical with, natural properties if, though actually constituted or realized by natural properties, moral properties can be or could have been realized by properties not studied by the natural or social sciences. [Moral properties might have been constituted by supernatural properties, for example.] Moral properties may well be constituted by natural properties; they may be nothing over and above organized combinations of natural and social scientific properties. (158)

Although Brink's language in this passage is tentative ("Moral properties may well be constituted by natural properties"), this is the position with which he most sympathizes and in effect endorses. Brink adds to this account of compositional naturalism that one and the same moral property may be constituted by different natural properties; for example, "The property of injustice . . . could have been realized by a variety of somewhat different configurations of social and economic properties" (158). This gives a certain sense to the claim that moral properties "supervene" on natural properties. Brink continues, "Moral properties supervene on natural properties because moral properties are constituted by natural properties" (158). The supervenience relation is a metaphysically necessary relation. If the natural properties G and H constitute the moral property F (and in this sense are the base properties upon which F supervenes), then in every metaphysically possible world in which x is G and H, x is F.

Brink's argument for his "compositional naturalism" is based on the essentialists' philosophy of language. Brink uses this philosophy of language to undermine the thesis of Moore and other logical realists that moral realism requires a *nonnaturalism* in ethics.

In chapter 1, I pointed out that Moore's argument that "moral realism implies nonnaturalism" is based on the "open question" argument and the charge of a naturalistic fallacy. Moore accepts a certain semantic thesis of the theory of reference that dominated analytic philosophy prior to the work of Marcus and others. The semantic thesis implies there are no relations of synonymity or meaning implication between moral and nonmoral terms. As Moore indicates, the "open question" argument shows that "pleasure" is not synonymous with "good" or any other natural predicate.[8] An open question is one about which it is possible for a competent speaker to doubt an affirmative answer. "Is pleasure pleasant?" is a closed question. Moore argues that for any natural predicate N and any moral predicate G, it is an open question as to whether G things are G just insofar as they are N. It follows from this semantic argument that "good" is not synonymous with any natural predicate, and therefore that goodness is not identical with any natural property. Because "good" has a sense and the sense of a term is its referent, "good" has a nonnatural property for its referent, the property ought-to-exist.

Brink undertakes to refute this argument, using the distinction between semantic content and cognitive significance made by the linguistic essentialists. Brink points out that Moore assumes that if two predicates are synonymous, then *all competent speakers associate the same properties with both terms.* Moore assumes that properties which are the referents (*semantic contents*) of the predicates are also the *cognitive significance* of the predicates. Thus, if "pleasant" and "good" refer to the same property, they have the same cognitive significance for me—which is just the property they designate. Brink notes that this "appears to be a consequence of the traditional theory of meaning according to which the meaning of a term is the set of properties that any speaker competent with the term associates with it [the term]" (157).

Given the distinction between cognitive significance and semantic content, however, the open question argument does not show nonnaturalism is true. "Good" and some natural predicate may refer to the same property but have a different cognitive significance. There may be no a priori connection between the cognitive significance of "good" and the cognitive significance of some natural predicate, for example, "pleasure," and it may require a posteriori knowledge to learn that they are coreferring or that the semantic content of the natural predicate constitutes the semantic content of the moral predicate.

A further feature of Moore's argument for nonnaturalism that is inconsistent with the essentialists' philosophy of language is his "semantic test of properties" (162). The semantic test implies that "meaning implication is a test of constitution or necessitation" (162). Thus, a moral property F is constituted by the natural properties G and H only if the moral property F is part of the meaning (semantic content) of the conjunction of the natural predicates "G" and "H." This is based on the idea that all necessary truths are analytic and thus that if the base property B necessitates the moral property M, then M is part of the meaning of "B." Given this semantic test, M is constituted by and supervenes on B only if "x is B" analytically entails "x is M."

Brink reconstructs Moore's argument as the claim that no natural sentence of the form "x is B" analytically entails a moral sentence of the form "x is M." In other words, a natural base property B necessitates and constitutes a supervening moral property M just in case it is part of the meaning of the base predicate "B" that B things are M. Because there are no such analytic entailments, however, it follows (given Moore's philosophy of language) that no natural properties constitute moral properties and that constitutional ethical naturalism is false.

Brink responds that Kripke and Putnam have shown that analyticity and necessity are distinct notions; analyticity is a semantic notion and necessity is a metaphysical (modal) notion. Given this, one cannot maintain that meaning implication is a necessary condition of a metaphysically necessary relation of constitution. The necessary connection can be synthetic (166) and a posteriori (175).

Such reasoning suggests that moral truths are synthetic, a posteriori, metaphysically necessary, and involve the "is" of constitution. "Institutionalized slavery is unjust" may be analyzed as saying that the property of institutional slavery constitutes the property of injustice, but injustice is not part of the semantic content of the predicate "institutionalized slavery." Correlatively, an a priori analysis of the semantic content of "institutionalized slavery" will not enable us to know the proposition expressed by "Institutionalized slavery is unjust." This proposition is know a posteriori, by examining the institutional structure and determining that it constitutes injustice.

Thus, Brink seems to arrive at an ethical naturalism, a compositional naturalism, and thereby rebuts Mackie's argument for queerness. Natural facts and the relation of constitution are not queer, and this challenge to moral realism seems to be met.

Brink misunderstands Moore on one point; Moore held that some necessities are *synthetic* and a priori. But we are examining Brink's essentialist ethics, and we may assume Brink's understanding of Moore. But even assuming this, does Brink's argument succeed?

23.2 A Critique of Brink's Compositional Naturalism

Note that Brink does not hold that injustice can be constituted *only* by institutional slavery; many different sets of natural properties can constitute injustice. For each such set S, if the properties in S are exemplified by x, then it is metaphysically necessary that x exemplifies injustice, such that injustice is composed of the properties in S. For example, the properties of institutional anti-Semitism or taxation without representation may also constitute injustice. Just as a table is constituted by a particular arrangement of microphysical particles but can survive changes in its particles or its arrangements, so injustice can be composed of different natural properties (157-58).

This theory seems problematic. If injustice is, as Brink says, "*nothing over and above* organized combinations of natural and social scientific properties" (158) such as the organized combination instantiated in the southern American states in the first half of the nineteenth century, then it seems to be *identical* with the organized combination of properties. This seems to be a general principle: If F is nothing over and above the organized combination of G and H, then F is identical with the organized combination of G and H. For F is "nothing over and above ( )" means "F is nothing but ( )," which means "F is identical with ( )." If F is not identical with the organized combination of the natural properties G and H, then F *is* something over and above this organized combination, and the part of F that is over and above the organized combination of the natural parts G and H will be (by definition) something that is not natural. (If it is natural, it will be part of the organized combination of natural properties that constitutes F.) On the other hand, if injustice is identical with this combination, it is *necessarily* identical with this combination, as Marcus's theory of the necessity of identity implies, and consequently injustice cannot be identical with a different combination of properties, say the combination instantiated in Nazi Germany.

These considerations about moral properties being "nothing over and above" organized combinations of natural properties suggest that Brink's naturalism is really an identity version of ethical naturalism, rather than a constitutional naturalism. But then it is difficult to see how Brink's theory could be plausible, for with which organized combination shall we identify injustice? Is injustice identical with the set of properties instantiated in all and only *institutions of slavery?* Or is injustice identical with the set of properties instantiated in all and only *anti-Semitic institutions?* Given that both institutions are unjust and are not identical with each other, it follows that injustice is not identical with either set of properties.

Perhaps we could retain Brink's constitutional naturalism if we said that the property of injustice is the disjunctive property, *being an institution of slavery or being a sexist institution or being an anti-Semitic institution and so forth*. Even if there are such things as disjunctive properties, which is doubtful, it is highly doubtful that moral properties are disjunctive properties. It seems quite clear that when we say that the Confederate States of America in the first half of the nineteenth century were unjust, we are not saying that they are either sexist or anti-Semitic or slave-owning or homophobic or taxed without representation, and so on.

Brink cannot be defended by invoking the idea that "a whole F is greater than the sum of its parts G and H," for Brink himself has already invoked this idea; he says the whole F is not just the parts G and H but is the *organized combination* of G and H. My criticism is of his particular version of the "whole is greater than the sum of its parts" theory. Brink is silent about the different metaphysical theories of the nature of properties (Is F a universal, and the organized combination of G and H a combination of particular properties, tropes? Or are all properties universals? Or are all properties particulars?—these questions are not addressed). Thus, it is not apparent which, if any, metaphysical theory of properties could avoid the problems about F, G, and H that I have mentioned.

I think Brink's theory is best revised to become a *nonnaturalist constitutional* ethics. Suppose we reject Brink's statement that injustice is "nothing over and above" the organized combination of the natural properties G and H. (I use "natural" as an abbreviation for what Brink calls "natural or social or economic.") Suppose we say that the whole property injustice contains an *extra aspect* that is "over and above" the *organized combination of natural properties* that constitute it. Although Brink does not say this, it seems to be a plausible way of viewing constitution theories.

Consider a table that is constituted by an organized combination of microscopic elements. Contrary to Brink's theory of constitution, the table is not "nothing over and above" this organized combination of atoms because it in addition has the nontrivially essential property of being designed as an artifact by the person x. This nontrivial essence is an "individuating essence" in Marcus's sense: it is partly definitive of the special character of the table and distinguishes the table from some other things of the same kind (the kind TABLE). The individuating essence of the table enables the table to retain its self-identity through changes and rearrangements of its parts.

Consider the property of institutional injustice (as distinct from unjust acts, unjust people, and so on). We may say that in some cases it is composed of the set of properties involved in institutional slavery, in other cases of the set of properties exemplified in anti-Semitic societies, and so forth. But injustice is not identical with either of these sets of properties. Injustice is composed (in each case) of some organized combination of natural properties *and an extra nonnatural property*, specifically, a nonnatural property of the various natural properties that partially constitute the different kinds of injustice. This property will be the nonnatural property *ought-not-to-be-instantiated*. This is a second-order property, a property of certain natural properties. There are different kinds of injustice, and the kinds are distinguished from each other by the different kinds of natural properties that exemplify ought-not-to-be-instantiated. Institutionalized slavery is one kind of injustice; this kind is the relevant set S_1 of properties that exemplify ought-not-to-be-instantiated. Institutionalized anti-Semitism is another kind of injustice: it is a different set S_2 of properties that ought-not-to-be-instantiated.

The genus institutional injustice, accordingly, is the complex property: being a kind of institution that ought not to be instantiated. The species of the genus are determined by the different kinds of institutions that ought not to be instantiated, racist, anti-Semitic, and so on.

No such genus/species distinction is possible on Brink's constitutional naturalism, if only for the reason that there is nothing to play the role of the genus. Because we cannot include a nonnatural property (ought not to be instantiated), we are left with the natural property, being a kind of institution. Because this would also be the genus of just institutions, we would have a contradiction; just and unjust institutions would be indistinguishable. Perhaps some other sort of constitutional naturalism would be a workable ethical theory, but it is difficult to see what it might be.

23.3 Constitutional Nonnaturalism and the Argument from Queerness

Given the problems with Brink's constitutional naturalism, it seems that his theory has not shown us how moral realism and naturalism can both be true. Thus, this particular response to the argument from queerness does not succeed, raising the question if a nonnaturalist ethics can rebut the argument from queerness. In this section, I shall show how constitutional nonnaturalism can be defended against the argument from queerness. Later in the chapter I shall show how a plausible *identity version of ethical naturalism* can be developed by a use of the essentialist method of linguistic analysis.

Before demonstrating how the nonnaturalist can refute the argument from queerness, I would first like to place the refutation of the argument from queerness in a larger context. A refutation of the argument from queerness can count as a sufficient reason for believing moral realism *only if* one first has a sound argument for (a) the thesis that commonsense moral beliefs imply moral realism and (b) an epistemic thesis that may be called *the principle of veridical seeming* (to be explained below).

(a) Regarding commonsense moral beliefs, Brink, Post, and other moral realists do not devote much of their philosophizing to arguing that common sense is committed to moral realism, but clearly such an argument is necessary if their position is to be tenable. Emotivists, prescriptivists, and constructivists such as Rawls and others have all argued that common sense is not committed to moral realism, and these arguments need to be addressed. I presented several arguments in part I for the thesis that first-order commonsense moral beliefs imply moral realism, and for this reason the thesis may be justifiably assumed in what follows. But this assumption is only one crucial assumption needed in the argument for moral realism.

(b) A second crucial assumption in the argument for moral realism is the conditional: if common sense is committed to moral realism, then it is rational to believe moral realism unless there is a compelling argument for moral antirealism. Mackie, Post, Brink, and others assume this conditional is true. But why should we believe it to be true? Why should what seems to be the case to us in our commonsense attitudes have any evidential force at all? If there is no compelling argument for moral antirealism and no compelling argument for moral realism, should we not remain agnostic on this issue, rather than abide by "what seems to be the case" to common sense? In the following I shall present an argument for this conditional.

I shall call the general principle of which this conditional is an instance *the principle of veridical seeming,* and the epistemic argument I shall present *the argument from veridical seeming.* Intuitively, the principle of veridical seeming is that we have reason to believe what seems to us to be true, unless there is good reason for us to distrust what seems to us to be the case.[9] The following argument can be shown to be sound:

1. Ordinary ethical sentences and commonsense first-level moral beliefs imply moral realism (or "Moral realism tacitly seems to be true in ordinary commonsense moral attitudes").

2. There are no empirical or a priori reasons to believe that first-level moral beliefs are all false.

Therefore,

3. It is more reasonable to believe moral realism than not to believe this.

First, I must show that this argument is valid. A skeptical claim that (1) and (2) do not entail (3) would be justified by the principle,

S. If p seems to be true, then, even in the absence of empirical and a priori reasons to not believe p, p's seeming to be true does not justify a belief in p.

Now what could justify a belief in the skeptical principle (S)? If we grant there are no a priori or empirical reasons to *not* believe (S) (other than the one I am about to prove), then the skeptic cannot appeal to the fact that (S) appears true to her to justify her belief in (S). For (S) rules out the epistemic legitimacy of this very appeal.

The skeptic might then introduce some reason R that is a reason to believe (S). If so, then it appears to the skeptic that R is true and that R justifies (S). But by (S), what appears to the skeptic to be the case gives the skeptic no reason to believe that it is the case. The skeptic (to be consistent with [S]) cannot trust her own beliefs and thus cannot trust any of her beliefs about the justification of (S).

This shows that the argument (1)–(3) cannot be refuted. But can I also show that we are justified in believing the argument-form instantiated by (1)–(3) is valid? Yes, for this argument-form is self-justifying. The argument seems to be valid, there are no a priori or empirical reasons to believe it is invalid, and therefore it is justified to believe it is valid.

Given this circumstance, there is no reason to believe that (1) and (2) are *defective justifications* for the thesis (3). There is no undermining defeater for belief in (3). So we have this argument:

1. Ordinary ethical sentences and commonsense first-level moral beliefs imply moral realism (or "Moral realism tacitly seems to be true in ordinary commonsense moral attitudes").

2. There are no empirical or a priori reasons to believe that first-level moral beliefs are all false.

Therefore,

3. It is more reasonable to believe moral realism than not to believe this.

4. There is no reason to believe that the conjunction of (1) and (2) is a defective reason to believe moral realism.

Therefore,

5. The belief in moral realism is indefeasibly justified.

This argument is valid, but is it sound? The two crucial premises are (1) and (2). I defended (1) in part I of this book. Thus, it is incumbent upon me to say something in behalf of premise (2). If (2) is rendered plausible, then moral realism is rendered plausible.

First, there are no a priori *analytic* reasons to believe that moral realism is false, for "There are objective moral facts" and "It would be the case that animals ought not to be tortured even if no humans believed this" are not implicitly logically self-contradictory; it cannot be shown, by substitutions of synonyms for synonyms, that the relevant negations of these sentences are substitution instances of first-order predicate logic with identity.

Second, there are no *synthetic* a priori principles that justify belief in the falsity of moral realism (no such principle has ever been offered, at least that I am aware of, and I cannot think of any such principle).

The arguments usually offered are empirical arguments. The main one is the argument from queerness developed by Mackie and endorsed by others. (I shall discuss below the other main empirical argument, the argument from moral disagreement.) In the following I shall show that a defender of a nonnaturalist constitutional ethics can refute Mackie's argument from queerness. (The third main empirical argument for moral antirealism, Harman's argument from "the explanatory impotence of moral facts," has been given plausible responses by Sturgeon, Sayre-McCord, and Brink, and I would refer the reader to their responses [see note 7 above]).

Mackie grants premise (1) of my argument for moral realism. He writes, "Belief in objective values is built into ordinary moral thought and language. . . . As such, [moral antirealism] needs arguments to support it against common sense."[10] Mackie's argument from queerness is in effect an attack on premise (2) of my argument; he wants to show there are empirical reasons to reject the moral realist thesis that is tacit in commonsense moral beliefs.

Mackie's argument from queerness is specifically designed to counter *nonnaturalist* theories of moral realism. (This is why the easiest response to his argument is to argue for a naturalistic moral realism, which I shall do in later sections. But here I shall defend moral realism in general by showing that Mackie's argument is ineffective even against a nonnaturalist moral realism.) One prong of his argument concerns the connection between natural properties and nonnatural properties. He writes, "A way of bringing out this queerness is to ask, about anything that is supposed to have some objective moral quality, how this is linked with its natural features" (41). Mackie notes that the connection cannot be one of entailment, logical necessity, or semantical necessity. But the constitutional nonnaturalist has a ready response to this claim: the connection is synthetic, metaphysically necessary, and a priori. The constitutional nonnaturalist will say we may plausibly consider the relation between moral and natural properties as a relation between properties and properties of those properties; that is, moral properties are second-order properties, properties of natural properties. For example, goodness is a property of the property *being scientifically knowledgeable.* The nonnaturalist may analyze "goodness" as meaning "ought to be exemplified," so that "scientific knowledge is good" means "scientific knowledge ought to be exemplified." It is not an analytic but a synthetic truth that scientific knowledge is good. And this truth is necessary and a priori. This synthetically necessary a priori relation is not one that Mackie even considered. Why not?

It seems that what lies behind Mackie's assumptions about queerness is a commitment to an extensional philosophy of language and a physicalist ontology. Linguistic essentialism, however, contains a battery of arguments for an intensional philosophy of language and for such abstract entities as possible worlds—I reviewed some of these in chapter 4. If our ontology is committed to such abstract entities as *the possibility of there being Fs,* then nonnatural moral facts such as *there ought to be Fs* are not queer. Indeed, if we reject Mackie's presupposition of physicalism and extensionalism, then the argument from queerness is a nonstarter.

Given the enormous influence of Mackie's argument, it is worth showing in detail that it is a blatant *petitio principii.*

Why does Mackie not consider the possibility that the relation between moral facts and natural facts is a relation of metaphysical necessity? Because he rules out such relations in advance. He writes, "If some supposed metaphysical necessities or essences resist such treatment [that is, reductive analysis in empiricist terms], then they too should be included, along with objective values, among the targets of the argument for queerness" (39). Now, as we have seen, Mackie can conclude that moral values are queer only by *assuming* there are no metaphysically necessary connections. In the passage just quoted, however, he asserts that the argument from queerness is *also* supposed to lead to the *conclusion* that there are no metaphysical necessities. The thesis that there are no metaphysical necessities is both an assumption and a conclusion of his argument from queerness. This vicious circularity vitiates any force his argument might have against moral realism.

Further, I should note that a premise of any argument for the queerness of metaphysical necessities would be that all *familiar* necessities are logical or semantic (analytic), and thus that metaphysically necessary connections are queer. If this particular argument is not to be a blatant petitio principii, however, Mackie would have to take on the entire tradition of linguistic essentialism from Marcus onward, which has provided numerous arguments that metaphysical necessities are quite familiar, both to common sense and to science. But this is not a task Mackie attempts to undertake.

Another part of Mackie's argument from queerness is his claim that "a faculty of intuition" is required if we are to apprehend objective values. The thesis that there is a "faculty of moral intuition" is one of the most famous strawmen in twentieth-century philosophy. Even the so-called intuitionists—Moore, Prichard, Russell, Ross, Ewing, and (perhaps) Butchvarov—did not postulate a faculty of intuition. Only Richard Price did in the eighteenth century. Mackie tries to make a great mystery out of how nonnatural moral values could be apprehended, but I suggest the mystery disappears once we eliminate the "perception" model of apprehending moral values. If moral values are nonnatural, they are apprehended analogously to how we come to have beliefs about the motives of people's actions. We can perceive people's behavior but not their motives. And yet we are constantly forming beliefs about their motives. We do this by tacitly inducing their motives from their perceived behavior. Likewise, when we come to believe that an action is wrong, we do not perceive its wrongness but come to believe it is wrong by inferring from the behavior we do perceive. (The inference relation is here a synthetically necessary relation.) In some cases, we ascribe wrongness to an action only if we also make a tacit inference about the motives of the act; in these cases, the acquisition of the belief about the moral value is relevantly similar to the acquisition of the belief about the motive. However, whereas we induce (in the sense of a tacit inference to the best explanation) from the behavior to the motive, we infer (grasping a synthetically necessary connection) the moral value from our inductively acquired beliefs about the motives, the action, and the action's consequences.

Furthermore, the apprehension of nonnatural moral values would be a special case of an apprehension of abstract objects, such as sets, numbers, universals, propositions, possibilities, and so forth. The apprehension of moral values can be seen to be queer only if we beg the question by assuming physicalism and nominalism—for example, that all we apprehend we apprehend by means of being causally affected by a physical object. The apprehension of moral values is queer only if *reductive* physicalism and nominalism are true. But reductive physicalism and nominalism have not been demonstrated to be true, and certainly not by Mackie.

Further, *nonreductive* physicalism can allow for nonnatural moral values, as Post has plausibly argued, and most physicalists today accept a nonreductive version.[11]

Mackie's additional argument is that objective moral values would be intrinsically motivating and action guiding, which is queer. "Something's being good both tells the person who knows this to pursue it and makes him pursue it" (40). Mackie's argument here runs together a host of distinctions, as Brink has shown in chapter 3 of his book *Moral Realism and the Foundation of Ethics.* Brink plausibly argues that there is an external connection between moral values and motives for acting. It does not analytically belong to the concept of a moral value that an apprehended moral value is motivating; more exactly, the concept C_1 expressed by "moral value" does not include the concept C_2 expressed by "The belief that something possesses a moral value is a sufficient motive for acting." If the moral value is motivating, that depends on such external considerations as the nature of the agent, the content of the moral theory, and so on. Further, the existence or possibility of existence of sociopaths shows it is possible to understand moral values intellectually and yet not find them motives for acting (this has been plausibly argued by Pritchard, *On Becoming Responsible*).[12] Even if, as I suggested in chapter 3, some moral statements do entail imperatives, it does not follow that understanding and believing these moral statements will motivate one to act on the imperative (I can believe "One ought to go to work" and understand that it implies "Go to work!" and yet feel unmotivated to act in accordance with the imperative.) Moreover, many moral statements do not imply imperatives: for example, "It is morally permissible to become a chemist" does not entail any imperative.

23.4 Moral Realism and the Problem of Moral Disagreement

In my argument for moral realism, I noted that we are justified in believing moral realism unless there are a priori or empirical reasons to think otherwise. I have argued that there are no a priori reasons to think moral realism is false and that the main empirical argument, the argument from queerness, is a petitio principii and in any case is directed against only one version of moral realism, the nonnaturalist version. Another main empirical argument against moral realism, one that I discussed in part in chapter 1 in regard to Moore's ethics, is the argument from moral disagreement. The conclusion I drew in chapter 1 is that Moore's principles entailed that human life is meaningful but absurd; if there are objective moral facts, there are no possible means of knowing them. The argument from moral disagreement as it is normally understood, however, is an argument that human life is objectively meaningless, that is, that there are no objective moral facts. This argument, of course, is not that there is moral disagreement, but that there seems to be *no possibility in principle of resolving moral disagreement.* The "argument from moral disagreement" is that the best explanation of this fact is that there are no objective moral values and therefore no fact of the matter as to which moral beliefs are true.

In response to this argument, I want first to make some comments about extant moral disagreements. First, there *is not* widespread moral disagreement, contrary to what philosophers and nonphilosophers alike often maintain. Virtually all people in virtually all cultures agree that murder, rape, stealing, lying, torturing children for fun are wrong. Virtually all humans agree about basic moral principles, such as that it is wrong to cause suffering needlessly, that love is morally better than hate, that wisdom is better than ignorance, and that it is good to heal the sick or injured, and so forth. Cases of moral disagreement are in fact isolated, even though they receive much attention (for example, the currently discussed issues pertain to abortion, death penalty, affirmative action, and so on). Indeed, there is more agreement in morals than in many other recognizably fact-stating disciplines. Philosophy of religion is fact stating; it is a fact that there is a god or it is a fact that there is no god. But fundamental disagreements about religious issues are more persuasive than those about morals. If you randomly take one thousand people on the earth you will probably find they all disagree about fundamental religious issues but all agree that it is wrong to cause suffering needlessly, wrong to steal, and so on. The same holds for psychology, economics, and other areas; there is more agreement about moral principles than about the psychological structure of the human personality or about how the economy works.

Another reason philosophers tend to overestimate the extent of moral disagreement is that they do not take into account the hundreds or thousands of "trivial and tacit" moral judgments we make every day, for example, that it is wrong to punch each person who walks by you in the nose, that it is right to behave in an amiable way to guests to whom one is introduced at a party, that it is wrong to drive one's car over one's neighbors' flower gardens, and so forth. If we add up these thousands of cases of tacit moral agreements that occur every day, they will outweigh extant moral disagreements by a very large ratio.

Second, virtually all instances of moral disagreement are about the relevant *nonnormative* facts, the relevant religious, natural, or social scientific facts. For example, the moral debate about abortion is primarily about the nonnormative issue of whether a fetus has a divinely implanted soul, which is a debate about factual religious claims. Disagreements we have with the Nazis largely concern the empirically false beliefs they held about Jews and Aryans; our disagreements with the nineteenth-century American slave owners primarily concern their empirically false beliefs about African Americans, and so on.

Where, then, do we find the flaunted "moral disagreements" supposed to constitute such a problem for moral realism? Butchvarov has made a good case in *Skepticism in Ethics* that it is intrinsically plausible that friendship, knowledge, pleasure, health, and existence are good and that enmity, ignorance, pain, sickness, and death are bad. There is virtually universal agreement about such noncomparative moral judgments, that is, judgments about what general kinds of things are good and what bad. But, as I suggested in chapter 1, the main cases of disagreement involve *comparative judgments*. Is friendship more valuable than knowledge, as Butchvarov maintains, or are Plato, Aristotle, Spinoza, and Hegel correct that knowledge is more valuable than friendship? Is pleasure more valuable than health or vice versa? There does seem to be widespread disagreement about *the hierarchy* of values. The argument from moral disagreement is best stated as an argument about widespread and seemingly intractable disagreements about comparative moral judgments.

In chapter 1 I suggested that the argument from moral disagreement would show (in the context of Moore's logical realist ethics) that moral realism is true (that human life has an ethical meaning) but that we cannot know which comparative moral judgments are true (and thus that human life is both meaningful and absurd). But outside the confines of Moore's logical realism, there is an answer to this argument that is consistent with human life being meaningful and not absurd. The seemingly intractable disagreements about comparative moral judgments are (in principle) a correctable epistemic feature of human moral life. The disagreements are due to a failure to realize that the relevant comparisons are made at too general a level for the comparison to have a truth-value. "Knowledge is more valuable than friendship" does not have a truth-value, but "Knowing the local phone directory by heart is morally better than having any friends at all" has the truth-value of false, and "Developing the special and general theories of relativity is more valuable than becoming casual friends for one day with one's neighbor's visiting cousin" has the truth-value of true. The same holds for "Pleasure is more valuable than health" and "Freedom is more valuable than love" and other such generalizations. There is no reason to think that just because we can construct ethical sentences of any degree of generality that they therefore all have truth-values.

To be convincing, the limited argument from disagreement should be an inductive argument that *there is no agreed-upon method* for resolving moral disagreements and therefore that it is likely there is no knowable method for resolving these disagreements. The further conclusion will then be that the best explanation of there being no knowable method for resolving disagreements is that there is nothing to be known, no objective comparative moral facts.

But this argument also fails because there is no agreed-upon method for resolving disputes in metaphysics, epistemology, religion, psychology, and so on, and this does not imply that it is likely that there is no knowable method for resolving disputes in these areas. The fact that there is no agreed-upon method for resolving disputes in these and other areas is best explained by the hypothesis that (1) there is a knowable method for resolving disagreements, but (2) the complexity and difficulty of the subject matter, combined with the limited epistemic abilities of the human species, have so far prevented humans from both learning *and* reaching agreement about this method.

In addition to these responses to the argument from moral disagreement, we may endorse some of the ideas that Brink presents. Brink addresses the argument from moral disagreement by noting that realism about a discipline does not require that all actual cognizers eventually reach agreement; rather, it is reasonable to expect agreement on all facts only if all cognizers (a) are fully informed, (b) are fully rational, and (c) have sufficient time for deliberation. In cases of moral disputes, very few people (if any) meet these three conditions. For example, although most people hold moral views about domestic and foreign policy political issues, hardly anybody is fully informed about the issues or is fully rational in his thinking about the issues or has sufficient time to deliberate about them. The explanation of moral disagreement by postulating that there are no moral facts would work only if there is pervasive disagreement *even after* the cognizers met these three conditions; but because these conditions are rarely, if ever, met, there is no reason to think that there is pervasive disagreement of this sort.

For these various reasons, the argument from moral disagreement fails to count as an empirical reason to defeat the justification for moral realism that is provided by our first-level commitment to moral realism. Because the other main antirealist argument, that from queerness, also fails, we have reasonably strong grounds for believing that human life has an objective ethical meaning.

But the grounds for this belief could be made stronger if we could show that *ethical naturalism* is true. In my response to the argument from queerness, I indicated how a constitutional nonnaturalism could be defended against it. But this does not imply that the preferred metaethical theory for the moral realist is nonnaturalism. Moral realism has stronger epistemic weight if it is combined with ethical naturalism. Some good informal and intuitive reasons for believing this are as follows.

Compare the conjunction *moral realism and nonnaturalism* with the conjunction *moral realism and naturalism*. Virtually all philosophers hold that some natural properties can be exemplified by some natural items independently of whether humans or other finite minds believe these items are exemplified. Call this position "minimal naturalism." Minimal naturalism is common to virtually every metaphysical theory (be it Platonic realism, Aristotelian realism, nominalism, scientific realism, physicalism, theism, phenomenalism, idealism). For example, even phenomenalists or idealists would grant that the natural property, *being a sense-datum and not a mind-independent physical thing,* is exemplified by some sense-datum even if the person experiencing it does not happen to hold the belief that this property is exemplified. If moral realism's metaphysical commitments are merely to this minimal realism, then the relevant metaphysical aspect of moral realism will be uncontentious. But if moral realism's metaphysical commitments are also to the thesis that there are objective nonnatural facts, then the metaphysical aspect of moral realism will be highly contentious and will have considerably less prima facie plausibility than the weaker metaphysical theory of minimal naturalism. This suggests that, *all else being equal,* the conjunction of ethical naturalism and moral realism has higher epistemic status than the conjunction of ethical nonnaturalism and moral realism. Of course, the nonnaturalist will deny that all else is equal because she will argue that ethical naturalism is false, perhaps even logically incoherent. Nonetheless, it is true that *if* a logically coherent and plausible ethical naturalism can be developed, then this form of moral realism, by virtue of having a metaphysical aspect that is uncontentious, is epistemically preferable.

This point may also be put by saying that the naturalist moral realist has one less position for which she needs to argue: The moral realist who is a nonnaturalist will not only have to argue, within the field of ethics, for her ethical theory, but will also have to take on the metaphysical task of showing that there are objective nonnatural facts in addition to natural facts. But because the ethical naturalist can take for granted that there are objective natural facts, she does not need to argue for her metaphysical theory and can confine herself to arguing for her ethical theory.

It seems to me that there is a plausible version of ethical naturalism, an *identity naturalism* rather than a constitutional naturalism, and thus that moral realism should be combined with identity naturalism rather than with the constitutional nonnaturalism I articulated in sections 23.2 and 23.3. This identity naturalism is what I shall call *global, naturalist perfectionism.* The remainder of this chapter is devoted to developing this perfectionist theory. The theory is partly based on Hurka's perfectionist ethics and will emerge as a criticism of the nonnaturalistic formulation he gives to perfectionism.

Normative Ethics

24. Hurka's Perfectionism and Linguistic Essentialism

In addition to arguing for ethical naturalism, I shall address issues about the ethical meaning of human life that so far have gone unaddressed in this book. Up to this point, the discussion has been confined to metaethics, specifically, to whether moral realism or antirealism is true. But what about normative ethics?

If we know that moral realism is true, we know *that* human life has an objective ethical meaning. But this will not tell us *what* this ethical meaning is. How should we live? What are the norms that govern the behavior of moral agents? A discussion of the meaning of human life is insubstantial without some arguments in normative ethics, so I shall argue for some theses in normative ethics, specifically, for a version of perfectionism that is partly influenced by Hurka's book *Perfectionism* (1993). This argument is a part of my project of discussing and evaluating essentialist ethics, for Hurka's ethical theory is based in large part on the essentialists' method of linguistic analysis, and my development and modification of his perfectionism will also be based on the essentialists' method.

The essentialist movement made possible a type of moral theory that had gone virtually undeveloped in the analytic tradition up until Hurka's *Perfectionism*. Perfectionist ethics (or at least what Hurka calls "narrow perfectionism," which is his topic) is based on the idea that the good is the development of human nature. Prior to essentialism, the idea of a thing's nature was seen as incoherent, obscure, or at least merely relative to a way of describing something. A main pre-essentialist position (whose main champion was Quine) was that necessity does not belong to objects (there is no necessity de re) but is relative to certain ways of describing objects. For example, relative to the description of humans as social beings, it is essential to humans to communicate. And relative to the description of them as animate beings, their essential nature is life. So the perfectionist idea of "developing human nature" has no univocal sense; it gives no one moral ideal, but an indefinite number of different and often conflicting moral ideals, depending on the description we use to pick out humans. Thus, perfectionism is not a viable moral theory if essentialism is false.

But the arguments for linguistic essentialism developed in the 1960s and 1970s provided the needed groundwork for a perfectionist ethics. Hurka writes, "Philosophers used to dismiss perfectionism by saying the concept of human nature is incoherent or obscure. This attitude is less common since Kripke."[13] Hurka does not elaborate, but one may ask exactly how essentialism or the essentialist's linguistic method enables us to make sense out of the concept of human nature.

Consider Hurka's interpretation of how the essential properties of humans and other things are known. He says there are two methods, the intuitive, associated with Kripke, and the scientific, associated with Putnam.

Hurka describes the intuitive method as involving thought experiments involving candidate members of a kind: "To learn whether its atomic structure is essential to gold, for example, we imagine a series of possible substances with gold's atomic structure but with a different outward appearance. If we judge all these substances to be gold, our judgement shows that its inner constitution is essential to gold and its phenomenal properties contingent" (34).

Hurka describes the scientific method of essentialism as determining what is postulated in explanations given by good scientific theories. Science tells us that the atomic structure of gold explains the phenomenal properties of gold, its yellowness, solidity, weight, and so forth. Because gold's atomic structure is explanatorily prior to its phenomenal properties, this structure is a nontrivial essence of gold.

It seems to me that Hurka is not entirely accurate in saying that Kripke adopted the intuitive method and Putnam the scientific method for knowing the essences of natural kinds. Rather, they both used a certain hybrid of the two methods Hurka distinguishes. For example, they both believed that we know by scientific investigation that a certain chemical structure explains the phenomenal appearance of gold, and that we know by modal intuition that this structure is essential to gold.

Hurka uses both his intuitive and scientific methods of knowing essences to determine the nontrivial essential properties of humans. Hurka uses these methods to arrive at the thesis that human nature consists of practical and theoretical rationality, a cardiovascular and digestive system, and so on. Because perfectionism is the thesis that goodness consists in developing human nature, Hurka will draw the conclusion that goodness consists in developing our practical and theoretical rationality and in developing our organic properties (becoming healthier).

How do Hurka's methods of knowing essences show that humans are essentially rational and have a certain organic structure? Regarding the intuitive method of knowing these nontrivial essences, Hurka briefly notes that we would not intuitively consider any beings to be human unless they were rational, that is, could form the relevant sort of justified beliefs and intentions to act. He writes, "If we imagine a species with no capacity for a mental life, or with none more sophisticated than other animals, we do not take ourselves to be imagining humans" (39). This seems to me a plausible reliance on our modal intuitions, given the defense of modal intuitions I gave at the end of chapter 4.

But Hurka's more substantial account appears in his description of the scientific method of knowing human nature, which in the present case involves the science of psychology. The essential property of humans that distinguishes humans from other animals is rationality. (Hurka defines "rationality" in terms of types of highly sophisticated beliefs and intentions that are not possessed by whales, dolphins, and so forth, which may be considered to have rationality in some different definition of the word.) Hurka plausibly takes as the relevant phenomenal properties of humans our observable *actions or behaviors.* He argues that psychological explanations posit rationality as the explanation of human action, much as chemical explanations posit the atomic structure of element 79 as the explanation of the phenomenal features of gold.

The premises of psychological explanations of human actions refer to human *beliefs* about scientific laws and sophisticated *intentions* for the distant future. These premises refer to practical rationality, a nontrivial essence of humans.

Theoretical rationality is also postulated in psychological explanations, for psychologists explain the beliefs that are relevant to actions in terms of humans having evidence that a certain activity is the most effective means to an end; *forming sophisticated beliefs, grounded in scientific evidence,* about the most effective means to an end is an instance of theoretical rationality.

This account seems plausible as far as it goes, but it seems to me that Hurka should say in addition that theoretical rationality is postulated to explain the observable human behavior evinced in writing books, teaching and learning in educational institutions, and talking about science and philosophy. In short, the most important phenomenal or behavioral evidence that humans have *theoretical reason* is not their practical behavior, but their theoretical behavior.

I want to reformulate Hurka's theory in terms of our understanding of linguistic essentialism, which Hurka intends to be applying to his ethical theory. We may say that the sentence, "Gold has the Aristotelian essence of having 79 protons" is analogous to the sentence, "Humankind has the Aristotelian essence of rationality and certain digestive, nervous, etc. systems." The reference-fixing description for the natural kind word "gold" is that this word refers directly and rigidly to whatever is causally responsible for the observable properties of being metallic and yellow and so on. The reference-fixing description for the natural kind locution "human nature" is that this term refers directly and rigidly to whatever nontrivial essences are causally responsible for the observable behaviors of humans.

Are the sentences in which these rigid designators appear cases of necessary a posteriori identifications or cases of necessary a posteriori nontrivially essential ascriptions? Although Hurka does not raise these issues, it seems the answer is that both sorts of sentences are involved:

(a) *A Posteriori Identifications.* As I have indicated, "human nature" is a directly referential rigid designator of a certain complex property, and the reference-fixing description is that "human nature" directly refers to whatever essential properties explain the behavior and physical appearance of humans. Let us use "organic structure F" to designate the digestive tract, sentient structure, and so forth that are Aristotelian essences of humans. "Human nature is rationality and F-organicity" then expresses the identity proposition *rationality and F-organicity is (identical with) rationality and F-organicity.* This proposition is known a priori. But the metalevel proposition that *"human nature" directly refers to rationality and F-organiticity* is known a posteriori. Empirical knowledge is needed to learn that rationality and F-organicity rather than, say, a robotic structure explain the phenomenal properties of humans.

(b) *A Posteriori, Nontrivial Essential Attributions.* If we consider any particular that exemplifies the property designated by "human nature," then this will be a nontrivial and Aristotelian essence of that particular. "Jane is rational and has F-organicity" expresses a singular proposition that is synthetic, metaphysically necessary, and a posteriori. Further, "All humans are rational and have F-organicity" is a nontrivial essential ascription, but it expresses a general rather than singular proposition.

How does the essentialist method of knowing the Aristotelian essences of humans enable a normative ethics to be developed? In Hurka's theory, this method enables him to reach such normative conclusions as that *right actions* are those that maximize the development of human rationality and F-organicity, and that *good states* are those in which humans' rationality and organicity are developed.

At this juncture, it seems we have a plausible beginning of a normative ethics that is known via the linguistic method of contemporary essentialism. It will appear, however, that there are some foundational problems in Hurka's theory of human nature that call into question whether his theory is really an instance of *perfectionism*. I shall argue that a solution to these problems is to adopt a naturalistic version of perfectionism.

24.1 Hurka's Theory of Human Nature

The basic problem with Hurka's narrow perfectionism concerns his procedure of formulating a definition of human nature. Hurka characterizes *narrow perfectionism* in terms of "the foundational idea that what is good, ultimately, is the development of human nature" (3). *Broad perfectionism* is a theory that is based not on the specific idea that the development of human nature is good, but on the more general idea that the good is the development of capacities or the achievement of excellence in art, science, and culture. Hurka proposes to construct a narrow perfectionism, and the key task is to formulate a definition of human nature: "To develop the best or most defensible perfectionism, we need, most fundamentally, the best concept of human nature" (9).

Hurka proposes two tests that a definition of human nature must pass to be "the best concept of human nature": (i) human nature must come out as morally significant and (ii) there must be intuitively plausible moral consequences of the definition. The definition must assign intrinsic value to certain properties; that is, the properties included in the definition of human nature must have intrinsic value, and they must seem to be morally worth developing. This implies that the properties are degreed properties, properties capable of admitting more or less, since a nondegreed property cannot be developed.

A definition of human nature will fail to pass the moral test if it succumbs to what Hurka calls the *wrong-properties objection*. This is the objection that a suitable definition of human nature cannot include properties that intuitively seem to be morally trivial (such as developing humans' essential property of occupying space) or morally bad (for example, being capable of killing members of one's own species).

Hurka examines several definitions to see if they pass the moral tests. Once he selects the best definition, he will proceed to construct the details of a normative ethics that is based on the idea that the moral goal is the development of human nature as specified in that definition. The definitions Hurka considers, and his reasons for rejecting most of them, are presented in what follows:

(D1) Properties Distinctive of Humans

The first definition Hurka discusses is that human nature is the set of properties possessed only by humans. He says this definition succumbs to the wrong-property objection. Humans uniquely make fires and uniquely kill things for sport. Hurka says these are not properties that are morally worth developing, and thus this definition of human nature is not suitable for a perfectionist ethics.

Hurka notes a second problem. The best definition of human nature must depend only on facts about humans. But the definition in terms of distinctive properties depends on facts about other species, for example, whether they possess rationality. This definition would imply the implausible consequence that we should conclude that human nature does not include rationality if we happen to determine that dolphins, for example, are rational (in the sophisticated sense of "rational" Hurka has in mind).

(D2) Properties Essential to Humans

A property is essential to the kind *human* if and only if every member of this kind possesses this property in each possible world in which it exists.

A property essential to humans depends only on facts about humans; we need consider only what properties humans possess in the possible worlds in which they exist.

Hurka says this definition also succumbs to the wrong-properties objection, for it includes the wrong properties in human nature. It includes morally trivial properties, such as being self-identical, being red if red, and being occupiers of space. These properties are not morally worth developing.

(D3) Properties Essential and Distinctive to Humans

A property F is essential and unique to humans if and only if (a) each human x possesses F in each possible world in which x exists and (b) only humans possess F in the actual world.

Hurka finds this definition unsatisfactory because it too succumbs to the wrong-property objection; it includes the properties of being able to light fires and killing for sport. A second problem is that this definition depends on facts about species other than humans; for example, if it turns out that some other species is rational, rationality is not a part of human nature.

(D4) Properties Essential and Necessarily Distinctive of Humans

A property F is essential to and necessarily distinctive of humans if and only if each human possesses F in each possible world in which she exists and there is no possible world in which anything other than humans possess F. This sort of property is analogous to Plantinga's "individual essences," except that they are natural kind properties.

Hurka notes that this definition excludes from human nature many morally valuable properties that are worth developing, for example, rationality. It is at least possible that there are other beings with rationality, and so rationality is not necessarily unique to humans.

Hurka concludes from this that the notion of distinctiveness must be rejected in attempts to come up with an adequate definition. He suggests we instead examine more closely the notion of essential properties and construct a satisfactory definition in terms of several nontrivial essences of humans.

(D5) The Essence-and-Life Definition

The essence-and-life definition is the one Hurka eventually concludes is the best definition. Hurka notes that each human has six classes of essential properties, distinguished by the range of objects that possess the property. These essences include trivial essences, Aristotelian essences, and individual essences. If ordered in terms of their extensiveness, they would appear as follows. The properties are

1. Essential to humans qua objects: Essential properties shared by all and only objects, for example, self-identity.
2. Essential to humans qua physical objects: Essential properties shared by all and only physical objects, for example, occupying space.
3. Essential to humans qua living things: Essential properties shared by all and only animate objects (for example, matter organized for functions of nutrition).
4. Essential to humans qua animals: Essential properties shared by all and only animals (Hurka offers no example of an essential property that is essential to animals but not to nonanimal living things).
5. Essential to humans but not to any other animals (rationality is such an essence, given that current empirical theory is correct in supposing that no other animals possess rationality in Hurka's sophisticated sense).
6. Essential properties that distinguish one human from another (for example, a person's genetic profile or a person's origination from these particular sperm and egg cells).

The definition that Hurka selects as the best definition of human nature includes the third, fourth, and fifth essential properties of humans; the essential properties we share with living things and animals and the essential properties that distinguish humans from other animals. By "the best definition" Hurka means the best definition for the purposes of constructing a theory of ethical perfectionism. Hurka rules out numbers 1 and 2 because he holds that our essential properties qua objects and qua physical objects are not morally significant; for example, self-identity and being spatially extended. But he holds that becoming healthy and developing our nature as animals (which Hurka never specifies), which are degreed properties corresponding to 3 and 4, and developing our practical and theoretical rationality (corresponding to 5) are morally significant. Hurka rules out 6, individual essences, because a person's genetic profile may include abilities for fire-lighting, stealing, or being a serial killer, and thus category 6 succumbs to the wrong-properties objection.

24.2 An Evaluation of Hurka's Theory of Human Nature

I shall argue in this section that Hurka's perfectionist ethics is implicitly self-contradictory, although many of the plausible theses he develops can be retained if his theory is reformulated to avoid the contradiction. We may approach this contradiction by first considering some remarks that merely seem to embody a contradiction (the real contradiction will lie in a related aspect of his theory). As I indicated, Hurka mentions two tests of a definition of human nature; these tests involve at least the following two considerations:

1. "Human nature must seem in itself morally significant."
2. "A perfectionist concept of nature assigns intrinsic value to certain properties" (9).

He also makes the following claim:

3. To include a property in human nature (in a definition) is not to make an evaluative claim; it is not to evaluate the property as "important or desirable," and so to use "prior evaluative standards." Rather, it is to make a descriptive or factual claim (18).

Are (2) and (3) mutually inconsistent? Does their conjunction imply that the perfectionist concept of human nature both assigns and does not assign value to a property F that it includes in its definition of human nature?

I think a charitable reading might resolve the problem in this way. Perfectionism (or, more precisely, narrow perfectionism, which is about human nature) is the thesis that developing human nature is good. Accordingly, if we make the descriptive or factual claim that human nature includes the property F, we can deduce from the perfectionist thesis that F (or developing F) is good. That is,

4. Developing human nature is good (the perfectionist assumption).
5. F belongs to human nature (taken as a descriptive or nonnormative claim).

Therefore,

6. Developing F is good.

Here we are interpreting (3) as (5). We are interpreting (1) as equivalent to (4), and we are interpreting (2) as the claim that the argument (4)–(6) is sound.

This seems to avoid the contradiction. Thus, it appears so far that there is no implicit contradiction in Hurka's theory.

But we have approached the contradiction. The contradiction lies in part in Hurka's procedure for formulating a definition of human nature, specifically, in his reliance on the two "tests": that the definition must make human nature seem morally significant and must entail attractive moral judgments. These tests are most clearly used in Hurka's employment of the "wrong-properties objection" as a criterion for rejecting various candidate definitions of human nature. Note Hurka claims that perfectionism is a freestanding morality; he says that if the perfectionist selection of a definition of human nature were not based on purely descriptive criteria, then perfectionism would not be a "free-standing morality" (18) but would depend on the "prior evaluative standards" (18) used to select the definition. Hurka's perfectionism, however, does depend on prior evaluative standards and is not a freestanding morality: the contradiction is that Hurka's theses jointly imply that perfectionism both is and is not a freestanding morality.

For example, Hurka writes that it counts as an objection to a certain concept of human nature that the "concept of nature includes properties that on their own seem morally trivial—if *it gives value to what, intuitively, lacks it.* This is a telling objection to the concept. A morality based on the concept will be hard to accept because it flouts *our particular judgements of value*" (9, emphasis added). The real foundations of Hurka's ethics are "our particular judgements of value"; his perfectionism stands on these prior judgments of value.

This fact is quite explicit in Hurka's statement: "We also want a concept [of human nature] that avoids the wrong-properties objection, by having fall under it only properties that seem in their own right worth developing" (10). If, however, we allowed prior moral criteria (embodied in what seems in its "own right worth developing") to determine our definition of human nature, then these moral criteria are the true basis of morality (not the ideal of developing human nature), and perfectionism then becomes equivalent to (a notational variant on) a moral system based on these nonperfectionist moral criteria.

Suppose we had the prior moral judgment that it is good to acquire philosophical knowledge. On this basis, we could define human nature (at least in part) in terms of humans' ability to acquire philosophical knowledge. "It is good to acquire philosophical knowledge" is then redundantly expanded to become, "It is good to develop the natural ability to acquire philosophical knowledge." We do not need any reference to human nature or developing natural abilities to state the moral truths, and so narrow perfectionism becomes an empty theory.

Hurka writes that one of the claims narrow perfectionism has on present moral thought is that "perfectionism, when combined with a well-grounded theory of human nature, entails attractive particular judgements. Many of us believe that states such as knowledge, friendship, and the completion of challenging tasks are good intrinsically, that is, apart from any satisfaction they bring. The best perfectionism entails judgements about these states that either match those we already make or take us beyond them in a way we can recognize as progress" (4–5).

Suppose we believe that knowledge, friendship, and the completion of challenging tasks are intrinsically good. We then select, among the several possible factual definitions of human nature, the one that entails, in conjunction with the assumption that developing human nature is good, that knowledge, friendship, and so on are good. What, then, is the justification for believing that knowledge and the others are good? The justification is not that it is entailed by the selected definition of human nature, in conjunction with the premise that developing human nature is good. For the beliefs about the goodness of knowledge themselves constitute the justification for selecting a certain definition of human nature. Because we independently believe that knowledge is good, we do not need the perfectionist assumption,

1. Developing human nature is good,

to justify this moral belief.

This argument can be presented more formally. Suppose we conjoined (1) with a definition of human nature that entails knowledge is good. Thus,

1. Developing human nature is good

and

2. Human nature includes rationality

jointly entail

3. Knowledge is good.

Now, despite the deduction of (3) from (1) and (2), (3) is not justified by this argument because it is an antecedently plausible moral thesis and serves to justify the selection of (2) as our definition of human nature.

Maybe there is a way to make Hurka's procedure seem plausible. Could not (3) *confirm* the conjunction of (1) and (2); perhaps the perfectionist theses are confirmed by our independent moral judgments.

This possibility is ruled out by the fact that (2) is a stipulative definition of human nature, not a real definition. We are stipulating that "human nature" means (2) because by virtue of this stipulation (3) can be derived. Because a stipulation cannot be true (stipulations have no truth-value), the stipulation cannot be confirmed.

Hurka's theory is in effect a version of *intuitionist ethics*, not perfectionist ethics. "Intuitionism" is here understood as the theory that normative ethics is based on articulating the more or less independent particular or general moral judgments that we make in our everyday lives and find intuitively or intrinsically plausible. Moral truths, according to intuitionism, are not justified by a systematic criterion, such as the principle of utility, a Kantian deontological principle, or the criterion of developing human nature. Rather, they need no justification other than themselves; our particular moral judgments (and our general moral judgments) are self-standing.

The underlying problem is that while claiming to offer a perfectionist ethics, Hurka in fact offers an intuitionist ethics. He correctly writes that human nature perfectionism has for its "foundational idea that what is good, ultimately, is the development of human nature" (3). But he abandons this foundational idea by basing his normative ethics on the foundational idea of intuitionism, that we determine what is good by relying on the various intuitive moral judgments we make in our daily lives.

Is this assessment unfair to Hurka's theory? Consider his three claims on behalf of perfectionism:

(i) He says, "That the human good rests somehow in human nature is, although elusive, also deeply attractive" (4). In order to make this thesis attractive, however, Hurka has to select from among a variety of definitions of human nature one that is designed to appeal to our antecedent moral judgments. What is attractive ultimately is not the perfectionist thesis about human nature, but these antecedent moral judgments. Indeed, because he himself argues that *most* of the definitions of human nature are not morally attractive, his theory suggests that it is largely false that the idea that developing human nature is attractive.

(ii) Hurka's second claim on behalf of perfectionism is that it entails attractive judgments. But this suffers from the same problem, for we begin with the theses we want to be entailed and then search for some definition of human nature that will entail these judgments. If our moral knowledge is already embodied in the entailed theses, the construction of some thesis about human nature that entails them is superfluous.

(iii) The third claim is that perfectionism systematizes our particular moral judgments. If we choose among the variety of definitions of human nature a certain definition that entails our particular moral judgments, then it might seem that we do have a systematization of our particular moral judgments. But the problem is that we are here stipulating that "human nature" is to refer to the human properties F, G, and H, rather than the human properties I, J, and K, because this stipulation enables us to deduce our antecedent particular moral judgments. But because stipulations lack truth-value, there is no systematization. An ethical systematization requires that (a) the theses being systematized be theorems of a theory of which the systematizing principles are axioms and (b) the axioms give us reason to think that the theorems are true. But in Hurka's case, the axioms lack truth-value and thereby provide no reason for us to think that the theorems are true. Condition (b) is not met by Hurka's perfectionism and so his third claim, about systematization, is false.

Thus, we are forced to the conclusion that Hurka has not developed a perfectionist theory. He has developed an intuitionist theory. This problem with Hurka's theory, however, is not as major as it might seem to some philosophers interested in developing a perfectionist ethics, because many of the other ideas developed in Hurka's book are particularly relevant to a perfectionist ethics and may be profitably used by a perfectionist theorist. The antecedent moral intuitions upon which Hurka relies accord in many cases with the theses that the perfectionist thinks are evidentially supported by genuine perfectionist premises. Apart from this kinship of Hurka's intuitionism with genuine perfectionism we should note that Hurka himself does not seem averse to intuitionist or pluralist ethics, as he himself remarks in his book, so the conclusion that his ethics is an intuitionism, with some ideas that a perfectionist could use, would not seem to be a major criticism of his theory. In spite of my criticisms of his foundations as being in fact intuitionist, Hurka's book seems to me to be the most important contribution to perfectionist ways of thinking since Aristotle's *Nicomachean Ethics*, and the perfectionism that I develop in what follows would not have been possible without it.

In the next section I shall show how a perfectionist ethics can be developed, using the tools of linguistic essentialism. I argue that there are reasons to believe that this perfectionism is a satisfactory normative ethics and provides us with an objective ethical meaning of human life.

25. Global, Naturalistic Perfectionism and the Method of Linguistic Essentialism

A perfectionist ethics can be developed if we use the method of linguistic essentialism to a greater extent than it is used by Hurka. Hurka uses the essentialist method only for the purpose of showing how we can know essential properties of humans. He does not apply this method to the moral terms "good" and "right." Hurka adopts a nonnaturalist position and takes "is good" to express the sense of "ought to be desired by agents" and "is right" to express the sense of "maximizes the good." Thus, in Hurka's theory, "x is good because it ought to be desired by agents" is an analytic, a priori, and necessary sentence. This nonnaturalist definition of "good" is partly similar to Moore's definition, where good means "ought to exist." It is also similar to the nonnatural constitutional ethics I outlined in my discussion of Brink's theory, where "good" expresses the second-order property ought-to-be-exemplified.

If we apply the essentialists' method of linguistic analysis to moral terms, we will be able to develop a plausible naturalistic perfectionism. Because the conjunction of ethical naturalism and moral realism is intrinsically more plausible than the conjunction of ethical nonnaturalism and moral realism, as I argued above, this naturalistic perfectionism will give us an even stronger reason to believe that human life has an objective ethical meaning.

Hurka believes that any naturalistic perfectionism is necessarily false because it fails to account for the intimate connection between evaluation and action. Hurka believes that to assent to a moral judgment "one must act as the judgement directs, or at least form the intention so to act when circumstances are appropriate" (28). Hurka believes that ethical naturalism entails that there is no such connection between evaluation and action. I believe he is correct, but I believe that no plausible ethical theory should entail there is such a connection. There is no such connection. Hurka's claim that assenting to a moral judgment *requires* forming an intention to act on it, when circumstances are appropriate, seems false. I assent to "I ought to get out of bed and start working on the next chapter of my book" and yet, feeling lazy and slightly guilty, lie in bed for another half an hour. In this case, I am not forming an intention to act when the circumstances are appropriate because the circumstances are *then* appropriate for me to so act—but I do not because I am too lazy. And I am sincerely assenting to the moral judgment, because I feel guilty for not forming an intention to act on the judgment. Hurka is assuming internalism about motives, but as I have earlier argued, and as Brink has argued in chapter 3 of his *Moral Realism and the Foundation of Ethics,* externalism about motives is the correct position.

I conclude that Hurka has given no convincing reason to think that a naturalistic version of perfectionism is untenable. In what follows, I argue for a version of naturalistic perfectionism that relies entirely on the essentialist method of linguistic analysis.

"Human," like "gold," "water," "cat," and "tiger," is a natural kind word. According to linguistic essentialism, it rigidly and directly designates a natural kind. A natural kind is a nontrivial essence or conjunction of such essences. In many cases, the reference-fixing description for a natural kind word specifies that this word refers rigidly and directly to the nontrivial essences that explain the phenomenal or observable properties that are normal to members of that kind. These nontrivial essences constitute the "kind of nature" of the things or, more briefly, the *nature* of the things. The reference-fixing description for "human" is that this natural kind word refers directly and rigidly to whatever nontrivially essential properties explain the phenomenal properties of humans (their physical appearance and their behaviors). These properties belong to some of the classes of essential properties Hurka mentioned, that is, what is essential to humans as physical objects, as living objects, as animals, and as distinctive from other animals.

I do not include what is essential to humans *as mere objects,* for these essential properties are either trivially essential properties (for example, being identical with Socrates) or logically necessary properties (being self-identical). Trivially essential and logically necessary properties do not explain the phenomenal properties of humans (their behaviors and physical appearance) and thus are not among the designata of the natural kind word "human."

According to the naturalist perfectionism I shall be defending, "goodness" refers to the natural property *being a development of things' natures.* What is said by the

statement, "Goodness is a development of things' natures" is an identity proposition, but we know that the statement expresses this identity proposition only a
posteriori (as I argue below).

The essences constituting the natural kind to which an object belongs do not
include all nontrivial essences of the object, for example, its individual essences.
Marcel Proust has the nontrivial essence, *writing in a cork-lined room in the actual
world* α, but this is not a part of Proust's "nature." (Of course, it is a part of Proust's
"nature" if we mean by this his individual essence, but I am using "Proust's nature"
to mean the nontrivial essences that make him a member of the natural kind
human.)

My argument will proceed by specifying various reference-fixing descriptions of
"good," "right," and so forth and showing that a posteriori considerations indicate
that such properties as *being a development of things' natures* satisfy these reference-
fixing descriptions. This method of ethical knowledge was first used (and discovered) by Adams, as I indicated in section 22, although I make several modifica-
tions and additions to his formulation of the method. Generally speaking, I shall do
what Adams did in arguing for his divine command ethical theory, namely, show
that a certain property satisfies the reference-fixing description for "wrongness"
(and analogously for "good," "bad," "right," and so forth). As I emphasized in the
section on Adams's theory, this method is the *linguistic essentialist* method of ethical
knowledge and is distinct from other methods, for example, the method of reflective equilibrium, rational psychotherapy (Richard Brandt's method), the phenomenological method (for example, as used by Butchvarov), and other methods.

My argument that the properties countenanced by global, naturalist perfectionism satisfy the reference-fixing descriptions for "good," "wrong," and so on cannot
be clearly presented unless we first have a reasonably precise idea of the sort of
property that I use "being a development of things' natures" to designate. I shall
first *explain* some of the main theses of global, naturalist perfectionism, and in the
next section begin presenting some *arguments* for this normative ethics.

According to naturalistic perfectionism, the reference-fixing descriptions for the
relational predicate "is more valuable than" imply there are two uses of this predicate. In one use it designates the relation *( ) is a greater degree of development of the
natural property F than ( )*. This relation obtains between different degrees of
development of a given essential property. An example is that Einstein's epistemic
states exemplify a greater degree of development of the essential property of
theoretical rationality than do the epistemic states of an average person.

The relational predicate "is more valuable than" also has a different use, in
which it designates the relation *( ) has a more developed kind of nature than ( )*.
An example is that a whale has a more developed kind of nature than a pebble on
a beach.

The second relation allows global, naturalistic perfectionism to provide a hierarchy of kinds of things based on the degree of value of different kinds of natures. In this sense of "more valuable than," a thing of kind K_1 is more valuable than a thing of kind K_2 if and only if K_1 is a more developed kind of nature than K_2. An explanation of this hierarchy will show what "more developed kind of nature" means.

The hierarchy is based on the fact that higher kinds of things include the natures of lower kinds of things as parts of their own nature. At the bottom of the hierarchy are mere physical objects: electrons, stones, mountains, stars, and so forth. The nature of a mere physical object consists of the nontrivial essential properties of *being spatiotemporally extended* and *having mass.* Because a mere physical object has a *developed kind of nature* (even though it is the least developed kind of nature of the various kinds of concrete objects), by virtue of having these two nontrivial essences, a mere physical object has *positive value* just by virtue of being a physical object. And because its nature consists of these two degreed properties, which vary in degree among different physical objects, a physical object can have more or less value than some other physical object. A physical object x that is more massive and spatiotemporally extended than another physical object y is (all else being equal) more valuable than y. The moon has more intrinsic value than a stone, and the Andromeda Galaxy (even abstracting from whatever life-forms it may include) has more intrinsic value than the moon. A physical object develops its nature by either enduring in time (and thereby becoming more temporally extended), expanding in space (and thereby becoming more spatially extended), or becoming more dense (and thereby becoming more massive).

Humans rarely have occasion to make intrinsic value judgments about mere physical objects, in that they are habituated to judging them only in terms of their extrinsic value as means to or conditions of the development of human beings. It would not be an exaggeration to say that theoretical discussion of the intrinsic values of mere physical objects is the least developed part (indeed, a virtually nonexistent part) of normative ethics. This is one respect in which *global,* naturalistic perfectionism departs from familiar types of normative ethics. It is "global" in that it is about the intrinsic value of all objects, including mere physical objects. (Hurka called his theory "narrow perfectionism" because it was only about the value of human beings.) Even most environmental ethics are not global in that they usually discuss the intrinsic values only of all animals or only of all living things or ecosystems.

I am *not* appealing to antecedent and independent "moral intuitions" to determine what is more valuable than what. If I followed Hurka's method, I would not be developing an ethical perfectionism but an ethical intuitionism. Rather, I am determining the values of things and their states by deducing their values from premises about the nontrivial essences that are the rigid designata of natural kind words. In global, naturalistic perfectionism, *material* or *substantive* moral theses about what is good or bad and what is better than what are deduced from premises about things' natures, and the evidence that the perfectionist theory (axioms and theorems) is a true normative ethics is that this theory satisfies the *formal* conditions laid down in the reference-fixing rules for moral words. (This aspect of the essentialist method of ethical knowledge will become clearer in the next several sections.)

To return to the subject of hierarchy, mere animate things (for example, plants, bacteria) have the next most valuable kind of nature. The nature of an animate thing includes the nature of a physical thing and *in addition* the nontrivial essences of *reproducing* and *obtaining nourishment*. (Here I side with the biologists who take bacteria, rather than viruses [which do not reproduce], as the most primitive known life-form.) This is the sense in which a mere animate thing has a more developed kind of nature than a mere physical thing. The development of the nature of an animate thing includes realizing its reproductive capacities (producing offspring), realizing its nutritive capacities (for example, performing photosynthesis), and in general maintaining and increasing these organic functions to the degree that is optimal for the health and reproduction of the organism.

Unless there are mitigating circumstances, the development of a mere physical thing's nature (for example, expanding in space) is less valuable than that of a mere animate thing's nature (for example, reproducing). It is bad that an ocean (considered only as a mere physical thing) increases its size and in so doing prevents the nutritive and reproductive functions of numerous plants that populate the shoreline. But the ocean contains plants and fish, and if its increase results in a significant development of the plant and fish life in the ocean, then the ocean's increase in size will be good overall, in spite of the harm done to shoreline plants. Moral considerations such as these are neglected in standard normative ethics, which tend to have humans as their sole subject matter, but are integral to global perfectionism.

Animals have a more valuable kind of nature than merely animate things. In addition to being essentially massive and spatiotemporally extended, nutrition-obtaining and reproductive, animals have a further nontrivial essence. But here numerous complications arise owing to the various species of lower and higher animals, ranging from the most primitive known kind of animal (some members of the parazoa family, which have only a thousand cells) to mammals. To avoid the complications of a theory that embraces the natures of all known species of animals, I will talk only about animals that are significantly different from mere organisms, which are at least the vertebrates (for example, fish, birds, amphibians, reptiles, and mammals). Vertebrates ("the higher animals") are distinguished from mere organisms by virtue of having the nontrivial essence of *the ability to move in order to satisfy their desires regarding what they can sense or imagine.* (Lower animals are self-realized in much the way mere organisms are, for lower animals have nutritive and reproductive abilities and differ from mere organisms in that they develop from egg and sperm cells and have double chromosomes. To simplify matters, I will use "animal" to refer only to the nature of the higher animals.) Some recent work by Arthur Falk has shown that the relevant properties—desire, sentience, and the ability to move so as to satisfy one's desires—present in humans are present in more primitive forms in much less developed animals, and we may with justification use "desire," "sentience," and so on to refer to the properties of a wide range of animals.[14]

The distinctive essence of animals is a degreed property, and its development consists in *movements that successfully fulfill the animal's desires regarding what it can sense or imagine.* Because successfully fulfilling a desire is a pleasurable feeling of satisfaction, our global perfectionism is able to explain why pleasure is intrinsically good, a normative fact that Hurka's "perfectionism" is unable to explain and is in fact inconsistent with (171).

Because animals have more valuable natures than mere animate things, the preservation of an animal is morally preferable to the preservation of a mere animate thing (all else being equal). It is good that a cow eats the grass it desires to eats, and thereby kills the grass, because a cow is a more valuable kind of thing than the blades of grass it eats.

The comparative principle at work here is based on a certain formal ethical principle, the *finite difference* principle, which differs from the *infinite difference* principle. According to the (false) *infinite difference* principle, any *one* thing or good state of a thing on a higher level of the hierarchy of kinds of things is more valuable than *all* the things or *all* the good states on a lower level of the hierarchy of kinds of things. One implication of an *infinite difference* principle is that all the plants on earth are less valuable than a single one of the billions of insects. Another implication is that the moral goal is always to increase the development of a thing of a higher kind, at the expense of anything lower, so that even the smallest increase in development of a single thing of a higher kind is more valuable than enormous increases in development of an infinite number of things of a lower kind. It is not this principle, however, but the *finite difference* principle that is the formal moral principal embodied in the reference-fixing descriptions of our comparative moral words. According to the *finite difference* principle, it can be true that the aggregate of all things, or all good states of things, on a lower level of the hierarchy can be higher in total aggregate value than some things or good states on a higher level. All the merely physical things in the universe are more intrinsically valuable than just one of the billions of bacteria that exist.

But this comparison is dependent on the abundance of bacteria and other life-forms; if the only animate thing in the universe was one bacterium, its value would not be outweighed by the aggregate value of all merely physical things. This is an instance of another formal principal, the *uniqueness* condition, which comes into play in comparing the value of things and is at the basis of the judgment that it is much worse to let the last members of a certain species die out than to let a few members of a highly populated and unendangered species die out (assuming the species are at approximately the same level of nature development.)

The *finite difference* principle also implies that in some cases, great increases in development of a large number of things of a lower kind add up to a greater amount of value than increases in development of some higher kinds of things. The flourishing of all plants on earth is of greater intrinsic value than the flourishing of just one of the billions of insects on earth. But the existence and flourishing of the billions of plants on earth is not intrinsically more valuable than the existence and flourishing of thousands of the scientists and philosophers that live in the twentieth century. (The existence of all plants is *extrinsically* more valuable than the existence of twentieth-century theorists because an earth without plants would not allow any higher kinds of things to exist.)

One species of physical things may have more value than another species if it is more developed in the relevant sense, and the same holds for different species of animate things. Regarding the species of animals, the most developed species is the human species. The nontrivial essence of rationality (as I shall later define it) is possessed only by humans, and this essential property is the most developed kind of essential property that belongs to anything's nature.

At this juncture, we have enough of an initial idea of global, naturalistic perfectionism to present the arguments that this normative ethics satisfies the reference-fixing descriptions for the words "good," "bad," "right," and "wrong."

25.1 Perfectionism and the Reference-Fixing Descriptions of Moral Words

The reference-fixing descriptions for moral words determine the rules by which competent language-users use these moral words, and these descriptions *in addition* constitute the cognitive significance of these words. Regarding cognitive significance, we tacitly or explicitly have in mind one or more of these several descriptive senses (the cognitive significance) when we use these moral words.

These moral words refer to certain properties, but an acquaintance with these properties is no more a part of the cognitive significance of these words than an acquaintance with *being H_2O molecules* is a part of the cognitive significance of "being water."

Competent language-users do not have in mind as the cognitive significance of "good" that "good" directly and rigidly designates the property *a development of things' natures*. Ordinary language analysts may correctly point out that this *is not* what we ordinarily would say "good" designates; but this only goes to show that ordinary language analysts failed to distinguish the cognitive significance from the semantic content of locutions.

In the following, I explain six reference-fixing descriptions relevant to the moral uses of "good," "bad," "right," and "wrong." I call them conditions because they are formal descriptive conditions that something must satisfy in order to be the designatum of "good" (or some other moral word). After I explain each reference-fixing description, I shall show how the properties mentioned in global, naturalist perfectionism satisfy these descriptions.

(R1) The Realism Condition

This reference-fixing rule of use of "good" states that "good" is used to refer to a property that is exemplified by items independently of whether or not we believe it is exemplified by these items (the same for "bad," "right," and "wrong"). If something is good, it is objectively good. I have already argued in several places in this book that first-level ordinary moral beliefs imply moral realism and thus I think we are justified in including the realism condition in the reference-fixing descriptions that govern the use of moral words.

Global and naturalist perfectionism conforms to the realism condition. If "good" in one of its uses refers to the property *a development of things' natures*, and, in another use, refers to *a developed kind of nature*, then our perfectionism meets this reference-fixing condition. For example, if on a certain occasion eighty million years ago a dinosaur developed its nature qua living thing by becoming nourished by the plants it was eating, the dinosaur exemplified this property independently of whether or not we believe it exemplified this property.

According to naturalist perfectionism, development-properties involve a species/genus distinction. The dinosaur being nourished by plants is a species of the genus *developing its animate nature*, and this genus in turn is a species of the higher genus *developing its nature*.

(R2) The Attitude Condition

A rule of use of "good" is that we predicate this word of things or states of things toward which we typically have emotionally positive attitudes.

When we predicate "good" of a *possible* and actualizable state of things, we typically desire to actualize this state or wish or hope that it is actualized or at least find its actualization acceptable or unobjectionable.

When we predicate "good" of *existing* states of things or of existent things, we are typically pleased, satisfied, joyous, or at least accepting of these states or things.

Predications of "bad" are typically accompanied by the corresponding negative attitudes.

Global, naturalist perfectionism satisfies the attitude condition; our positive attitudes associated with predications of "good" are attitudes toward developments of things' natures or toward things that have highly developed kinds of natures.

There are many examples of this, but we may choose a seemingly controversial one. When I praise a teacher for being a good teacher, I am praising her for teaching effectively and promoting significant learning in students. Teaching effectively is a way of developing a part of her nature (her theoretical and practical reason), and promoting learning is promoting the development of the students' natures (their theoretical reason).

This example, which is typical of perfectionist ethics, may face this objection: Is "good" in the phrase "a good teacher" a moral use of "good" or a nonmoral, task-related sense of "good"? I think it is a moral use of "good," for there are the following connections: Suppose we believe that Jane lives a morally good life. If asked to give evidence for our belief, we would include in our evidence that she has chosen teaching as a career and that she is an effective teacher. If she were a *criminal* or a *poor* teacher, *these* facts would not count as evidence that she lives a morally good life. Task-related senses of "good" ("a task well done") can be types or species of the moral sense of "good." It is morally good to do well a task (profession, job, social function) whose defined goal is to develop people's or other things' natures.

It is easy to think of examples of nature developments that meet the attitude condition, but the real test comes from putative counterexamples, such as the following. We admire or respect Jane for learning calculus (which is a development of her theoretical reason) and believe that her learning calculus is a good state of affairs. But suppose Jane is responsible for the welfare of children in a day care center and they all died because she spent her time studying calculus rather than caring for them. In this case, we would be outraged at Jane's developing her theoretical reason. Does not this show that developments of natures do not satisfy the attitude condition?

The answer is negative because a state of a thing that is a development of something's nature can be part of a more complex state of things that consists of a greater amount of *prevention* of nature development than it does of nature development. The predicate "badness" in one of its moral uses refers to the property *being a prevention of the development of things' nature* or, more exactly, *being more of a prevention of the development of things' nature than a development of things' natures.* The complex state of things Jane-learning-calculus-and-thereby-allowing the-children-to-die is bad (prevents more than it develops) even though one part of this complex state, Jane's learning calculus, is good (is a development). Just as bad states can contribute to the overall goodness of a whole, so good states can contribute to the overall badness of a whole.

Joseph Ellin makes a good point that the cases of animals killing and eating each other seem to many to be counterexamples to a naturalistic perfectionism.[15] A wolf

realizes its essential nature by killing and eating a caribou; the wolf realizes goodness by developing its nature, but what about the caribou? Clearly, the caribou's
premature and painful death is bad. So how can the wolf's development of its
nature be considered good? Certainly, the caribou would not agree to that proposition, so to speak.

These sorts of questions cannot be adequately answered unless we consider the
overall state of affairs, the wolf-eating-the-caribou. Is this complex state of things
more bad than it is good or vice versa? There is no clear answer here without
considering extrinsic matters. Is the wolf population too great for its territory? Are
the caribou dying out, and will they soon be extinct? Is there no other way for the
wolf to be nourished? Or is the caribou population becoming so great that unless a
few were killed by wolves, the caribou would eat up their own food sources and all
die from starvation? Whether this state of affairs is overall good or bad depends on
whether answers to these other questions are affirmative or negative. There is also a
possibility that there is a *moral tie* here: the good belonging to this state of affairs
may equal the bad. The ambiguity in our emotional attitudes to this state of affairs
reflects the fact that it is not clear (without further information) whether it is
overall good or overall bad or is a moral tie. Further, if it is overall good, this may be
by only a slight degree; it is just barely more good than bad. This would also reflect
our emotionally ambiguous attitude to a state of affairs of this sort.

But note that it would have been better if a different sort of universe U_1 had
existed instead of the universe U that in fact exists, a universe U_1 in which all
animals were vegetarians, in the precise sense I have argued elsewhere.[16] This
counterfactual moral truth is a part of "the probabilistic argument from natural
evil" against the existence of God, for no all-good and all-powerful being would
have created animals that had to cruelly murder and devour one another just in
order to survive.[17] But given that (a) our universe U with its many kinds of
carnivores does exist, and that (b) it is better that these carnivores exist than all die
out, and that (c) many animals will die out from scarcity of food if some of their
kind are not killed, it is (just barely) overall good in some cases that some animals
be eaten by others.

Another possible objection to the claim that a naturalist and global perfectionism satisfies the attitude condition concerns our attitudes to death. We typically
have negative emotional attitudes to cases of premature death. We regard premature deaths as intrinsically bad. It may be objected to global, naturalist perfectionism that it is theoretically ad hoc to characterize a thing's premature death as bad in
virtue of the fact that it is *a prevention of the development of the thing's nature.*

This is not ad hoc because it follows logically from a naturalist global perfectionism and characterizes exactly why premature death is intrinsically bad. Prematurely dying or ceasing to exist is the prevention of a thing developing its nature

as a physical thing and higher sort of thing. Being a physical thing entails being a spatiotemporally extended thing. Qua spatiotemporally extended thing, I develop my nature by becoming *more* spatiotemporally extended, which entails becoming *more* temporally extended (lasting longer). Premature death prevents this temporal development, *and thereby prevents any further development of all the higher parts of my nature.* This explains why premature death is bad.

But this may suggest a further counterexample to the claim that naturalistic perfectionism conforms to the positive and negative attitudes relevant to our predications of "good" and "bad." We have a negative attitude to fatness that is justifiable insofar as being fat is unhealthy. Naturalist and global perfectionism, however, implies that developing my spatiotemporal extension is good. Because I can increase my spatial extension by becoming fat, should I become fat?

Global, naturalist perfectionism implies that increase in spatial extension is intrinsically good; but for humans, this increase—if it involves becoming fat—is typically accompanied by a decrease in the degree of development of a person's nature as a living thing. Becoming unhealthy is a decrease in the effectiveness of my organic functioning. Because my nature as a living thing has higher value than my nature as a physical thing, increases in spatial extension that involve becoming fat are typically part of a state of affairs that contains more bad than good and thereby is a bad state of affairs. Thus, it is false that global perfectionism implies that humans should become as fat as possible.

This point, along with the point about increasing my temporal extension, is evidence against Hurka's claim that a plausible perfectionist ethics cannot include humans' *physical* nature in the definition of human nature.

One moral use of "bad" is to refer to the property *being more of a prevention of a development of natures than a development.* A related use of "bad" is to refer to *being a decrease in degree of a degreed essential property that belongs to a thing's nature.* Becoming unhealthy is bad not merely in that it prevents an increase in the effective functioning of an organic degreed property, but is a decrease in this effective functioning.

"Bad" and "good" also have additional uses in which they are predicated of things to which we have negative or positive attitudes (as distinct from states of things). How can a naturalist global perfectionism explain our positive attitudes to Jane when we assent to the sentence "Jane is good" or "Jane is a good person"? Our perfectionism implies that the first sentence expresses the singular proposition *Jane highly develops human nature (her own and others)* (or Jane has a highly developed nature and highly develops the nature of other things). Inductive evidence suggests that, as a matter of fact, it is to such "developed people" as Jane that we have attitudes of admiration or respect or approval.

But what of the increases in development of the nature of insects, weeds, and the like, to which we typically do not have positive attitudes? Does this show that perfectionism fails to satisfy one of the reference-fixing descriptions for "good"?

The reason we do not have positive attitudes toward developing weeds and insects is that we normally regard these developments only as parts of more complex states of affairs to which we have a negative attitude, such as states of affairs that frustrate our desires (our nature qua animals) to inhabit a suitably clean, healthy house, walk through a forest without being stung or poisoned, or cultivate an aesthetically satisfying garden. (It may be the case, however, that humans' disenchantment with weeds is not based on any good attitude to the plant kingdom, in which case moral progress would involve changing our value judgments about weeds and manicured gardens and other unnecessary attempts of humans to dominate or control the plant world.)

But what about love and friendship, to which we have positive attitudes? How are these developments of our nature? They are developments of our animal natures; humans qua animals have the degreed essential property of being able to move so as to satisfy their desires regarding sensed or imagined things. One of our desires is to relate to other people in a friendly or loving way and to have them relate to us in a friendly or loving way.

But are not love relationships of intrinsic positive value *apart from* the fact that they satisfy our desires to love and be loved? It seems to me this is not the case, for if a species of animals had an essential aversion to love relations and lived fully satisfied lives without them, then love relations among members of this species would have negative value. The primary reason love is good is that it satisfies our desires to love and be loved.

I said that "humans qua animals have the degreed essential property of being able to move so as to satisfy their desires." Is increasing the degree of this essence increasing the *ability* to move in a satisfying way or is its increasing the quantity or quality of the satisfying *movements?* In general, are developments increases in the *capacity* to do something or are they increases in the *occurrent realizations* of a fixed capacity? Essential developments are both, but most cases of development are increases in occurrent realizations of a fixed capacity.

A serial killer has the desire to murder people; this desire (as is any desire) is part of the killer's essence qua animal. Does it follow from perfectionism that it is good that he moves so as to satisfy this desire? By now, we should know how such objections to perfectionism are answered: We consider the overall state of affairs, the killer murdering Jane, Bob, Beth, and Richard, and recognize that this state of affairs is bad. One of its parts is good, the killer moving so as to satisfy his desires, but we are unable to imagine this part without imagining the horribly bad other parts of this state of affairs, the murders of the victims, so this entire state of affairs appears to us to be repugnant.

(R3) The Justification Condition

Robert Adams suggested that understanding the nature of wrongness would give us one more reason, rather than one less reason, to not want to perform the wrong action. This condition is clearly satisfied by perfectionism, for if we understood that wrongness was decreasing or preventing the development of things' natures, that would give us one more reason, not one less reason, to not want to engage in actions we regard as wrong. (The same holds, conversely, for right or good states.)

This is not, however, what I have in mind as reference-fixing description (R3), the justification condition. This condition is that "good" is used to refer to a property F, such that a possible state of affairs' exemplification of F is typically regarded as a sufficient justification for some agent to actualize that state of affairs.

Note that the justification condition does not imply internalism about reasons (in Brink's sense). Description R3 does not say that "F is good" analytically entails "There is sufficient justification for an agent to actualize F." The reference-fixing concept of "good" instead implies that expressions of the form "F is good," if believed to be true by humans, are typically regarded by humans as stating sufficient justification for an agent to actualize the property F. This is a form of externalism about reasons.

Global perfectionism satisfies this condition because if a possible state of affairs is believed de re or de dicto to have the property *being a development of things' natures* (or, more fully, being more of a development than a hindrance of things' natures), then actualizing that state of affairs is typically regarded as a sufficiently justified action. The belief de re that something has this property is crucial to this case, given the distinction we are using between cognitive significance and semantic content. The cognitive significance of "The F-ness of x is good" may be a belief de dicto involving the reference-fixing descriptions governing "good," and the belief that the F-ness of x is a development of x's nature may be a belief de re. This may be explained as follows.

Belief de dicto does not allow intersubstitutivity in all epistemic contexts; the sentence, "David believes it is sufficiently justified to become a chemist because the advancement of chemistry is good" does not in general allow a substitution of "a development of things' natures" for "good," given that David may not know that the semantic content of "good" is a development of things' natures. If "x believes de dicto that S" is true, x must recognize that the proposition he believes is expressible by the sentence S.

But belief de re allows intersubstitutivity in all epistemic contexts because "goodness" and "developing things' natures" have the same semantic content, even though David does not know this. David is epistemically related (de re) to the proposition, *It is sufficiently justified to become a chemist because the advancement of chemistry is a development of things' natures.* If "x believes de re that S" is true, it is sufficient that x believe the proposition expressed by the sentence S, even though x may not realize that the sentence S expresses this proposition. (Analogously, David believes de re that H_2O is H_2O when he believes that "water is water," even though he may not recognize that "water is water" expresses this proposition.)

The justification condition is met if the possible states of affairs typically believed to be sufficient justifications for actions are believed de re to be developments of things' natures, even though the associated de dicto beliefs are merely that these actions are generally approved of, are desirable, are what ought to be realized, and so forth. In many cases, however, the justification condition is met by a de dicto belief that a possible state of affairs is a development of things' natures. We may have in mind as sufficient justifications for acting that some state of affairs consists in a forest or ecosystem developing its nature by becoming more healthy, a horse developing its animal nature by having room to run and exercise, a human having enough material goods so he can devote his time to developing his nature as a theoretically rational person, and so on. (It is worth emphasizing that "typically" does not imply "always," for it is built into the rules of use of moral words that there can be some moral failures, for example, due to sociopathology or other defects of human moral nature. Thus, my frequent use of "typically" in discussing these rules of use.)

Are there counterexamples to the claim that global perfectionism satisfies the justification condition?

It is the nature of the AIDS virus to grow and multiply. Is enabling this virus to develop its nature a justified action? We already know the global perfectionist answer; a virus has less intrinsic value than humans, and thus a greater amount of goodness is realized by preventing the virus from realizing its nature and thereby allowing the relevant humans to realize their nature. The virus growing, considered by itself, is good, but the more complex state of affairs of which it is a part is bad.

Another possible counterexample is this: There is an air mattress lying on the floor, and it is not blown up. Becoming more spatially extended is a development of its nature as a physical thing, so extending the mattress by blowing it up is actualizing a good state of affairs. It may be alleged that global perfectionism implies the absurd conclusion that increasing the mattress's spatial extension is a morally sufficient justification for my engaging in the action of blowing it up, and therefore that I ought to go around blowing up any deflated mattresses I see.

Global perfectionism accounts for this putative counterexample by noting that the more complex state of affairs, *my blowing up the mattress in order that the mattress may increase its spatial extension,* is bad. It is bad because I should be spending my time bringing about nature developments that are significantly more valuable than developing the mattress's physical nature.

(R4) The Consensus Condition

Part of the reference-fixing descriptions of our moral words is that there be large-scale agreement about which states and things have the properties designated by "good," "bad," and so forth. This does not mean there is a certain body of items all agree upon, but that there are significant overlapping agreements among most people.

The primary evidence about the moral beliefs people hold is their *behavior*, not what they report verbally when they are asked about their moral beliefs. Frequently, the behavior and verbal reports of people differ. For example, biographical materials about Nietzsche show that he actually lived by and intuitively believed the moral views he condemned in his books; that is, he was a compassionate, sensitive, and gentle man who often took pity on people. The appeal to behavior has added importance when we recognize the distinction between the cognitive significance and semantic content of people's utterances, and the fact that belief in global, naturalistic perfectionism is manifested more often in belief de re (exhibited in behavior) than in belief de dicto (exhibited in verbal reports "about what I believe").

Our naturalist perfectionism satisfies the reference-fixing description (R4), for there is widespread agreement (both de re and de dicto) that developments of things' natures are good and preventions of this development bad. Such nature developments as the acquisition of knowledge, the satisfactions of humans' and other animals' desires, the various practical accomplishments that are developments of practical reason, becoming healthy, the flourishing of wildlife, the endurance of the mountains, and so on are regarded as good and their opposites as bad.

Notice that I am not including within the reference-fixing description for "good" a list of kinds of goods—knowledge, friendship, health—for this would make our normative ethics an intuitionist ethics rather than a perfectionism. If I did include this list, I would begin with an antecedent intuitive knowledge of what is good, a knowledge embodied in the cognitive significance of our moral words, and our ethical theory would simply be an articulation of these moral intuitions. Our normative ethical conclusions, in this case, would *not* be derived from premises about the development of things' natures, and statements about "developing something's nature" would be as redundant in our normative ethics as they are in Hurka's. For this reason, I must reject Robert Adams's inclusions of examples of kinds of wrong actions in the reference-fixing concept associated with "wrong" (see section 22); Adams's normative ethics presupposes an antecedent knowledge of what is wrong and is not derived from premises only about *contrariety to divine commands*. In this respect, Adams's ethics tends to be an intuitionist ethics, not a divine command ethics. *Formal* moral principles, such as the *finite difference* principle, are embodied in reference-fixing descriptions for moral words, but *material* principles about what is good and bad and what is better than what are instead deduced from premises about things' natures. (Accordingly, our statement that Adams discovered "the linguistic essentialist method of ethical knowledge" is more accurately put by saying that he discovered some parts of this method but that fundamental corrections of and additions to his theory need to be made before we have a theory of the linguistic essentialist method of ethical knowledge.)

To clarify further this crucial aspect of the linguistic essentialist method, I should emphasize that the examples of good and bad items, or kinds of goods and evils, that I just mentioned and that I mentioned in discussing reference-fixing conditions (R1) through (R4) are not analytic or a priori parts of the reference-fixing conditions. Rather, they are offered as evidence that global, naturalist perfectionism satisfies these conditions. Consider the proposition,

P. The state of affairs *Dinosaurs developed their natures regardless of whether humans believed they did* satisfies the moral realist condition (R1).

The mentioned state of affairs is known a posteriori and the concept of this state of affairs includes a concept of a kind of good (developing an animal nature), but neither of these concepts is contained analytically or a priori in any of the reference-fixing descriptions (R1)–(R6) for our moral words. This kind of good is deduced from the axioms of global, naturalist perfectionism (some of these axioms being that all things [concrete objects] have natures in the sense of nontrivial essences that constitute their natural kind, that goodness is identical with developing these nontrivial essences, and so forth). An example of this kind of good, *dinosaurs developing their animal nature,* is mentioned in proposition (P) for the purpose of providing evidence that global perfectionism meets the reference-fixing conditions (R1) for the word "good."

The next two reference-fixing descriptions pertain to uses of "right" and "wrong." The rules I have already listed, (R1) through (R4), are not very controversial (except for the realism condition, and I have presented several arguments on its behalf in chapters 1–6), but rules (R5) and (R6) are more controversial in that they imply that *both* consequentialist and deontological moral properties are instantiated. Consequentialists might want to deny that any deontological properties are instantiated, and some deontologists might want to deny that any consequentialist properties are instantiated. But it seems to me that the inductive evidence about our moral talk and beliefs evidence suggests that both sorts of properties are instantiated, and this is the major source of moral dilemmas.

(R5) The Consequentialist Condition

The rule of use of "right" (in its consequentialist sense) is that this word is predicated of voluntary actions that maximize the good. The predicate "right" expresses a relational property that is formally characterized as *maximizing the good* or, more exactly, as *having the highest expected value;* the expected value is a function of the act's possible outcomes and of their probabilities of being realized. (As I understand the consequentialist condition, the value of the act itself is one of the components—and sometimes the sole component—included in the aggregate amount of value realized by the act.)

Note that the rule of use of "right" includes the concept of the good, so that this rule of use is conceptually dependent on the concepts in rules (R1)–(R4) that pertain to the word "good."

The expression "is wrong" (in its consequentialist use) is predicated of a voluntary action that is not maximizing, and this predication is normally associated with attitudes of condemnations or other negative attitudes.

There is evidence that global, naturalistic perfectionism satisfies condition (R5). For example, people admire or approve of Einstein's theoretical efforts, Beethoven's musical efforts, Sylvia Plath's literary efforts, and these efforts maximize (or at least are believed to maximize) the development of human nature, which includes the creator's nature as well as the audiences' natures. Many other examples could be adduced: doctors are respected for maximizing health, some psychologists are respected for maximizing happiness (the satisfaction of desires), and firefighters and rescue workers are admired for maximizing the temporal extension of people qua physical beings (that is, "saving their lives," as these right actions are normally called).

(R6) The Deontological Condition

The rule of use of the *noun phrase* "a right" (for example, "a right to life") is different from the rule of use of the *verb phrase* "is right." "A right" has a deontological sense and, unlike "is right," does not mean *maximizes the good.* The noun phrase "a right" refers to a state of a thing, such that voluntary destructions or impairments of this state are typically objects of disapproval, outrage, condemnation, and other negative attitudes. ("State of a thing" is meant in the broadest possible sense to include voluntary or involuntary actions, emotions, dispositions, static physical conditions, movements, and so on; that is, it refers to any property or relation of a thing.)

According to global, naturalistic perfectionism, the phrase "a right" directly and rigidly designates the property *being a necessary condition of developing something's nature.* For example, life, liberty, free speech, freedom of inquiry, freedom from physical harm by others, control over one's body, and so forth, are all conditions of developing human nature. All rights are defeasible; your right to life is defeated if the only way to stop your random spree of murdering humans is to kill you.

Global perfectionism implies that nonhuman animals as well as humans have rights. But they do not have equal rights; for example, "Nonhuman animals have rights" does not imply "It is always wrong to use nonhuman animals in medical experiments, such that their health or life ought never be sacrificed for the sake of advancing the health of humans." Humans' rights to life and health defeat the rights of animals with less developed kinds of natures. In general, the rights of higher kinds of things defeat the rights of lower kinds of things. It would be wrong to use animals in medical experiments if such use were not necessary to bring about vital advances in medical knowledge relevant to humans' health.

The right of an individual x (of a certain natural kind K) to do F defeats the right of another individual y (of the same natural kind K) to do G if (all else being equal) x's doing F is a realization of a higher kind of natural essence than is y's doing G. Your right to develop your theoretical reason defeats my right to satisfy my desire to amuse myself with material luxuries. But in cases in which y's being prevented from doing the action G of the lower kind would deprive y of abilities to do actions of a higher kind as well, y's right to do G is not defeated. Your right to pursue knowledge does not defeat my right to life because my being alive, although a lower kind of natural essence than theoretical reason, is a necessary condition of me developing all my higher kinds of natural essences.

The finite difference principle, however, shows there are many exceptions to these general hierarchy-based principles. For example, foxes' rights to life are not defeated by humans' desires to wear furs as luxury items. The right to life of a less developed kind of thing (the fox) morally outweighs a certain trivial and super-fluous desire of a more developed kind of thing (the human's desire to wear furs). If it were necessary for humans to wear furs as clothing to survive, the foxes' right to life would be defeated, but this is not necessary, and so it is wrong to kill foxes for their furs.

In some cases, rights and consequentialist considerations about maximizing the good clash and produce moral dilemmas. One of the most important moral di-lemmas concerns vegetarianism. Because humans can survive without eating ani-mals and eating meat is not necessary to human health or happiness, it might be thought that global perfectionism implies that it is morally obligatory to be vege-tarian. But in fact, global perfectionism implies a moral dilemma about this issue. If all humans became vegetarians, millions of animals that would otherwise be born and live to maturity would be deprived of the chance for life, health, and happiness. These animals' living a healthy and happy life until their maturity, when they were killed painlessly, would be a more valuable state of affairs than their not living at all. Thus, reasoning on consequentialist grounds, the raising of happy animals to be eaten by humans counts as a right action—it maximizes the good. These animals, once alive, however, have a right to life that is not defeated by a human's morally insignificant desire to enjoy the taste of meat. This deontological consideration clashes with the consequentialist consideration and produces a genuine moral dilemma (that is, there is no moral fact of the matter as to whether we ought to raise and eat happy animals or not bring them into existence and eat only plants). Global perfectionism does imply that the unhealthy and painful conditions in which cows, pigs, chickens, and so on are typically raised are bad and that farmers are doing something wrong in raising the animals in these conditions.

Global, naturalist perfectionism also implies that plants and physical things have natural rights. A tree has a right not to be cut down, even though this right can be defeated if this is necessary as a consequence of the rights of a more developed kind of thing. Humans have a right to pursue the development of their theoretical reason, and if this requires that trees be used for books, then the tree's right to life is defeated. A mountain has a right to its natural integrity; it is wrong to dig a tunnel through a mountain unless the tunnel is required by more significant rights of a more developed kind of thing.

It may be objected to naturalist, global perfectionism that plants and physical objects are not typically regarded as having rights, and therefore that this normative ethics does not satisfy the reference-fixing description of "a right." I would respond that the reference-fixing description of the word "a right" is merely formal and does not include a list of the kind of things that have rights, so global perfectionism is not inconsistent with a rule of use that limits rights to humans or to humans and animals.

It may nonetheless be objected by some ethicists that the reference-fixing description of "a right" does include limitations on the application of this word, and that its application is limited to humans or to animals or at least to living things.

I believe the inductive evidence about the use of "right" suggests that there is no such limitation built into its reference-fixing description. First, note that the rights of plants and physical objects are habitually defeated by humans' rights to life, health, happiness, knowledge, and so forth, and *for this reason* the rights of plants and physical objects are typically not a topic of moral deliberations. There is no cause to stop and deliberate about a piece of fruit's right to life because this right is obviously defeated by humans' right to life. Second, on the relevant occasions, the rights of physical things and plants are recognized. Humans' predominate way of relating to plants and physical things is to use them. This prevents humans from contemplating plants and physical things as something other than mere materials for human usage, and this contemplation is required to recognize they have rights. On such occasions of contemplation, however, their rights typically are recognized. For example, when humans are sitting on top of a mountain contemplating the beauty of nearby mountains and forests, they are in a position to recognize the intrinsic value of these things, and on these occasions they do tend to recognize the rights of the mountains and forests to their natural integrity or life. For example, the thought of cutting down a forest or strip mining one of the mountains to produce unnecessary luxury items would typically be found to be morally repugnant on these occasions. The fact that humans are typically disturbed by such thoughts on these occasions is best explained by the fact that they recognize that the mountains and forests have rights to be left alone and not to be destroyed needlessly by humans.

Some consequentialists and deontologists may object to the claim that the reference-fixing descriptions of our moral words specify *both* consequentialist and deontological uses of these words. But this objection seems inconsistent with the inductive evidence. Some evidence is that the predicates of voluntary actions "is wrong" and "is right" have deontological uses as well as the consequentialist use mentioned in (R4). In the deontological use of "is wrong," an action is wrong if it violates something's rights and is right if it respects things' rights.

Consequentialists would object that human moral life does *not* involve a deontological use of "wrong action" in addition to the consequentialist uses of "wrong action." But it seems the consequentialists are wrong; consider, for example, the statement, "It is wrong to steal." What is the cognitive significance and rule of use of "wrong" in this sentence? "Wrong" does not mean here that stealing *fails to maximize the good* in the relevant situation. Rather, it means that stealing is an action that *violates a person's right,* namely, their right to private property. The same holds for "It is wrong to rape," which does not mean that raping somebody does not bring about the best consequence in the relevant situation. Evidence for the claim that it is wrong to rape Jane is not that this brought about the second-best consequence in the situation, rather than the first-best. Neither does it mean that rape is a kind of action that tends not to bring about the best consequences. Rather, "It is wrong to rape" means that the act of rape has the property of violating the person's right to control her body.

But it also seems evident that this is not the only use of "is wrong." Deontologists who claim that our moral life does not involve a consequentialist sense of "is wrong" seem to be mistaken. Consider the statement, "Rimbaud was wrong to stop writing poetry and devote the remainder of his life to making as much money as possible." Here "wrong" has the consequentialist sense of an action that fails to maximize the good (to maximize the development of Rimbaud's and other humans' natures). Here Rimbaud is not violating anybody's rights. Further, "It is wrong to lie around lazily all day" does not mean that some right is being violated; it means that this activity manifestly fails to bring about the best consequence open to the agent.

I believe the explanation of most moral dilemmas is that one and the same action simultaneously instantiates "is right" in a consequentialist sense and "is wrong" in the deontological sense (or vice versa). This fact explains most of the data discussed in the articles in *Moral Dilemmas,* edited by Christopher Gowans. For instance, Marcus mentions in "Moral Dilemmas and Consistency" the example, originally given by Plato, of a person who has promised to give a cache of arms back to a person who is intent on mayhem. The decision to not give the arms back "is right" in the consequentialist sense (it maximizes the good or minimizes the bad) but "is wrong" in the deontological sense (because it violates the relevant person's right to have promises made to him abided by). This is a dilemma in that there is no common criterion to resolve the issue—consequentialist and deontological criteria of rightness and wrongness are incommensurable. (This does not mean that we cannot know the true answer to the dilemma, but that there *is* no true answer, and knowing this is knowing all there is to know about it.)

Concluding Remarks about Rules R1–R6

Part A of this chapter is about metaethics, part B about normative ethics. The division corresponds roughly to the distinction between the issue of whether or not human life has an ethical meaning (part A) and the issue of what this meaning is (part B). It is pertinent at this juncture to make some concluding remarks about the role the reference-fixing rules (R1)–(R6) play in the arguments constitutive of normative ethics.

The argument I presented has the following structure. We know by empirical induction that (R1)–(R6) are the reference-fixing descriptions for "good" and other moral words; the descriptions (R1)–(R6) require that it be an empirical discovery as to what properties satisfy these descriptions and are the referents of moral words. I further argued that we know by empirical induction that properties involving developments of things' natures satisfy the reference-fixing descriptions.

It might be objected that this "method" of doing normative ethics is misguided from the very beginning. How can mere facts about the senses of words determine what is good and bad? How can the sense of a word make it right or wrong for me to do something? If it turned out that, upon investigation of natural language, that "good" meant random killing, would it follow that it is good to engage in random killing? Consider this argument:

1. The referent of the moral use of "good" in natural languages is *a development of natures.*
   Therefore,
2. Moral goodness is a development of natures.

What shall we make of this inference? On the one hand, it seems valid if "good" is used in the conclusion in the same way it is used in natural languages. But it seems invalid if we allow that the conclusion is a sentence in a metalanguage and that all competent speakers of natural languages may be systematically mistaken in their (de re and de dicto) beliefs about goodness. I think we should allow these latter conditions and thus that the inference of (2) from (1) is invalid. If we add to (1), however, the premise consisting of a relevant version of "the argument from veridical seeming" presented in section 23.3, then we may validly infer the conclusion

3. We are justified in believing that moral goodness is a development of natures.

It might be objected that even if a pertinent version of "the argument from veridical seeming" is sound, and even if I have presented some evidence that (1) is true, I have not shown that other types of normative ethics, for example, a Kantian-type ethics, egoism, or utilitarianism, or a social contract ethics, or a pluralism of Pritchard's sort are false. Specifically, the objector may continue, I have not shown that other normative ethics do not satisfy the reference-fixing descriptions (R1)–(R6) or that there is a better fit between perfectionism and these descriptions than other types of normative ethics.

I agree that I have not demonstrated this, but I believe I have put the ball in the court of the defenders of these other sorts of normative ethics. I have argued that global, naturalist perfectionism satisfies these rules, and the burden of proof is on the defenders of other sorts of normative ethics to show that their theory equally or better satisfies these rules than perfectionism. But I would briefly note that many of these normative ethics seem ruled out on the face of it. For example, social contractarianism appears to fail to satisfy the *realist* condition (R1). And utilitarianism (at least in its traditional forms, in which happiness is the good) seems to fail to satisfy the *attitude* condition because its range of goods seems much too limited to accommodate all that we approve as morally good; egoism fails for the same reason. Further, utilitarianism appears inconsistent with the *deontological* condition. Kantian ethics fails to satisfy the *consequentialist* condition. If some nonperfectionist ethics is to satisfy all these rules, it would at least have to be in a form modified from its standard way of being formulated. It seems to me doubtful, however, that any nonperfectionist ethics satisfies these rules as well as global, naturalist perfectionism, and that there is justification to believe that this perfectionism is the most adequate type of normative ethics.

26. The Supreme Ethical Meaning of Human Life

According to global, naturalist perfectionism, the objective ethical meaning of human life is to develop things' natures, the nature of humans as well as that of other objects. (Here "human life" is used in its intuitive sense in the phrase "the meaning of human life"; I am not referring merely to human organic processes.) For any x, if x is a human, then the ethical meaning of x's life is to develop the natures of things.

The ethical meaning of human life cannot just be to develop the nature of humans, for humans can realize more goodness by striving to develop the natures of humans, nonhuman animals, plants, and mere physical things, than just humans alone. Furthermore, the ethical meaning of my life cannot just be to develop my nature, for in some cases I can bring about more goodness by striving to develop the nature of other things at the expense of my personal development. The extreme case would be to sacrifice my life for the sake of other people, animals, and so forth if this would bring about significantly greater goodness than the further development of my own nature.

The questions, "What should I do with my life?" and "How should I live?" are answered in a general way by saying, "You should choose the way of life that would most contribute to developing the nature of all things."

A person who lives an exceptionally meaningful life is a person who contributes more to the development of things' natures than is normal, whether this is done by the person developing her own nature to an especially high degree or by contributing an exceptional amount to the development of other things' nature (typically, one will involve the other, for example, as in the case of Albert Einstein or Charles Darwin). This fits in with the empirical data about what people typically believe to be meaningful lives. We typically regard such people as Plato, Galileo, Susan B. Anthony, Martin Luther King, Gandhi, Georgia O'Keeffe, Peter Singer, Joseph Salk, Virginia Woolf, Louis Pasteur, Florence Nightingale, Beethoven, Stephen Hawking, Bertrand Russell, and the like as living the most meaningful lives, which fits in with perfectionist ethics.

Of special interest is the supreme ethical meaning of human life. By this, I mean the supreme *distinctively human good*. The nontrivial essence that is distinctively human, that is, that distinguishes humans from other animals, is reason. "Reason" is an ambiguous word and only in a certain sense of "reason" does it designate the distinctively human essence.

"Theoretical reason" (as I use this phrase) refers to the ability to know the nomological reasons why something exists (or why things of a certain kind exist) or possesses certain properties; that is, it is the ability to construct deductive or inductive arguments whose premises include at least one law of nature and which explain the proposition that serves as the conclusion. The conclusion is a proposition asserting that something exists (or things of a certain kind exist) or possesses certain properties.

In short, theoretical reason is the capacity to explain why things are and why things are the way they are. The maximal development of theoretical reason is to know the reason why *everything* exists and why *everything* possesses the properties that are in fact possessed. The maximal development is (at least) to know the reason for every fundamental state of affairs that has a reason; it may be that some states of affairs have no reason, such as the fact that the universe exists, and being able to pick out these states of affairs would be a part of the maximal development of theoretical reason.

Although the standard naturalist view is that the supreme explanatory laws explain why there are some fundamental kinds of things (for example, atoms), rather than explain *why the universe exists at all* (rather than nothing), it is at least epistemically possible that humans can attain the latter sort of explanatory knowledge, which would be the greatest explanatory knowledge that is conceivably possible. For example, it is at least epistemically possible we can know a certain law of nature that explains why this universe exists. Perhaps such a law would be a complete "wave function of the universe," which is a supreme law of nature that involves the unification of Einstein's general theory of relativity with quantum mechanics. Stephen Hawking mentions such a complete law. He says that the "sum over all the possible histories of a universe" will give us a law that describes everything in the universe: "Each history in the sum over histories will describe not only the space-time but everything in it as well, including any complicated organisms like human beings who can observe the history of the universe."[18] This law will also explain why our universe exists, for (as Hartle and Hawking say), this law will give "the [probability] amplitude for the universe to appear from nothing."[19] We do not know (yet) such a complete wave function of the universe, but it is epistemically possible that we may some day know such a law, and if we do know this law, we will have realized the supreme good of theoretical reason.

The distinctively human essence is reason, which is practical as well as theoretical. What is the supreme good of practical reason? The phrase "practical reason," if it refers to a distinctively human essence, cannot refer just to the ability to know the best means of attaining one's goals, for some nonhuman animals have this ability as well. The ability to know the best (most effective) means to attaining one's goals may be called "instrumental reason," as distinct from practical reason. Distinctive to humans is the ability to know the most effective means to attain the *morally best goal.* The best goal is the realization of the greatest amount of goodness, that is, bringing about the greatest development of things' natures. The morally best goal, in other words, is *to develop the nature of the whole universe,* the conjunction of all things. In determining the best goal, I do not take into account just humans, but all humans, all other animals, all plants and other organisms, and all physical things.

Each human has a distinct set of individual abilities and exists in a unique set of circumstances, and the most effective way for each human to attain the best goal will differ from human to human and from circumstance to circumstance. Typically, I can best contribute to developing the nature of the universe by concentrating on a small part of the universe that is within my spatiotemporal reach, particularly, the development of my own nature and the nature of the people, animals, plants, and physical things in my surroundings.

The supreme good of theoretical reason is the same for every human, even though it will be true only for some humans that pursuing the supreme good of theoretical reason is the best way they can contribute to developing the nature of the universe. By contrast, the supreme good of practical reason is only formally similar for every human; what is common is merely the formal structure of acting on one's knowledge of the best means of developing the nature of the universe. Practical reason involves knowing both long-term goals, for example, writing the Ring Cycle of operas (one of Richard Wagner's goals), discovering a cure for AIDS, raising a family, and so forth, but also the day-to-day goals that contribute to the realization of these long-term goals. And there are good goals that do not fit into such lifelong projects; saving someone from drowning may be my best goal in a certain circumstance, even though this is not a part of any of my specific long-term projects (unless I am a lifeguard).

Practical reason involves at least some knowledge of my *individual essence,* a property that I possess in each possible world in which I exist and that nothing else possesses in any world. My individual essence involves my DNA and my origin. I possess a nontrivial essence that nothing else can possess, namely, having an origin from this sperm and egg cell and having this DNA. Developing my individual essence involves realizing my genetically endowed abilities in ways allowed by my environment. The phrase "my good" may be used to refer to the development of my individual essence.

What is the relation of "my good" (or "an individual's good") to the referent of "goodness," *developing things' natures?* Developing the capacities given to me from my genetic endowment are objectively good (that is, "good" in the sense of naturalist perfectionism) *if and only if* they are developments of my essence qua physical thing, qua animate thing, qua animal, or qua a distinctively human animal. I ought to develop my individual essence in this way if and only if the total state of affairs that results from me developing my individual good contains more goodness than badness (with the deontological qualifications mentioned in section 25). My nature qua animal involves the capacity to move so as to satisfy my desires, but if one of my desires and special abilities is to attain power ruthlessly, by any means at all, then acting so as to satisfy this desire, although it realizes my individual good, is nonetheless something I ought not to do because the total state of affairs that will probably result will contain more badness than goodness.

Now a person's genetic profile will often give them special abilities, for example, as a musician, theoretician, carpenter, politician, homemaker, and so forth, and if the person can best increase the total amount of goodness in the universe by realizing their special abilities, then *knowing this* will be a conclusion reached by their practical reason and will constitute a development of their nature as practically rational beings.

Practical reason, however, is not simply *knowing* the most effective means by which I can develop the nature of the universe. Practical reason essentially includes the ability *to act* so as to attain the best end by the best available means; practical reason is developed only if this ability to act in the best way is realized in actions.

A person has *practical wisdom* (in the moral sense, as distinct from the "technical know-how" sense) *only if* she knows her special genetically endowed abilities and knows whether and how the realization of some of them will contribute most to developing the nature of the universe (and acts accordingly). Further, her acting on this knowledge will contribute more than is normal to the development of the universe. She has practical wisdom *if* she also has a significantly above average ability to discern other people's special abilities and how they can best contribute to developing the nature of the universe (and realizes this ability in her communicative relations with others). The fact that practical wisdom consists of these two things is evinced by the general view that a "wise woman" or "wise man" is somebody who lives a specially good life and is someone to whom one can go for advice about how one should live and how one's life fits into the overall scheme of things.

In actual fact, there are several people who have practical wisdom even though they do not theoretically believe (or even know about) global, naturalistic perfectionism. Their behavior shows they have the intuitive understanding that is sufficient to satisfy the global, perfectionist criteria of a wise person. Even if they are monotheists, they do not need to refer to God or God's plan in order to explain to others how living a certain way best contributes to developing things' natures. Practical wisdom, in other words, does not entail theoretical wisdom. (Put less contentiously, I can consistently say of some person x, that x has practical wisdom and yet disagrees with my philosophy of religion and my normative ethics.)

There is a relation between the goods of theoretical and practical reason. For people with the relevant abilities and who are in the relevant circumstances, it may be that the morally best goal is to engage in theoretical activity; for some, the best goal will be to engage in the theoretical activity of trying to discover the explanation of why the universe exists and communicating the results of their work to others. Here the practical question, "What should I do?" is answered by "pursuing the supreme good of theoretical reason." But for most people, the most effective way to develop the nature of the universe will be to make some other pursuit(s) the primary focus of their lives.

Does global, naturalist perfectionism provide criteria for ranking *people* in terms of their value (and *lives* in terms of their value)? Like all other normative ethics, be they utilitarian or social contractarian or whatever, perfectionism does provide such ranking criteria. (Note that "egalitarianism" is typically used to mean that all people have *equal rights*, for example, equality of opportunity, equal treatment under the law, and so forth. It is not used to mean that all people and ways of life are of *equal value,* which is manifestly false. The various theories of normative ethics that are accepted by philosophers today all imply that Albert Einstein was a better person than Adolf Hitler and that Einstein's way of life was more valuable than Hitler's way of life.)

According to naturalistic perfectionism, the criteria for value-rankings involve development of natures. There are three senses of "the morally best person":

(i) *The best realization of the distinctively human essence.* The person who knows that her morally best goal is to develop her theoretical reason and who actually does develop her theoretical reason is a better or more valuable kind of person (in one sense of "better person") than other kinds of people. This person develops both aspects of the distinctively *human* essence, theoretical and practical rationality, and thus has the most developed essential property that distinguishes humans from other animals. Among theoreticians, the more fundamental and comprehensive the explanatory knowledge that the person discovers, the better the person. The best possible person is someone who discovers why the universe exists.

This is a major way in which perfectionism differs from other normative ethics, such as utilitarianism. For utilitarians, the best person is one who produces the greatest happiness of the greatest number (at least according to one version of utilitarianism). Other normative ethics, such as Kantian or social contractarian ethics, also imply that the morally best person is the person who is most altruistic or most advances the civil rights of other people. But perfectionism has the consequence that the morally best person is the one who has the most developed human essence, which involves discovering the most fundamental explanatory knowledge.

This perfectionist conclusion does not widely diverge from the majority of humans' moral views. For example, such people as Albert Einstein and Stephen Hawking are widely admired and even revered as people who are superior to the average person. (Again, this does not mean they have superior *rights* than the average person but superior natures.) For another example, monotheists typically regard the people to whom God (who functions in monotheism as the supreme explanatory factor—the Causal Explanation of the universe) has revealed himself as the best sort of person. Jesus, Paul, Mohammed, and so on are revered by people in the relevant religious traditions, and the hundreds of small and local religious cults that spring up for a short period of time typically revere their leader as having supreme theoretical wisdom, even though their understanding of what a "theory" is may be rather limited. Indeed, it seems arguable that perfectionism better fits in with the majority of people's views about who are "the best people" than does utilitarianism or Kantian ethics or other types of normative ethics.

(ii) *The best realization of human nature.* Human nature includes not only the distinctively human essence, rationality, but also the essence of humans qua animal, qua organism, and qua physical thing. "The best human" in this second sense is somebody who has realized to the best degree all of her essences, who not only has theoretical and practical wisdom, but also has moved so as to satisfy her main desires, is healthy and has reproduced, and lives a long life (the most morally relevant part of our physical essence of *being spatiotemporally extended*). The philosophers F. P. Ramsey and Gareth Evans developed their reason but died prematurely, were not healthy, and did not reproduce. A more likely candidate for "best person" in this second sense of a "full or complete human" is Bertrand Russell, who lived to an old age, lived a healthy life, satisfied his major desires in life (perhaps his failed marriages and difficult relations with his children would count as his major weakness in this area), and developed his practical and theoretical reason. Einstein is another good candidate for the best person in this sense, and the astronomer Margaret Geller may also be. The morally best person in this second sense is both theoretically and practically wise, happy, healthy, and long-lived.

(iii) *The person who contributes most to developing natures.* This third sense of "the morally best person" pertains to the moral intuitions to which utilitarians, Kantians, social contractarians, and so on appeal. In this third sense, the morally best person is the one who has contributed most goodness to the universe, who has done most to develop the nature of things. Because humans are the highest kind of thing, as far as we know, the morally best person in this third sense will likely be a benefactor of humanity. Here the examples include such people as Gandhi, Martin Luther King, and Susan B. Anthony. Discoverers of vaccines—for example, the polio vaccine—such as Jonas Salk also are candidates for contributing the most to developing humans' natures. But the examples of Einstein and Hawking also come to mind in this third sense of "best person," for they are also benefactors of humankind by contributing a significant amount to the development of other people's theoretical reason.

But we cannot concentrate only on benefactors to humans. Perhaps Peter Singer, the most influential person in promoting the welfare and rights of animals, will ultimately have contributed more to the development of the universe than benefactors merely of humans. Perhaps Singer's book *Animal Liberation* will (over the centuries) have increased the happiness, health, and lives of animals to such an extent that it adds up to a greater amount of goodness than the human development that will be the total consequence of (say) Gandhi's actions.

I have discussed the supreme theoretical and practical goods and the three senses of "the morally best human being." These remarks all need to be qualified by deontological considerations, which will imply that it is not always "right" in the deontological sense to do what is "right" in the consequentialist sense (maximize the development of the nature of the universe). Such considerations play a part in practical deliberations about what I ought to do. But this does not alter the fact that the morally best goal is to develop the nature of the universe because deontological considerations may be understood as "side constraints" on our pursuit of this supreme practical goal.

What is the real importance of the theory of the *meaning of human life* that is emerging from this discussion? If someone asks us, "What is the meaning of human life?" and we answer, "To maximize the development of the nature of the universe," they may answer, "All right, so that's the meaning of human life. So what? I don't see any reason to care about developing the nature of the universe. In fact, I don't give a damn about whether the nature of the universe is developed or not developed. Why *should* I live my life in accordance with the objective ethical purpose of human life?" This person is in a genuine existential predicament, but of a different sort from that of the *Steppenwolf* character I discussed in chapter 3, who did not believe there was an objective ethical meaning to human life. In the present case, we have a person in an "existential predicament" because he finds no good reason to care about the objective ethical meaning of human life.

Here we may appeal to the two classes of reasons to justify this person's caring about the ethical purpose, nonnormative reasons and normative reasons.

There is a nonnormative reason *if* the person has a desire to live an ethically meaningful life, and the reason will be that living this life will fulfill the person's desire for meaning and make him happy in this respect.

Although "satisfying one's desire for a meaningful life" is a nonnormative reason (specifically, a psychological reason) to endeavor to develop the nature of the universe, it is not by itself sufficient to make a person happy. In his discussion of the question "What is the meaning of life?" one of the points Ellin makes is that the happiness I can attain by virtue of living, and believing I am living, a meaningful life is *only one kind of happiness* and is quite consistent with being unhappy in other respects.[20] "Living a happy life" is not equivalent to "living a meaningful life." For example, Ingmar Bergman, the writer and director of films about the issue of life's meaning, lived a very meaningful but very unhappy life (as his autobiography shows). This is probably true of many artists, poets, and others.

I would add that living an ethically meaningful life does not automatically bring pleasure or emotional contentment *even in respect of one's meaningful activities.* Contributing to the development of the universe's nature often involves tremendous, even painful effort, the overcoming of great difficulties, sacrifices of one's other desires, and frequently or sometimes encounters with major failures of one's projects. The happiness that comes from living an ethically meaningful life is rather a sense of a deep, underlying fulfillment that is defined in terms of (a) a dispositional belief that one is doing something worthwhile, (b) preferring to be living the kind of life one is in fact living, rather than some other kind of life, and (c) being satisfied with the fact that this is what one needs to do to develop the universe's nature. Successes and the enjoyable aspects of striving for certain goals will bring feelings of emotional pleasure, but the "happiness" that a meaningful life brings is not primarily defined in terms of feeling pleasurable emotions. (This expands on the definition of the animal essence of "moving so as to satisfy one's desires" given in section 25.)

Although *satisfying a desire* is developing one's nature and thus is good, the appeal to satisfying this desire is "nonnormative" in the sense that we are not appealing to this desire because it is morally good to satisfy it, but because it appeals to the person's desire to be happy, independently of whether or not fulfilling this desire is good. In a sense, then, it is an appeal to the person's "self-interest," rather than to his "conscience."

There is also a *normative reason* to live an ethically meaningful life, a reason that a person may have in addition to, or instead of, the above-mentioned nonnormative reason. Suppose a person has no nonnormative reason to live an ethically meaningful life; she still has a normative reason to care about living an ethical life, namely, that this is what she should do. "She ought to live in accordance with the ethical purpose of human life" is a normative reason to live meaningfully.

But is it begging the question to answer the question, "Why should I be moral" by answering "Because you are morally obligated to live morally"? It may seem to be a question-begging answer, but I do not believe it is. This is no more a question-begging answer to the question "Why should I care about ethical meaning?" than is the contrary assumption that *the class of reasons to which one can appeal in answering questions of this sort includes only nonnormative reasons.* (Pritchard makes this point at greater length in chapter 12 of his *On Becoming Responsible.*) If, in asking this question, you make a condition of answering the question that the person cannot appeal to a certain reason that belongs to the class of legitimate reasons to which one can appeal when asked "Why should I do x?", then your questioning involves a theoretical fallacy. The class of reasons for justifying actions *in fact* includes both normative and nonnormative reasons, and a person is legitimately allowed access to all members of this class if asked to justify undertaking a certain action (or way of life). The statement, "You ought to do x because you ought to do x" can be misleading because the issue is then phrased in a way that is designed to make it seem like a blatant petitio principii, but the above way of analyzing the issue shows that appealing to normative reasons is legitimate.

Global, naturalistic perfectionism enables us to answer another one of the "so what?" responses to assertions about the meaning of human life. One "so what?" response is directed at theses that imply that human lives have no place in the larger scheme of things. "Human life is condemned to triviality, and no objective meaning will enable us to escape this triviality."

But global perfectionism implies that we *do* have a place in the largest scheme of things, namely, the whole universe. Our moral place in the universe is to develop the nature of the whole universe. We are global beings in the sense that our ethical concerns and purposes properly relate to everything. Thus, the ethical purpose of human life is the opposite of a trivial purpose, for it relates to all things that have value, the aggregate of things that comprise the universe. Consequently, by choosing to live an ethical life, one escapes triviality and becomes connected to the most significant scheme there is, the global drama of struggling to develop the nature of the entire universe.

It may be objected that we can be connected to a grand scheme only if there is an ethical purpose to the universe as a whole, and there is no such purpose (given our rejection of monotheism).

There is a legitimate sense, however, in which there is an ethical purpose of the universe. A good state is *a state that ought to be realized,* and "a state that ought to be realized" is equivalent to "a moral end" or "an ethical purpose." The maximally good state is the development of the universe's nature. The universe has a nature (recall that I use "the nature of the universe" to mean the natures of the conjunction of all things), and humans can contribute to developing the nature of the universe. Because *a development of things' natures* is the referent of the term "good," it follows that there is a natural ethical purpose to the universe.

This purpose is immanent to the universe; it is not given to the universe by some supernatural agency that is external to the universe. The universe was not created and designed by God for the sake of realizing *God's* moral purpose. In this case, the universe would not have the ethical purpose because the purpose is God's purpose, and the universe would merely be a realization of God's purpose. But according to global, naturalist perfectionism, the universe itself has an ethical purpose. "There is an ethical purpose to the universe" expresses the same proposition as (but has a different cognitive significance than) "The universe has a nature that is developed to some degree and can be developed to an even greater degree."

Does this immanent purpose to the universe enable us to conclude that global perfectionism implies a "big picture theory of the meaning of life." Ellin lists four conditions for "a big picture theory of the meaning of life":

1. It must explain the purpose of human life.

(Global perfectionism meets this condition because it explains the purpose of human life as the development of the nature of the universe.)

2. It must enable anyone to explain the major events in his or her life by reference to this purpose.

(This condition is met because the major events in my life either contribute to the development of the universe's nature or fail to do this.)

3. It must justify suffering (including death), that is, show how or why suffering contributes to the purpose and is necessary in the larger scheme of things.

(This condition is not met, except in a partial way. As I argued in chapter 5, there is much gratuitous suffering and gratuitous premature death in the universe. These sufferings and premature deaths, so far from *contributing* to developing the universe's nature, in fact decrease or prevent its development. Some cases of suffering, however, are ethically justified in that they are required to produce an equal or outweighing good.)

4. It must explain the purpose of life in a way that seems good; it must reconcile us to life.[21]

(Global perfectionism does meet this condition in Ellin's intended sense; he means to rule out such intuitively abhorrent cases as our purpose being to serve as food for extraterrestrials. But in another sense, global perfectionism may not fulfill condition #4; if we allow people from the various religious traditions to insist that we can be reconciled to life only if their various religious tenets are met, global perfectionism will not satisfy condition #4. But this is not the intended sense of condition #4, which is intended to rule out purposes that seem obviously repugnant to all or virtually all people. For example, if global perfectionism implied that our purpose is to destroy the earth until it becomes uninhabitable by any living creatures and to then destroy the entire human species, then perfectionism would fail to meet condition #4.)

Although the sort of ethical meaning that is implied by global, naturalist perfection will not satisfy people with certain kinds of religious needs or wishes, global perfectionism does lead to a certain kind of religious outlook, namely, *a naturalistic pantheism*, which is the topic of the Conclusion of this book.

Conclusion   Naturalistic Pantheism

27. Naturalistic Pantheism and Global, Naturalistic Perfectionism

It might appear that our conclusion is that human life lacks a religious meaning but possesses an ethical meaning. But our negative conclusion is merely that it lacks a *monotheistic* religious meaning. This conclusion is consistent with the thesis that the religious meaning of human life is described by a naturalistic pantheism. According to naturalistic pantheism, everything ("pan" = all) is holy.

"Holiness" has a different sense in naturalistic pantheism than it does in monotheism. According to monotheism, holiness implies supernatural purity and maximal metaphysical greatness: perfect goodness, omniscience, omnipotence, eternality. This is the fundamental sense of holiness for monotheism. The derivative sense of "holy" in monotheism applies to people and places (holy man, holy ground) which stand in a certain relation to the being that has fundamental holiness.

Naturalistic pantheism, which involves a type of religious attitude different from that of monotheism, implies that all is holy. Because all things include the bad as well as the good, "holiness" does not mean what it does in monotheism. The attempt to combine pantheism with the monotheistic sense of "holiness," which implies the omniattributes, results in absurdity, as in Plantinga's (mis)definition of "pantheism" in *A Companion to Metaphysics:* "Pantheism is the doctrine that all is God—not, absurdly, that each thing is God, but that the totality of things is somehow God. ('Somehow', since it is not easy to see how the totality of things could be able to do or know anything at all, let alone be almighty and all-knowing.)"[1]

222

Contra Plantinga, pantheism is not the doctrine that all things are "holy" or "divine" in the monotheistic sense of these words. According to naturalistic pantheism, "holiness" means *has all naturally instantiated values*, negative as well as positive. (In chapter 6, I often used "valuable" in one of its senses, that is, good, but I am using it here in a broader sense in which it includes both negative and positive values.) The holy, what has all naturally instantiated values, is all things. A thing is a concrete object (a mere physical thing, a mere organic thing, or an animal), and a value is naturally instantiated if and only if it is instantiated by some concrete object. The statement that the holy has all naturally instantiated values does not mean that each thing has all naturally instantiated values. Rather, it means that (i) for each value F that is naturally instantiated, there is some part of the holy that instantiates F, (ii) each part of the holy instantiates some value, and (iii) all and only concrete objects are parts of the holy.

Because holiness includes all naturally instantiated badness as well as all naturally instantiated goodness, the holy is both horrifying and awesome.

The holy is the conjunction of all things: Jane and Jack and Fido and this lizard and that tree and that star, and so forth. The conjunction of all things is awesome in respect of the conjunction of all positive values that are naturally instantiated, and the conjunction of all things is horrible in respect of the conjunction of all negative values that are naturally instantiated. This means, in effect, that the holy deserves the emotional response of horror in respect of all the decreases and preventions of developments of things' natures; it deserves awe and admiration in respect of all the developments of the natures of things and the conjunction of all things with a developed kind of nature.

There is an additional element to the awesome aspect of the holy, which implies that the holy at its base level is purely good. Each thing, if it is a physical thing, animate thing, animal or human, is good intrinsically in that it exemplifies a kind of nature; each kind of nature (for example, physicality, organicity) is a kind of natural development and thus a kind of goodness, because goodness = natural development. A good is a kind of nature (for example, animality) or a development of a kind of nature (for example, an animal's satisfying its desires).

This implies that there is one sense in which it is better that there is something rather than nothing. It is better that there be things of some natural kinds rather than no things at all. But it does not imply that it is better that there are these things than *any* other conjunction of possible things (or kinds of things), or that it is better that the history of these things is better than *any* other possible history of these things. Further, the fact that it is better that there are things rather than nothing does not imply, "Regardless of what things there are, and regardless of the history of these things, it is better that there are things rather than nothing." For suppose all that exists is a tiny rock (or rocklike) enclave inside of which there exists a human child (or something human childlike in the relevant respects) all of whose bones are broken, who is dying of starvation and thirst, and whose agony is so great that she is literally crazed with pain. This universe exists for two days and ceases to exist when the humanlike being dies. Here are two kinds of things, a rocklike thing and an intelligent organism, which are good inasmuch as they are developed kinds of nature. But the evil consisting in the prevention and decrease in the development of the organism's animate, animal, and rational nature outweighs the good of the existence of an inanimate kind of thing and a rational kind of thing. This indicates that "it is better that there be things of some natural kinds rather than no things at all" is consistent with the falsity of some (other) sense of "it is better that there is something rather than nothing," namely, the sense "it is better that there be things of some natural kinds rather than no things at all, *regardless of the history (actual circumstances and behavior) of these things.*" What is the distinction involved?

It is based on the fact that there are two criteria of goodness, but only one of badness. A thing's possession of a kind of nature (for example, animality) is intrinsically good and not intrinsically bad. And a thing's development of its kind of nature (for example, an animal's satisfying its desires) is intrinsically good. Badness consists only in preventions and decreases of the development of things' natures (for example, an animal's desire for food being unfulfilled). (This was argued in chapter 6.) Now if we consider things only in respect of their possession of a kind of nature, then we can say that (in this respect) it is better that there be something rather than nothing. Indeed, this is a necessary truth. But if we consider instead the total situation produced by the degreed developments of these things' natures and the preventions and decreases of these things' nature, the total situation may have more negative value than positive. It would then follow, as a matter of logic, that this situation ought not to exist. If the total situation S has negative value, this implies S ought not to be. This in turn implies that (a) it is better that there be nothing at all rather than S and (b) it is better that there be another total situation S' *rather than S or nothing,* such that S' is any total situation that has (overall) positive value.

If the total situation that exists has overall positive value, that does not imply that the bad in the universe is morally justified or that each bad is necessary for some equal or outweighing good. Many preventions or decreases in the development of things' natures are gratuitous evils. What it means is that despite the gratuitous evils, the total situation produced by the existence and history of the kinds of things is more good than bad, and in this sense has "(overall) positive value" and ought to exist. (Of course, this is not simply a matter of counting the goods and evils because we need to consider the total situation as an "organic whole" in G. E. Moore's sense.)

We are not in an epistemic situation to know for certainty whether the total situation that exists is more good than bad. But I think it is fair to say that if the rest of the universe is not radically different from the tiny part of the universe about which we know, then it is more probable than not that the total situation is overall good (even if the good just barely outweighs the bad).

Given this, what are the appropriate attitudes to the holy? There are several. It is appropriate to have positive appreciations of the facts that (a) there are some *kinds of things* rather than nothing, that (b) there are some *developments* of the natures of the inanimate, animate, animal, and rational things that exists (for example, some desire-satisfactions), rather than no developments, and that (c) the available evidence, admittedly very limited, suggests that the *total situation is more good than bad* and thus ought to exist rather than nothingness.

But it hardly follows that the emotional attitude to the holy that takes into account everything relevant to the appreciation of something is unambiguously positive. There is no Spinozist "intellectual love of God" as the supreme pantheistic attitude. This would require a blindness to the gratuitous evil that exists. The most appropriate emotional appreciation of the holy in *all* its respects, good and bad, requires an emotion of profound ambivalence. One is in a state of ambivalence between horror and awe, or joy and despair, when one contemplates the whole. One feels horrified awe at the universe or a joy tinged with sadness and despair.

Because the word "awful" in its ordinary use is ambiguous, sometimes used in the sense of "horrible" and sometimes in the sense of "awesome," we may use "awful" to express both these senses and say simply: the holy is awful. *Webster's New World Dictionary* lists as two different senses of "awful" *highly impressive* and *appalling,* which arc appropriate predicates of the holy.

Regarding joy and despair, we may say the holy is "good in some respects but still tragically hopeless." The importance of despair in naturalist pantheism—and the different role it plays in pantheism and monotheism—is discussed further in a later section. But here I note that these results show that naturalistic pantheism is immune from the Freudian charge of "wish-fulfillment" which Freud argues is the psychological origin of religion.

What is the argument for the existence of the holy? The moral realist and global, naturalistic perfectionism articulated in chapter 6 entail naturalistic pantheism. The ethical theory I developed entails that each thing has value, and this entailment (conjoined with the premise that some things exist) entails that the concept of holiness is instantiated.

"The holy" has the same designata as "all things," but the two expressions have a different cognitive significance. The cognitive significance of "the holy" has elements that are common to the various uses of "the holy" across religious traditions, monotheism, polytheism, naturalistic pantheism, and so on. These elements are of necessity vague or ambiguous, given the disparity of the religious traditions. These items are that the holy is in some sense "more valuable than anything else" and is in some sense "more real than anything else." The vague or ambiguous expressions "more valuable than" and "more real than" have been given familiar precise senses in the "perfect being" theological tradition of Judeo-Christianity. In naturalistic pantheism, they mean that the holy is the conjunction of *all concrete things* (and thus there is no thing—no concrete object—apart from the holy that is real) and the conjunction of *all that is positively or negatively valuable* (and thus that no concrete object apart from the holy has any value).

The cognitive significance of the naturalist pantheist use of "the holy" is also its reference-fixing description, which is that "the holy" directly and rigidly refers to the conjunction of all things that exemplify positive and/or negative value. Because the reference is rigid, "the holy" picks out the conjunction of all things in the actual world in respect of every possible world to which it refers.

"The holy" is a referentially used definite description in Marcus's sense, not in Donnellan's. In Donnellan's sense, the same definite description can sometimes be used attributively and sometimes referentially (for example, "the man in the corner who is drinking a martini"), but in Marcus's sense a referentially used definite description is constantly used referentially and behaves like a name.

The rigidity of "the holy" reflects the fact that the modal difference between absolute actuality and relative actuality is of crucial religious significance. The actual world α is the only world that is absolutely actual (this means that only α *is actual*), but each world is relatively actual in that it is actual at itself (that is, for each world w, w *would have been actual had it been actual*). But the actual world is not to be confused with the holy; the actual world is the maximally true proposition W; for each proposition p, W includes p as a conjunct or includes the negation of p as a conjunct, such that W includes only true conjuncts. But a maximally true proposition is an abstract object, and the holy is the conjunction of all and only concrete objects. Thus the holy *corresponds* to (or is a truth-maker of) a part of the actual world, namely, the relevant propositions about the natures of things or the developments (or preventions or decreases in developments) of the natures of things. (Because correspondence is a symmetrical relation, if a proposition corresponds to a situation, that situation corresponds to the proposition.)

The fact that "the holy" is a rigid designator, a referentially used definite description, shows that *the contingent fact of existing* is a metaphysically necessary condition of being the holy. If it is true that something does not exist but might have existed, then its failure to possess the ontological status of existence deprives the possible thing of any claim to being a part of the holy. Of course, the phrase "the holy" might have designated a different conjunction of things, if a different possible world had been actual (just as "water" might have designated XYZ rather than H_2O, if XYZ had satisfied the reference-fixing description of "water"). But given the contingent ontological facts, only these things—the existent ones—have the good (or bad) luck of being the designata of "the holy."

Thus, "the holy" does not designate different things in respect of different possible worlds. It designates only the things that have the world-indexed property of existing-in-α, where α is the actual world. Things that merely might have existed do not have a high enough ontological status to be parts of the holy.

"The holy is all things" is necessarily true if "all things" is used in a directly referential way. Because "the holy" is a directly referential expression, a referentially used definite description, this sentence will be necessarily true if "all things" also is directly referential. Sometimes "all things" is directly referential and has existential import (contra the definition of this phrase in modern logic textbooks). For example, "All people on the block are old" uses "all people" in a directly referential way, as I have argued elsewhere.[2] The de re proposition expressed by "The holy is all things" (given that "all things" is directly referential) is true in each possible world in which this proposition exists, but it exists only in the worlds in which all and only the actually existent things exist, because it contains these things as parts. ("The holy is all things" is an informative sentence because "the holy" and "all things" have a different cognitive significance.)

If "all things" is used in the way that is standard in logic textbooks, then "The holy is all things" is contingently true. For there are some possible worlds that include all the things that exist in α and in addition some other things. In these worlds, it is false that all things with the world-indexed property of existing in α— the designata of our use of "the holy"—are all things.

Because the fact that *the property of holiness is exemplified* is known by being deduced from global, naturalistic perfectionism and because this normative ethics is known to be true only a posteriori, "The holy is all things" is known a posteriori to express a true proposition.

In one sense of the question, "Why is holiness exemplified?" the answer is that something exists and that global, naturalistic perfectionism is true. But in another sense, the question is about why the things that, in fact, are the designate of "the holy" exist rather than some other things or nothing at all. The second sense of this question pertains to the supreme good of theoretical reason.

The supreme good of theoretical reason is knowing the explanation of the holy. By knowing the explanation of the holy, I not only know the holy (as that which is explained) but also know why the holy exists. I know why there is something rather than nothing, and why this universe exists rather than something else.

Note that this contrasts with monotheism, which implies that knowing the holy is knowing the *explanans* of the universe; the explanans is God or God's decision to create the universe. But in naturalistic pantheism, knowing the holy is knowing the *explanandum*, the universe itself. The explanans is not the holy; rather, it is some law of nature, for example, a wave function of the universe. The holy belongs to this explanative knowledge as the conclusion of the argument ("the universe exists"), rather than as the premises (which refer to the relevant law of nature).

For example, if the wave function of the universe developed by Hartle and Hawking explains why the universe exists, then we would have this explanation of why the holy exists:

EXP.

WF. $\psi[h_{ij},\phi] = N \int \partial g \, \partial \phi \exp(-I[g,\phi])$

Therefore, it is probably true that:

H. The holy exists.

The integral is a path integral over all finite four-dimensional space-times g with matter fields ϕ that have the three-dimensional space h_{ij} and matter field ϕ as a boundary. The square of the modulus of the amplitude, $|\Psi[h_{ij},\phi]|^2$, gives the probability that there begins to exist (uncaused) a universe with the three-dimensional space h_{ij} and matter field ϕ. As Hartle and Hawking say, the wave function equation (WF) is "the [probability] amplitude for the universe to appear from nothing."[3] (In this equation, N is the normalization constant. I is the Euclidean Einstein action. It is obtained by replacing the time t with $(-i\tau)$ in the normal Einstein action and adjusting the sign so that I is positive. The four-dimensional space-times summed over have a positive definite signature.) The explanation is probabilistic because the wave function, when squared, gives a high probability that a universe of our sort will "appear from nothing." Although it is doubtful that (WF) is the correct explanation (for example, the unification of Einstein's general relativity with quantum mechanics has not yet been accomplished, and this unification is assumed, not proved, in [WF]), if (WF) is the correct explanation, then knowing (EXP) is the supreme moral goal of human life.

The supreme ethical purpose of human life is equivalent to the purpose of increasing the goodness of the holy, to make the holy more impressive and less appalling. This is tantamount to maximizing the development of the nature of the universe (the nature of all things).

In this section, I have given a relatively formal explanation of naturalistic pantheism. In the next several sections, I shall discuss its intuitive content, in a way that makes manifest its distinctive religious nature.

28. Independent and Dependent Naturalist Pantheism

The fact that the holy includes negative as well as positive values is something that naturalistic pantheism shares with polytheistic religions. The Greek Homeric religion, the ancient Egyptian religion, the Babylonian religion, and so forth all imply that the deities do evil things as well as good things and that the holy character of these deities embraces their evil dispositions as much as their good dispositions.

For polytheism, as well as for naturalistic pantheism, there is no "problem of evil." The existence of natural evil and moral evil (as they are called in the philosophy of religion), far from being evidence against the existence of the holy (as it is in monotheism), is instead part of the evidence for its existence. When Plato redefined "the holy" or "the divine" to imply perfect moral goodness in *The Republic*, he introduced "the problem of evil" into the philosophy of religion, rendering the religious worldview both logically and evidentially in conflict with the observed fact, or so at least I argued in chapter 5. Plato's redefinition of "the holy" to include perfect goodness is probably his most influential mistake (at least in the area of the philosophy of religion).

Naturalistic pantheism is not experientially or intellectually "derivative from" Judeo-Christian monotheism or any other sort of theism but has an independent source in an independent type of religious experience and thought. We can distinguish several sorts of pantheism and distinguish independent naturalistic pantheism, the sort I am describing, from a naturalistic pantheism that is dependent on religious notions taken from traditional monotheism.

There is supernatural pantheism, nonnatural pantheism, and naturalist pantheism. Supernatural pantheism is exemplified by the later Fichte, Schelling, Hegel, Bhat Shankara and other Hindu and Mahayana Buddhist writers. This view holds that the universe, in some sense, is identical with a supernatural mind, even though it normally appears not to be identical with this mind. Nonnatural pantheism is exemplified by the works of Plotinus, Spinoza, John Leslie, Michael P. Levine, by my book *Language and Time*, and by my article "An Analysis of Holiness."[4] Spinoza is mistakenly regarded as a naturalistic pantheist by many philosophers, the exception being the majority of Spinoza scholars (for example, Edwin Curley, Harold Joachim, and others); as Curley notes, by "God or Nature" Spinoza is in fact referring to a platonic realm of abstract objects. Spinoza's "finite modes" would correspond to our *concrete things*, but Spinoza denies that the conjunction of all finite modes is the holy. Perhaps we could say that what we call "the holy" is the conjunction of all *the finite modes* of the attributes of Extension and Thought in Spinoza's metaphysics. But for Spinoza, the holy is instead the platonic realm, a view he shares with Plotinus, Leslie, and others. Spinoza held a *non*naturalist pantheism (much as Moore's platonic realism committed him to a nonnaturalist moral realism).

In "An Analysis of Holiness" I argued the *existing* of the universe is holy and in the conclusion of *Language and Time* I implicitly suggested that the presentness (= *existing* in the present tensed sense) of all concrete and abstract objects is holy. Taking the existence of the universe as the proper object of pantheistic awe is a view also reflected in Milton Munitz's writings, especially the last chapter of his *Logic and Existence*. Munitz denies that the existence of the universe is a property, or at least a normal sort of property, such as redness, but his view suggests a nonnatural pantheism inasmuch as the Existence of the universe is not identical with the natural universe. I discussed Munitz's interesting theory in more detail in "An Analysis of Holiness."

Michael P. Levine's book *Pantheism* (1994) compares various concepts of pantheism, theism, monism, and other ideas. Levine's discussion is clearly relevant to any pantheistic philosophy, but his ideas seem to diverge from our naturalistic pantheism in that he characterizes pantheism in terms of a "divine Unity" and regards this divine Unity as a morally good order of reality. Levine says that "living in accord with the Unity is ethically good and violating it in some way, going against it etc., is ethically wrong. . . . what is morally correct will be in accord with the Unity."[5] This differs from naturalistic pantheism, which implies that all is holy and that all ways of living are in accordance with the holy or "the divine," both good ways of living and morally bad ways of living because each thing, no matter how it lives, is just as much a constituent of the holy as any other thing. Levine's pantheism is nonnatural because the holy is identified with a morally good order rather than with the natural universe.

Two books that come closer than any other to a naturalistic pantheism are my *The Felt Meanings of the World: A Metaphysics of Feeling* (which is based on a theory that rejects moral realism) and John Post's *The Faces of Existence* (which is based on a moral realist theory).[6]

The Felt Meanings of the World can be regarded as a pantheistic philosophy of religion only with some important qualifications. For one thing, it does not fall in the category of an analytic philosophy of religion. In this early work, I attempted to develop a philosophy that falls outside of the current divide between "analytic philosophy" and "continental philosophy" and that unifies both sorts of philosophizing into a different and new way of thinking. Bruce Wilshire wrote, "A colleague has called *The Felt Meanings of the World* the most important book in phenomenology yet written by an American. I tend to agree."[7] I would say the book is neither phenomenological nor analytic. Panayot Butchvarov correctly described the goal I had in mind when he wrote in his review that *The Felt Meanings of the World* "presents a picture of our cognitive relationship to the world that is radically different from virtually all other such pictures."[8] What is germane to my present discussion is whether the book can be interpreted as presenting a naturalistic pantheism. At the time of its writing, I did not see this book as a version of naturalist pantheism, but in hindsight it seems to have many points in common with pantheism. Moral values are rejected in favor of objective "ways of being important," and the target of the relevant emotions (awe, reverence, despair, and so on) is not the *conjunction* of all things, but *the whole* of all things, where "the whole" refers to a concrete thing that is distinct from all other things and that stands to them in the relation of being composed of them. This whole, the "world-whole," is a natural aggregate composed of all the natural things that presently exist, and the "global affects" described in the book can be viewed as the variety of affects a pantheist could experience. The "metaphysics of feeling" developed in this book can be interpreted as a naturalistic pantheism based on the tensed theory of time and moral antirealism.

John Post's *The Faces of Existence* may be regarded as presenting a naturalist pantheism based on the tenseless theory of time and moral realism. In fact, an analytic philosopher who is a pantheist may rightly regard Post's book as the most fruitful and valuable book on the philosophy of religion since Spinoza's *Ethics.* I want to make several qualifications to my characterization of Post's theory as pantheistic.

Post's theory best exemplifies a "dependent naturalistic pantheism," and I shall discuss his pantheism at some length in order to distinguish it from the "independent naturalist pantheism" I am articulating.

I need to distinguish the dependent naturalistic pantheism articulated in chapters 1–7 of Post's book from the versions of nontraditional monotheism Post discusses in chapter 8. Post's project in chapter 8, entitled "God," is to formulate various types of philosophical theologies that are consistent with physicalism. Post distinguishes two nonreferential versions of monotheism and one referential version.

One nonreferential version of monotheism may be called "normative monotheism," although Post does not use this phrase. According to this version, which treats "God" as nonreferential, "God is the maker of heaven and earth" is objectively true, even though "God" fails to refer. Normative monotheism implies that this sentence is objectively true in that it expresses objectively correct moral values and a certain way of life. The moral values it expresses are monotheistic values, and normative monotheism requires us "to see what there is as essentially good." In response to a possible objection that monotheistic moral values are not instantiated, Post suggests we may adopt a second version of nonreferential monotheism, one which construes "God exists" as meaning simply that moral realism is true, without specifying which moral values are instantiated.

The referential version of monotheism that Post outlines comes close to being a sort of pantheism, even though Post denies this version is pantheistic. Post's referential version of monotheism implies that "God" refers in some predications but not in others. We treat "God" as referring to the Universe in negative predications; God or the Universe is immutable, not in time, not dependent on anything, and so forth. Post denies this theory is pantheistic because he takes "pantheism" to mean that the Universe has some positive monotheistic properties. He writes, "Pantheism not only identifies God with the Universe but holds that therefore all and only the positive predications that can be true of God are those that can be true of the Universe, including 'God is the proper object of our worship, reverence, and awe' " (362).

Yet it is not this sense of "pantheism" that I have in mind when I say that Post's book can be viewed as presenting a naturalistic pantheism. Chapter 8 of the book is less about naturalist pantheism than are chapters 1–7, which are ostensibly not about the philosophy of religion but other subjects, such as explanation, physicalism, and values. Chapters 1–7 in fact articulate in great detail a philosophy of religion to which Post gives no name but which may be called a "dependent naturalist pantheism."

The naturalist pantheism articulated in these chapters is a dependent pantheism in the sense that it is derived from the religious categories of monotheism. Post writes that the universe is

(a) the symbol and source of truth, beauty, and goodness, if only because facts about its aspects or its parts determine such matters. We may go further and recall that by Chapter 3 the universe is also (b) the eternal, immutable, uncreated, independent, self-existent, explanatorily necessary First Cause of all that is. For many, (a) and (b) will be more than enough to justify according the universe the role of divinity—of such divinity, at any rate, as we were ever entitled to believe in or ever will be . . . the universe *is* the divine. (325)

Although Post does not include himself among the "many" who unreservedly endorse this "dependent pantheistic" theory, he gives the best articulation of this sort of pantheism that is available in the literature. Post gives special meanings to the terms "eternal," "explanatorily necessary," "First Cause," and so forth that differ from the monotheistic meanings and that can be truly predicated of the natural universe, conceived in accordance with a tenseless theory of time.

Post argues that religion should accord with the science of the day. Just as Aquinas saw that Christianity should be formulated to accord with the Aristotelian science of his day, so religion should now be formulated to accord with the scientific and physicalist worldview of the twentieth century. Accordingly, Post gives a meaning to the traditional monotheistic predicates "First Cause," "explanatorily necessary," "immutable," and so on that are consistent with contemporary science. Two of the basic ideas are "First Cause" and "immutable," in terms of which we can understand his definitions of the other predicates.

The Universe is the First Cause, but not in the normal sense of an efficient cause. Post first notes that an ultimate explainer in a parade of explanations is some explanatory factor E that explains other facts in the parade but is not itself explained. He introduces the novel principle,

P. If x explains y, then all the wholes of which x is a part also explain y.

It follows from this principle that the Universe is the ultimate explainer of everything that has an explanation. For every other ultimate explainer is a part of the Universe, the greatest whole. From Post's principle (P), it follows that the Universe explains everything that is explained by any other ultimate explainer. Because the Universe itself has no explanation, it is an ultimate explainer.

But the Universe is not just one ultimate explainer among many; it has the unique status of being the First Cause. Post defines a cause as an explainer, and the Universe is the First Cause or First Explainer in the sense that it is the whole of all the ultimate explainers plus anything else that has no explanation. In this way, the description "the First Cause" can be redefined in a way to make it consistent with a naturalist pantheist view of the universe.

The First Cause is the Universe. But what is the Universe? According to Post, the Universe is the spatiotemporal whole of which every physical existent is a part. The Universe is distinct from the manifest universe; the manifest universe is the physical universe as conceived through present-day scientific categories. The Universe is the real physical universe, the universe that science aims to know and to which its theories are successively better approximations.

The Universe is *immutable* in that it is not subject to change. The Universe is a four-dimensional spatial-temporal whole. What changes are spatially three-dimensional objects that persist through time, but the four-dimensional space-time does not itself persist through time or acquire and lose properties. It is also tenseless, timeless, and eternal in senses relevant to a four-dimensional space-time ontology.

If we identify this Universe with God, as Post suggests we might, we have a version of naturalistic pantheism. We can say with truth that the Universe or God is the First Cause, immutable, eternal, timeless, and necessary; because the Universe instantiates the suitably redefined predicates that the monotheistic god was said to instantiate, we can justifiably identify the Universe with God.

This religious view has some plausibility, assuming the tenseless theory of time is true. But the relevant point I wish to make is that this view is not the *independent* naturalistic pantheism articulated in the previous sections. Independent naturalistic pantheism is not experientially or intellectually "derivative from" Judeo-Christian monotheism or any other sort of theism but has an independent source in an independent type of religious experience and thought. Naturalist pantheism is not constructed by saving whatever can be saved from monotheism, consistent with twentieth-century science. There is no need for the ontological predicates of monotheism—being the First Cause, immutability, explanatory necessity, being eternal, and so forth—to be instantiated in order for independent naturalist pantheism to be true.

A certain passage in Post's *The Faces of Existence* suggests that he is partly aware of this independent sort of naturalistic pantheism. He writes, "The totality of natural fact might suffice to determine that certain value terms are true of the universe—say, that it is beautiful, terrible, awesome, eerie, intriguing, astonishing, and more. . . . In addition, the universe could have meaning in the sense that it is the appropriate object of certain emotions—not only, on occasion, of terror or awe but of acceptance and even reverence" (324–25). Post does not clearly segregate this independent pantheism from the dependent sort, however: he proceeds to assert in the next paragraph that if we regard the universe in addition as an "eternal, immutable, uncreated, independent, self-existent, explanatorily necessary First Cause," then the universe may be regarded as being "divine."

An independent naturalist pantheism is approached more nearly by some writers on the "Great Goddess religion," writers such as Marija Gimbutas and Donna Wilshire.

Although Gimbutas has not convincingly shown that there is archeological evidence of such a religion in prehistory (the consensus of archeologists is that Gimbutas's claims are mistaken), there are a few practitioners of a Great Goddess religion now, and that seems sufficient for such a religion to exist. We can abstract from questions of archeological accuracy in Gimbutas's writings and extract the religious content. She writes that the Great Goddess is plausibly identified with Nature:

> [It is] appropriate to view all of these Goddess images as [representing] aspects of the one Great Goddess with her core functions—life-giving, death-wielding, regeneration and renewal. The obvious analogy would be to Nature itself; through the multiplicity of phenomena and continuing cycles of which it is made, one recognizes the fundamental and underlying unity of Nature. The Goddess is immanent rather than transcendent and therefore physically manifest . . . [and is] in animals, plants, water, mountains, and stones. The Goddess may be a bird, a deer, a vase, an upright stone, or a tree.[9]

If the Great Goddess is this bird and that deer and that vase and that stone and that tree, and so on, for each concrete thing that exists, then the Great Goddess is identical with what independent naturalistic pantheism calls "the holy."

Donna Wilshire also writes in a way that is suggestive of an independent naturalistic pantheism. She says that "the Great Mother Goddess Hera" is not a supernatural person governing nature but a metaphor for nature itself. She writes, "The Goddess's Inner Wisdom tradition promotes awareness that all life is of and in this material world-universe (not some immaterial otherworld 'out there'), that all life is sacred (not fallen, illusory, or evil), and that life is meant to be lived and shared ecstatically (not dutifully). In this Old Way one can fearlessly embrace All-

That-Is and passionately accept one's full Self, one's whole body, all emotions and dreams."[10]

This material world-universe is sacred for what it is, because it consists of stones, deer, and people, and not because it satisfies any monotheistic ontological predicates, such as being a First Cause or immutable or eternal or explanatorily necessary. According to dependent naturalist pantheism, "the holy" would be defined in terms of the ontological predicates (immutable, and so forth) of the monotheistic god, without the personal predicates (loving, good, and so on). Naturalistic pantheism would in effect be monotheism without the personal element.

As I have suggested, however, an independent naturalistic pantheism derives from its own religious sources, feelings of harmony with, horror, despair, awe, and joy at all the good and bad natural things and states of natural things that exist. We do not retrieve whatever we can from the concept of the supernatural and apply it to nature; rather, we begin from within the nature that affects us and is manifest to us and includes us, and experience it, and from these experiences one derives the concepts of what constitutes the holy.

Certain poems express an independent pantheism that is clearly distinct from a dependent pantheism. A type of natural pantheist religious experience is expressed in these lines from "Meditation at Oyster River" by Theodore Roethke:

> Now, in this waning of light,
> I rock with the motion of morning;
> In the cradle of all that is,
> I'm lulled into half-sleep
> By the lapping of water,
> Cries of the sandpiper.
> Water's my will, and my way,
> And the spirit runs, intermittently,
> In and out of the small waves,
> Runs with the intrepid shorebirds—
> How graceful the small before danger!
>
> In the first of the moon,
> All's a scattering,
> A shining.[11]

Here there is no reference to such monotheist sentiments as worship or the feeling that a loving person is watching over one or even any sense that there are any minds other than the minds of organisms. There are no dependent pantheistic sentiments about an eternal, immutable, necessary, self-explanatory universe that is a "First Cause." The sentiment is independently pantheistic because there is an emotional response to "all that is," understood as all that there is in the universe or nature: all matter and organisms throughout all of space and time.

Roethke is feeling in harmony with all that is; he feels himself to be a part of all that is, a part that is harmoniously related (at least in certain respects and at that time) to all other parts: "I rock with the motion of morning; / In the cradle of all that is."

Further, Roethke's poem evinces a positive appreciation of the universe that is not dependent on believing that there is a good moral order of the universe, that everything is ordered to the good. The feeling of being a harmonious part of all-there-is requires that there be enough good in all-there-is so that the realization of my nature can (*at least at some times and to some degree*) be allowed by the way things are. It also requires only that other things manifest some degree of harmony in this sense, that all things are interrelated in such a way that they permit or promote the development of some things' natures to some degree. These requirements are consistent both with there being gratuitous evil and with there being more evil than good in the universe.

The holy is harmonious in some respects and dissonant in others. The pantheist feeling of harmony is an emotional response to the holy in its harmonious aspect. The emphasis in the feeling of harmony is on the positively valuable aspect of all there is. Roethke is appreciating the beauty of the water, the moonlight, the natural skill and grace of the shorebirds. He is quite conscious that the holy wears another face besides the harmonious and beautiful. He writes in "Journey to the Interior,"

> As a blind man, lifting a curtain, knows it is morning,
> I know this change:
> On one side of silence there is no smile;
> But when I breathe with the birds,
> The spirit of wrath becomes the spirit of blessing,
> And the dead begin from their dark to sing in my sleep.

There are two sides of silence, the wrathful, dark side where death has negative value, and we cannot at these times be reconciled with death. This aspect of all-there-is is the dissonant aspect: various parts of nature destroy, harm, or impede the realization of other parts of nature. But there is also a positive side of silence, where there is a smile; in respect of this side, the opportunity I have to participate in all-there-is feels like "a blessing" and is something good. In this respect, I feel fortunate, for sometimes and in some respects I and other parts can realize their natures constantly with one another. I feel harmonious with the birds and the rest of nature, and I am reconciled with the fact that all that lives must die. Death destroys me and in this respect is bad, but it allows new life-forms to be born, evolve, and participate in all-there-is, and in this respect death is good.

I would suggest that the most rational way for me as pantheist to be reconciled with death is to realize how insignificant my life is in the grand totality that constitutes the holy. My self and my life are but a drop in the oceanic spread of space and time, and the cessation of my self is the cessation of something that has very little value in comparison with the total aggregate value of everything else. A true emotional crisis would be rationally elicited by a belief that the whole universe is about to cease to exist, for in this case all that is valuable would disappear. But an emotional crisis at the thought of one's own death seems to be an egocentric delusion based on an overestimation of the value of one's self.

It seems that Einstein felt in some respects a natural pantheist attitude. He writes,

> A human being is part of the whole, called by us "Universe"; a part limited in time and space. He experiences himself, his thoughts and feelings as something separated from the rest—a kind of optical delusion of his consciousness. This delusion is a kind of prison for us, restricting us to our personal desires and to affection for a few persons nearest to us. Our task must be to free ourselves from this prison by widening our circle of compassion to embrace all living creatures and the whole of nature in its beauty. Nobody is able to achieve this completely but the striving for such achievement is, in itself, a part of the liberation and a foundation for inner security.[12]

Although Einstein aptly expresses the sense of transcending the narrow circle of what we experience to be important—ourselves, family, career, and so on—he seems guilty of adopting the wish fulfillment approach to religion, in which religion is defined as a route to happiness. Perhaps, more charitably, he can be interpreted as expressing one aspect of the natural pantheist attitude—feeling compassion, focusing on the beautiful aspect of nature and the positive feeling of liberation. One may feel compassion, for example, for the twenty million people who died of the plague in the fourteenth century, but one cannot blind oneself to the horribleness of the fact that this gratuitous natural evil exists at all. Insofar as inner security is a goal, it cannot honestly be attained by focusing only on the positive side of nature, "the whole of nature in its beauty." Given that the universe is awesome, beautiful, horrible, and grotesque, inner security can be attained only by realizing one's insignificance and thus that the good and bad things that happen to one (including one's death) do not matter very much in the broad scheme of things. One feels secure in the face of fate because one is too unimportant for anything very important (bad or good) to happen to oneself.

There are other ways for a naturalist pantheist to attain a religious peace of mind, but it is important to note that peace of mind is not "the ideal state" for the naturalist pantheist, for peace of mind can be attained only by not taking into account the horrifying aspect of the holy. At some times and in some respects, the naturalist pantheist will justifiably achieve a peace of mind, but to live a genuine religious life, the pantheist at other times must not be at peace with the way things are. A religious state of mind that is equally as "ideal" as peace of mind is to be deeply saddened or fundamentally discontent at the way things are.

Is the harmonious and discordant universe enough to satisfy human religious needs? Is even the positively valuable aspect of Nature enough? To quote from another Roethke poem, "I'm Here":

> Is it enough?—
> The sun loosening the frost on December windows,
> The glitter of wet in the first of morning?
> The sound of voices, young voices, mixed with sleighbells,
> Coming across snow in early evening?

We may take these few lines of verse as suggesting to us several different questions.

First, is holy Nature enough to satisfy the religious desires of *each actually extant human*? The answer is clearly no; most humans with religious needs have a monotheistic need to relate to a Good and Loving Supernatural Person who governs Nature. (Not all humans have religious needs or desires. This is clear from empirical observations of human behavior, and only a religious ideology—for example, Christianity—would require one to believe that "despite the evidence" all humans have a religious need. Some people have no desire to relate to the holy in any of its senses, be it monotheistic, pantheistic, or whatever. Perhaps someone like W. V. O. Quine would have such a nonreligious personality, as is suggested by his autobiography. Perhaps most atheists have no religious desires, although some clearly do [even if they are unfulfilled, as with Nietzsche and Camus].)

Second, is holy Nature enough to satisfy all humans in some possible world *in which they had no religious delusions,* that is, recognized that supernaturalism and other false religious beliefs are in fact false? The answer again is no, for some humans clearly do have a need to relate to a monotheistic god even if they believe that no such god exists.

Third, is holy nature enough to satisfy the religious desires of *the naturalist pantheist*? The naturalist pantheist believes that the holy is horrific. Does the naturalist pantheist desire or need to relate to what is horrible? In one sense, the answer is yes: the pantheist wants to *contemplate* the Holy in its horrifying aspect as well as in its sublime aspect. Watching a documentary film on the Nazi extermination camps or a documentary on the slaughterhouses for cattle and pigs currently operating in America counts as a religious activity for the naturalist pantheist. The Horrible is as much a part of all-there-is as the beautiful and majestic, and a pantheist desires to appreciate what-is.

The question, Does the naturalist pantheist desire or need to relate to what is horrible? has a negative answer if the question is taken in a noncontemplative respect. Perhaps it goes without saying that the pantheist does not desire herself or others to be gratuitously *harmed or destroyed* by the horrifying aspects of Nature; she does not desire herself or others to die of AIDS, become insane, or be raped. In this respect, the naturalist pantheist has an *aversion* to the Holy as much as an attraction to it. In naturalist pantheism, we need to talk about both "religious desires" and "religious aversions."

In monotheism, there is a place for religious aversion; for example, the Christian religion, on some interpretations, implies that Satan and some atheistic humans have an aversion to God in that they do not want to submit to God's authority (the "sin of pride"). But this aversion to the holy is a *defective* way of living religiously in monotheism; it is living in a religiously improper way. In naturalistic pantheism, however, an aversion to the holy is a proper and appropriate way to relate to the holy, for the horrible facet of the holy deserves aversion or repugnance. Indeed, the naturalist pantheist must have an ambivalent attitude to the holy.

The naturalist pantheist will thus answer the Is it enough? question by saying the Holy qua sublime or good is enough to satisfy her desires to relate in a positive way to the Holy, and that the Holy qua horrifying is enough to produce aversion in her to the Holy.

The Is it enough? question also has a different answer when we contrast the despair/joy affects with the horror/awe affects. There is another important sense in which holy nature is not enough to satisfy. In despair, I feel dissatisfied at the universe's lack of nature development. This is different from horror. In horror or repugnance at the universe, there is no belief that changing the universe for the better is a *hopeless* task. But in despair, the actual degree of nature development in the universe is deemed hopelessly insufficient. There is nothing I could do to bring this nature development to a point that is satisfactory to me. This may be because the kinds of things that exist are insufficiently developed kinds (there appears to be nothing more developed in the universe than *mere humans*). If all that exists are humans, lizards, and stars, then the natural kinds belonging to the holy are too insignificant for any activity regarding them to be worth the effort. And one may also be in despair because, even if the kinds of things are sufficient, their actual or present degree of development is hopelessly insufficient, and no activity could increase their development to a degree that would make any activity worth the effort. Despair is not a deluded affect; one cannot "refute" the beliefs upon which it is based by pointing out that there are some activities one can undertake to better the universe. For the despairing person takes as her ideal of goodness something that is higher than anything that actually exists or is attainable. If such an ideal matters to one, then despair is indeed the appropriate attitude. Despair can be alleviated if the person chooses to have a lower standard of goodness matter to her; what matters to her will become the attainably good, not the unattainably good.

In monotheism, depression or despair is seen as a "distance from the holy," as something from which one is alleviated by a proper appreciation of the holy. Monotheism holds out the promise to depressed and despairing people that there is indeed hope and happiness after all, if only one has faith in the monotheistic god. But naturalist pantheism is not offered as a panacea for despair, an opium for the masses, or a magical fulfillment of one's deepest wishes. Rather, naturalistic pantheism sanctifies and justifies the despair of the depressed person. Despair is an end in itself, for the holy is fully understood only if despair is included among one's responses to it. It is indeed true that there are ideals of goodness that are actually unattainable and unrealizable, regardless of one's efforts. To remain blind to this fact in order to "be happy" implies a failure to view the universe from all true standpoints.

Despair contrasts with joy, an equally important naturalist pantheist attitude. In despair, one is comparing the universe with the Ideal; but in joy, one is comparing the universe to nothingness—there being no things at all. There being things at all, rather than nothing, is taken to be a matter for rejoicing. In addition, one may rejoice at the actual instances of goodness, the actual ways things develop their natures. Further, one may also rejoice that the limited evidence we possess seems to suggest that the totality is more good than bad, and therefore that it is better that this totality exist rather than nothingness.

But there is more to be said about the Is it enough? question. Note that in his poem, Roethke is really asking if the beauty or sublimity of Nature is enough to satisfy his desires to relate positively to something holy. Roethke is asking whether all the religious desires he has, which may include monotheistic as well as naturalist pantheistic desires, are satisfied by the sublimity of holy Nature. And here the answer is no; Nature in its sublime aspect cannot satisfy a monotheistic religious need. In "Meditations of an Old Woman: First Meditation," Roethke suggests that he has both monotheistic and naturalist pantheistic religious needs, and so he is only sometimes religiously satisfied:

> A flame, intense, visible,
> Plays over the dry pods,
> Runs fitfully along the stubble,
> Moves over the field,
> Without burning,
>> In such times, lacking a god,
>> I am still happy.

Here is the basic joy that this universe exists at all, rather than nothingness. And here we see Roethke in transition from a despairing atheism at the "death of God" (the loss of monotheistic belief) to a way of viewing things in a naturalist pantheist light.

The "death of God" despair has cognitive import for naturalist pantheism, for it shows that the holy *is not* the maximally good or perfect being, something that is capable of making me completely fulfilled and happy; there is conceivable something that is better than holy Nature. If one's ideal is that there exist a reality that is enough to make one *continuously* and *fully* satisfied, then naturalist pantheism will justify an attitude of despair. The religions of the supernaturalists are designed precisely to ward off this despair. A reasoning based on wish fulfillment may go like this: "A continuous and complete satisfaction cannot be attained on earth, in this life; therefore it must be attained in a heavenly afterlife." In supernaturalist religion as in no other place do we see how humans' desire for happiness affects their belief-formations.

An independent naturalist pantheism has its basis in a certain sort of religious experience, just as monotheism has a basis in a sort of religious experience, for example, St. Paul's on the road to Damascus. For the pantheist, these experiences are of Nature.

Summary

In this book, I have aimed to accomplish several goals:

1. First, I have endeavored to establish a certain thesis about the history of analytic philosophy. I have shown in some detail how the ethics and philosophies of religion of four main movements in analytic philosophy are based on the philosophies of language of these movements. This helps to dispel the old objection to analytic philosophy (still prevalent in many quarters) that in its practicing of the "analysis of language" it is antithetical to addressing the basic questions about ethical and religious meaning. I have not tried to dispel this objection in the manner *normally* attempted by analytic philosophers in the past couple of decades or so, namely, by pointing out that since the 1970s analytic philosophers have written extensively about ethics and the philosophy of religion *in addition* to writing about the philosophy of language. Rather, I have argued that the "analysis of language" is the *method* used by many analysts to derive conclusions about ethics and religion and, moreover, that this concern with the perennial questions has been a focus of analytic philosophy from its inception with the logical realists and logical positivists. In contrast to the standard histories of analytic philosophy (John Passmore's, J. O. Urmson's, Munitz's, and so forth), I have emphasized that analytic philosophy, even in respect of its main movements that have focused on the "analysis of words," is no less concerned with the meaning of human life than is existentialism or traditional philosophies such as Plato's, Aquinas's, Spinoza's, and Hegel's.

2. A second but less broad-based aim in the history of analytic philosophy was to

present a history of linguistic essentialism that is more accurate than the "standard" history, which is focused on Kripke and others. I have argued that the theories of rigid designation, direct reference, the causal theory of reference, reference-fixing descriptions, cognitive significance, metaphysical necessity, and so on were originally developed not by Kripke, Donnellan, and Kaplan (as the standard history claims), but by Marcus, Plantinga, and Geach.

3. A third and related aim pertaining to the history of contemporary analytic philosophy was to present a *more complete* account of linguistic essentialism by making more explicit how certain philosophies of religion and ethics belong to this movement. The connection of Plantinga with essentialism has been well known for decades, so my attempt to contribute something novel in this regard consists in identifying a certain area in *ethics* (occupied by Adams, Brink, Feldman, Hurka, and others) that is a part of the movement of linguistic essentialism. Intuitionism is associated with logical realism, emotivism with logical positivism, prescriptivism with ordinary language analysis, and the essentialist ethics of Adams, Brink, Hurka, and others should be likewise associated with linguistic essentialism.

The above-mentioned three goals are the most significant ones of this book in the area of the history of analytic philosophy; again I would like to add the caveat that this book presents a history of only a highly selective part of analytic philosophy, and this book should *not* be seen in any sense as a history of analytic philosophy.

The remaining goals I attempted to accomplish in this book do not belong to the history of analytic philosophy but to ethics and philosophy of religion:

4. One goal was to argue for the metaethical thesis that moral realism is true. My criticisms of the antirealist positions of the logical positivists (chapter 2) and the ordinary language analysts (chapter 3), as well as of the more recent positions of Mackie and others (chapter 6), are intended to elaborate upon or supplement the many arguments already given in the literature by contemporary moral realists such as Brink and Butchvarov.

5. A fifth goal pertains to *the method* of normative ethics. I have tried to make explicit and develop at length the "linguistic essential method" of ethical inquiry, first formulated and used by Robert Adams. I have put this method to a relatively extensive use in constructing a global, naturalist perfectionism, and I hope this "linguistic essentialist method" will be seen by ethicists as a viable option to the currently popular method of "reflective equilibrium."

6. A sixth goal concerns the arguments I gave in chapter 6 about normative ethics. I began by presenting some ideas in Thomas Hurka's *Perfectionism*, arguably the most important book on perfectionist ethics since Aristotle's *Nicomachean Ethics*. By means of altering, developing, and criticizing Hurka's version of perfectionism, I constructed a theory of global, naturalistic perfectionism that seems to

me to be more plausible than other normative ethics currently being discussed. Several decades ago, John Rawls extensively revived the "social contract" tradition in ethics, and I hope Hurka's book will similarly revive the perfectionist tradition in ethics. I prefer to see my global, naturalist perfectionism as a "second step" in the revival of perfectionism, following Hurka's "first step," rather than as a "criticism" or "refutation" of Hurka's first step.

7. Another goal was to show in more detail than normal why the philosophies of religion of the positivists and ordinary language analysts are mistaken and to further support the now widely accepted view that statements about objective religious meaning have both sense and truth-values.

8. A more specific goal in the philosophy of religion was to construct a new and sound version of the "logical argument from evil," a version that is able to undermine Plantinga's widely accepted free will defense. If this version is sound, there appears little, if any, rational justification for continued belief in Judeo-Christian monotheism.

9. A positive, constructive goal in the philosophy of religion was to break new ground by developing an independent naturalist pantheism. The two more or less "provincial" alternatives within which Anglo-American analytic philosophers have been confined in this century, "Judeo-Christian monotheism or atheism (narrowly defined as disbelief in Judeo-Christian monotheism)," have been worked to death in the literature, and some fresh ideas are needed. I have joined John Post in exploring naturalistic pantheism as an alternative, and I developed an independent naturalist pantheism that contrasts with the dependent naturalist pantheism I argued was implicit in Post's writings.

10. A final goal is my endeavor to write a book on "the meaning of human life" that shows how this extremely vague and equivocal phrase can be defined in precise terms, so that it reduces to certain exactly specified topics in metaethics, normative ethics, and the philosophy of religion. Contrary to the prevailing opinion among both laypersons and philosophers, the topic of "the meaning of human life" *can* be dealt with in a logically rigorous and conceptually precise way. We no longer need to answer the clichéd question, What is the meaning of human life? with jokes because we can explicate this question in terms of univocal and precise questions in the fields of ethics and the philosophy of religion.[13]

The various goals at which I have aimed in this book are interrelated in a way that I hope is fruitful and thought provoking. I have addressed the questions about ethical and religious meanings by means of a historical approach, by way of explaining, criticizing, and developing the ideas in four main movements of analytic philosophy, logical realism, positivism, ordinary language analysis, and linguistic essentialism. The reader will note that the answers I have offered to the questions about ethical and religious meanings fall within the framework of linguistic essentialism. The theory in this book may thus be regarded not only as a partial history of analytic philosophy, but as a development of one of its current movements, linguistic essentialism. My journey through a part of the history of analytic philosophy in this book has brought me to a final position that consists of versions of linguistic essentialism, moral realism, global perfectionism, and naturalistic pantheism.

Notes

Preface

1 Stephen Hawking, *A Brief History of Time* (New York: Bantam Books, 1988), 174–75.
2 E. D. Klemke, "Living without Appeal: An Affirmative Philosophy of Life," in *The Meaning of Life*, ed. E. D. Klemke (New York: Oxford University Press, 1981), 163.

Chapter 1. Logical Realism

1 The quotation from Moore's letter is taken from Thomas Baldwin, "Moore's Rejection of Idealism," in *Philosophy in History*, ed. Richard Rorty, J. B. Schneewind, and Quentin Skinner (Cambridge: Cambridge University Press, 1984), 370.
2 G. E. Moore, "The Nature of Judgement," *Mind* n.s. 8 (1899): 176–93.
3 Bertrand Russell, *The Principles of Mathematics*, 2d ed. (New York: Norton, 1938), 42.
4 Ibid., 47.
5 Ibid.
6 Ibid., 44.
7 Russell, "A Free Man's Worship," in *The Meaning of Life*, ed. E. D. Klemke (New York: Oxford University Press, 1981), 56.
8 Moore, "The Value of Religion," in *G. E. Moore: The Early Essays*, ed. Tom Regan (Philadelphia: Temple University Press, 1986), 108, 120.
9 According to the big bang theory, all natural causes can be traced back to the big bang, which itself has no natural cause. For a discussion of whether it is reasonable to believe the big bang is uncaused or caused by God, see William Lane Craig and Quentin Smith, *Theism, Atheism and Big Bang Cosmology* (Oxford: Clarendon Press, 1993).
10 For some more sophisticated contemporary discussions of the argument from design, see Alvin Plantinga, *God and Other Minds* (Cornell University Press, 1967), and Richard Swinburne, *The Existence of God* (Oxford University Press, 1979).
11 Moore, "The Nature of Judgement," in *G. E. Moore: The Early Essays*, 78–79.

12 Moore denies he is an atheist and suggests he is agnostic, but this denial is fatuous because he claims that God exists only if he is not the cause of anything. No theist would call such an impotent being "God."

13 See Moore's *Principia Ethica* and *Ethics* and his "Mr McTaggart's Ethics," *International Journal of Ethics* 13 (1903): 341–70, "The Conception of Intrinsic Value" and "The Nature of Moral Philosophy" in *Philosophical Papers* (New York: Harcourt, Brace, 1922), and "Is Goodness a Quality?" *Aristotelian Society Supplementary* 11 (1932): 116–68. Also see his ethical discussions in his "A Reply to My Critics," in *The Philosophy of G. E. Moore*, ed. P. Schilpp (Evanston: Northwestern University, 1942).

14 Moore, "The Value of Religion," 116.

15 Moore adopts this terminology in *Principia Ethica*, esp. 110ff.

16 For a critical discussion of Moore's distinction, see the essays by Broad, Frankena, Paton, and Edel in *The Philosophy of G. E. Moore*.

17 Moore, *Principia Ethica*, 16–17.

18 See Max Scheler, *Formalism in Ethics and Nonformal Ethics of Values* (Evanston: Northwestern University Press, 1973), and Panayot Butchvarov, *Skepticism in Ethics* (Bloomington: Indiana University Press, 1989), 98–101. Butchvarov correctly denies that he and others are "intuitionists" in the improper sense that they postulate a faculty of ethical intuition. "Ethical intuitionism" in the *proper* sense means the conjunction of moral realism with the thesis that some ethical truths are "evident of themselves" in some sense of this phrase.

19 H. A. Prichard, "Does Moral Philosophy Rest on a Mistake?", in Melden, ed. *Ethical Theories*. (Prentice-Hall 1967, Englewood Cliffs, New Jersey), pp. 532–3, n. 8.

20 Thomas Nagel, "The Absurd," in Klemke, *The Meaning of Life*, 155.

21 Matthew Arnold, "Dover Beach," from last stanza, in M. Danziger, *A Poetry Anthology* (New York: Random House, 1968), 465.

Chapter 2. Logical Positivism

1 Ludwig Wittgenstein, *Philosophical Remarks* (Oxford: Basil Blackwell, 1975), 200.

2 Moritz Schlick, "Positivism and Realism," in *Logical Positivism*, ed. A. J. Ayer (New York: Free Press, 1959), 86.

3 Rudolf Carnap, *Philosophy and Logical Syntax* (London: Psyche Miniatures, 1935), sec. 1.

4 Otto Neurath, "Protocol Sentences," trans. G. Schick, in Ayer, *Logical Positivism*, 202.

5 Carnap, "Uber die Aufgabe der Physik und die Anwendung des Grundsatzes der Einfachstheit," *Kant-Studien* 28 (1923): 90–107. My use of "explicit definitions" corresponds to Carnap's in "Testability and Meaning" and the preface to *The Logical Structure of the World* (1961) as well as to the usage of most writers on positivism, e.g., the essays by Pap and Hempel in *The Philosophy of Rudolph Carnap* and Frederick Suppe, *The Structure of Scientific Theories* (Urbana: University of Illinois Press, 1977). But in Carnap, *The Logical Structure of the World*, 65–67, and Ayer, *Language, Truth and Logic* (New York: Dover Publications, 1952), chap. 3, what I am here calling "explicit definitions" are called "definitions in use."

6 Carnap, "Testability and Meaning," in *Readings in the Philosophy of Science*, ed. H. Feigl and M. Brodbeck (New York: Appleton-Century-Crofts, 1953), 47–92, esp. 52–53.

7 Ayer, *Language, Truth and Logic*, 146.

8 John Wisdom, "Gods," *Proceedings of the Aristotelian Society* (1944–45). My statement of the parable follows Anthony Flew's in Flew, Robert Hare, and Basil Mitchell, "Theology and Falsification," in *Philosophy of Religion*, ed. William Rowe and William Wainwright (New York: Harcourt Brace Jovanovich, 1989).

9 R. B. Braithwaite, "An Empiricist's View of the Nature of Religious Belief," in *Philosophy of Religion*, ed. S. Cahn (Harper and Row, 1970), 162.

10 For further argument along these lines, see Quentin Smith, "An Atheological Argument from Evil Natural Laws," *International Journal for the Philosophy of Religion* 29 (1991): 159–74.

11 The atheistic argument is straightforward and intuitive, but the theistic counterargument has the appearance of being contrived or at least convoluted. See, for example, Alvin Plantinga, "The Probabilistic Argument from Evil," *Philosophical Studies* 35 (1979): 1–53, and William Alston, "The Inductive Argument from Evil," in *Philosophical Perspectives* 5 (1991). I think many theists would admit this is the weakest point in current analytic theism.

12 Aquinas, *Summa Theologica* (New York: Benziger Brothers, 1948).

13 Ayer, *Language, Truth and Logic*, 111.

14 Ayer, in *The Logic of God*, ed. John Hick (New York: Macmillan, 1964).

15 For a more sophisticated analysis of the PV, see John Post, "Paradox in Critical Rationalism and Related Theories," *The Philosophical Forum* 3 (1971): 27–61.

Chapter 3. Ordinary Language Analysis

1 For a critical discussion of some of these formulations, see Carl Hempel, "Empiricist Criteria of Cognitive Significance: Problems and Changes," in *Aspects of Scientific Explanation*, ed. C. Hempel (New York: Free Press, 1965), 101–22.

2 John Wisdom, "Metaphysics and Verification," *Mind* (1938): 454.

3 C. L. Stevenson, "Persuasive Definitions," *Mind* (1938): 339–40. For further discussion of Wisdom's and Stevenson's articles, see J. O. Urmson, *Philosophical Analysis: Its Development between the Two World Wars* (Oxford: Clarendon Press, 1956), chap. 11.

4 Rudolf Carnap, "Logical Foundations of the Unity of Science," in Herbert Feigl and Wilfred Sellars, *Readings in Philosophical Analysis* (New York: Appleton-Century-Crofts, 1949), 410.

5 P. F. Strawson, "Carnap's Views on Constructed Systems versus Natural Languages in Analytic Philosophy," in *The Philosophy of Rudolph Carnap*, ed. P. Schilpp (La Salle, Ill.: Open Court, 1963), 505.

6 J. L. Austin, *Sense and Sensibilia* (Oxford: University Press, 1962), 63.

7 Strawson, "Carnap's Views," pp. 513–14.

8 J. O. Urmson, for example, regards this article as the first publication of the ordinary language movement. *Philosophical Analysis*, 172ff.

9 John Wisdom, "Philosophical Perplexity," in *The Linguistic Turn*, ed. R. Rorty (Chicago: University of Chicago Press, 1967), 101.

10 Ludwig Wittgenstein, *Philosophical Grammar*, trans. A. Kenny (Berkeley: University of California Press, 1974), 59–60.

11 Wisdom, "Philosophical Perplexity," 104.

12 Gilbert Ryle, *The Concept of Mind* (New York: Barnes and Noble, 1949), 126.

13 Ryle distinguishes between "use" and "usage" in his article "Ordinary Language," but we need not follow his practice for our present limited purposes.

14 Ryle, *The Concept of Mind*, 22–23.

15 Wittgenstein, *Philosophical Investigations*, trans. G. E. M. Anscombe (New York: Macmillan Co., 1953), #116.

16 Wittgenstein, *Philosophical Investigations* #120.

17 D. Z. Phillips, *Religion without Explanation* (Oxford: Basil Blackwell, 1976), 41.

18 Wittgenstein, "Religious Belief," in *Philosophy of Religion*, ed. Rowe and Wainwright (San Diego: Harcourt Brace Jovanovich, 1989), 277. Reprinted from *Lectures and Conversations*, ed. C. Barret (Berkeley: University of California Press, 1966).

19 Phillips, *Religion without Explanation*, 147.

20 Norman Malcolm, "The Groundlessness of Belief," in *Reason and Religion*, ed. Stuart C. Brown (Ithaca: Cornell University Press, 1977), 144.

21 D. Z. Phillips, *The Concept of Prayer* (New York: Schocken Books, 1966), 35.

22 Phillips, *Religion without Explanation,* 150.

23 Rush Rhees, *Without Answers* (London: Routledge and Kegan Paul, 1969), 131–32.

24 Wittgenstein, *Philosophical Investigations,* 226.

25 Quoted in W. T. Stace, *Mysticism and Philosophy* (Philadelphia: Lippincott, 1960), 228.

26 Wittgenstein, "Religious Belief," 277.

27 Wittgenstein, *Philosophical Grammar,* sec. 133.

28 Peter Winch, "Understanding a Primitive Society," in *Religion and Understanding,* ed. D. Z. Phillips (Oxford: Basil Blackwell, 1967), 11–12, 22 (emphasis added).

29 Peter Winch, *The Idea of a Social Science* (London, 1958), 100–01.

30 Milton Munitz, *The Question of Reality* (Princeton: Princeton University Press, 1990), 97.

31 Stephen Toulmin, *Am Examination of the Place of Reason in Ethics* (Chicago: University of Chicago Press, 1986), 144.

32 Carnap, *Philosophy and Logical Syntax,* 24.

33 R. M. Hare, *The Language of Morals* (London: Oxford University Press, 1952), 69.

34 P. H. Nowell-Smith, *Ethics* (Baltimore: Penguin Books, 1954), 21.

35 Charles Stevenson, "The Emotive Meaning of Ethical Terms," 417.

36 Jean-Paul Sartre, *Being and Nothingness,* trans. Hazel Barnes (New York: Pocket Books, 1966), 76.

37 Jean-Paul Sartre, *Baudelaire,* trans. Martin Turnell (New York: Pocket Books, 1966), 65, 29.

38 Hare, *Freedom and Reason* (Oxford: Clarendon Press, 1963), 2.

39 Hermann Hesse, *Steppenwolf,* trans. Basil Creighton (Middlesex: Penguin Books Ltd., 1965), 7–8, 9, 13–14.

40 Hare, "Nothing Matters," in *The Meaning of Life,* ed. E. D. Klemke (New York: Oxford University Press, 1981), 242.

41 Austin, *Philosophical Papers* (Oxford: Oxford University Press, 1979), 59.

42 Colin Wilson, *The Outsider* (Boston: Houghton Mifflin Co., 1956), 11.

43 Samuel Beckett, *Three Novels* (New York: Grove Press, 1955), 180, 190.

44 Hare, *The Language of Morals,* 25.

45 Ibid., 8.

46 Ibid., 97.

47 Austin, *Sense and Sensibilia,* 136.

48 Austin, "A Plea for Excuses," in *Philosophical Papers,* 185.

49 Malcolm, "Moore and Ordinary Language," in *The Linguistic Turn,* ed. R. Rorty, 120.

Chapter 4. The Essentialists' Method of Linguistic Analysis

1 See Quentin Smith, "Marcus, Kripke and the Origin of the New Theory of Reference," in *Synthese* 104, no. 2 (August 1995), ed. James H. Fetzer and Paul W. Humphreys, 179–89; "Marcus and the New Theory of Reference: A Reply to Scott Soames," ibid., 217–44; "Direct, Rigid Designation and A Posteriori Necessity: A History and Critique," in *The New Theory of Reference,* ed. James H. Fetzer and Paul Humphreys (Kluwer Academic Publishers, 1998). The two articles in *Synthese* are reprinted in *The New Theory of Reference.*

2 See *Synthese* 104, no. 2 (August 1995), ed. James H. Fetzer and Paul W. Humphreys, and *The New Theory of Reference,* ed. Fetzer and Humphreys.

3 Jaakko Hintikka and Gabriel Sandu, "The Fallacies of the New Theory of Reference," *Synthese* 104 (1995): 271.

4 David Kaplan, printed on the back cover of the paperback edition of Ruth Barcan Marcus, *Modalities* (New York: Oxford University Press, 1993).

5 Michael Devitt, "Against Direct Reference," in *Midwest Studies in Philosophy* 14, *Contempo-*

rary Perspectives in the Philosophy of Language II, ed. P. French et al. (Notre Dame: University of Notre Dame Press, 1989), 220.

6 P. T. Geach, "The Perils of Pauline," *Review of Metaphysics* 23 (1969): 287–300.

7 Terence Parsons, "Ruth Barcan Marcus and the Barcan Formula," in *Modality, Morality, and Belief,* ed. W. Sinnot-Armstrong (Cambridge: Cambridge University Press, 1995).

8 Stig Kanger, *Provability in Logic* (Stockholm: Almquist and Wiksell, 1957).

9 Nino Cocchiarella, "On the Primary and Secondary Semantics of Logical Necessity," *Journal of Philosophical Logic* 4 (1975): 13–27; "Logical Atomism, Nominalism, and Modal Logic," *Synthese* 31 (1975): 23–62; Jaakko Hintikka, "Standard vs. Nonstandard Logic, Modal and First-Order Logics," in *Modern Logic: A Survey,* ed. E. Agazzi (Boston: D. Reidel, 1980), 283–96; "Is Alethic Modal Logic Possible?" *Acta Philosophica Fennica* 35 (1982): 89–105.

10 Richard Montague, "Logical Necessity, Physical Necessity, Ethics, and Quantifiers," *Inquiry* 4 (1960): 259–69.

11 Saul Kripke, "A Completeness Theorem in Modal Logic," *The Journal of Symbolic Logic* 24 (1959): 1–14; Jaakko Hintikka, "Modality and Quantification," *Theoria* 27 (1961): 119–28.

12 Devitt, "Against Direct Reference," 220.

13 Ruth Barcan Marcus, "Modalities and Intensional Languages," *Synthese* 13 (1961): 303–22, 309–10. This is reprinted with some changes in her *Modalities* (Oxford: Oxford University Press, 1993).

14 Marcus, *Modalities,* 10.

15 Marcus notes that her semantics corresponds in part to Carnap's semantics in *Meaning and Necessity* (1947).

16 Marcus, *Modalities,* 195. This quote is from Marcus's later essay "Possibilia and Possible Worlds."

17 Ibid.

18 David Kaplan, "Demonstratives," in *Themes from Kaplan,* ed. J. Almog et al. (New York: Oxford University Press, 1989) [circulated as a mimeograph since 1977], 493.

19 Marcus, *Modalities,* chap. 15.

20 Jaakko Hintikka, "The Modes of Modality," *Acta Philosophica Fennica* 16 (1963): 65–79. See page 72 of the reprint of this article in Michael Loux, ed., *The Possible and the Actual* (Ithaca: Cornell University Press, 1979).

21 Kripke, "Speaker's Reference and Semantic Reference," in *Contemporary Perspectives in the Philosophy of Language,* ed. P. French, et al. (Minneapolis: University of Minnesota Press, 1977).

22 Alvin Plantinga, "De Re et De Dicto," *Nous* 3 (September 1969): 235–58, 244.

23 Alvin Plantinga, "World and Essence," *The Philosophical Review* 74 (October 1970): 461–92.

24 In *Language and Time* (New York: Oxford University Press, 1993), I argued that what Plantinga calls "states of affairs" must, on pain of contradiction, be identical with what he calls "propositions."

25 Geach, "The Perils of Pauline," 289. I discussed Geach's theory more extensively in my articles in Fetzer's and Humphrey's *The New Theory of Reference* (1998).

26 H. P. Grice, "Vacuous Names," in *Words and Objections,* ed. Donald Davidson and Jaakko Hintikka (Dordrecht: D. Reidel, 1969), 118–45.

27 Plantinga, "The Boethian Compromise," *American Philosophical Quarterly* 15 (1978): 129–38, 138.

28 Marcus et al., "Discussion of the Paper of Ruth B. Marcus," *Synthese* 14 (1962): 132–43, 141.

29 See Quentin Smith, "The Conceptualist Argument for God's Existence," *Faith and Philosophy* 11 (1994): 38–49; Selmer Bringsjord, "Are There Set Theoretic Possible Worlds?" *Analysis* 45.1 (1985); Christopher Menzel, "On Set Theoretic Possible Worlds," *Analysis* 46.2 (1986).

30 Marcus, *Modalities*, 54.

31 Mohan Matten, "Ostension, Names and Natural Kind Terms," *Dialogue* 23 (1984): 44.

Chapter 5. Essentialist Philosophy of Religion

1 Alvin Plantinga, *The Nature of Necessity* (New York: Oxford University Press, 1974), 220, 221.

2 Peter Van Inwagen, "Ontological Arguments," *Noûs* 11 (1977): 375–95.

3 Kripke, *Naming and Necessity*, 14.

4 Richard Purtill, "Plantinga, Necessity, and God," *The New Scholasticism* 50 (1976): 59.

5 Plantinga, "Existence, Necessity, and God," *The New Scholasticism* 50 (1976): 71.

6 See almost any volume of *International Journal for the Philosophy of Religion, Religious Studies,* and *Faith and Philosophy* published during the 1980s or 1990s.

7 Plantinga, "Is Theism Really a Miracle?" *Faith and Philosophy* 3 (1986): 109–34.

8 Plantinga, *The Nature of Necessity*, 220–21.

9 Thomas Morris, *Anselmian Explorations* (Notre Dame: University of Notre Dame Press, 1987), 190.

10 The text has an ungrammatical "had"instead of a "has," which may be a misprint.

11 Richard Gale, *On the Nature and Existence of God* (Cambridge: Cambridge University Press, 1991), 228–37.

12 For further arguments against the theist modal intuition, see Post's discussion of Grim, in John Post, *Metaphysics* (New York: Paragon House, 1991), 160–65.

13 Plantinga, "Tooley and Evil: A Reply," *Australasian Journal of Philosophy* 60 (1981): 66–75, 74.

14 Plantinga, *The Nature of Necessity*, 172.

15 Ibid., 180.

16 Plantinga, "Tooley and Evil: A Reply," 67.

17 John Mackie, *The Miracle of Theism* (Oxford: Oxford University Press, 1982), 174.

18 Plantinga, "Is Theism Really a Miracle?" 109–34, 126.

19 Plantinga, *The Nature of Necessity*, 187.

20 Robert Stalnaker, "A Theory of Conditionals," in *Studies in Logical Theory*, ed. N. Rescher (Oxford: Blackwell, 1968), and David Lewis, *Counterfactuals* (Cambridge: Harvard University Press, 1973).

21 Plantinga, *The Nature of Necessity*, 178.

22 R. M. Adams, "Middle Knowledge and the Problem of Evil," *American Philosophical Quarterly* 14 (1977): 109–17; Anthony Kenny, *The God of the Philosophers* (Oxford: Oxford University Press, 1979), 62ff.; William Hasker, *God, Time, and Knowledge* (Ithaca: Cornell University Press, 1989), 18–52; William Lane Craig, *Divine Foreknowledge and Human Freedom* (Leiden: E. J. Brill, 1991), 237–78.

23 Plantinga, "Reply to Adams," in *Alvin Plantinga*, ed. J. Tomberlin and P. van Inwagen (Dordrecht: D. Reidel, 1985), 374.

24 Craig, *Divine Foreknowledge and Human Freedom*, 261.

25 Stalnaker, "A Theory of Conditionals," 108.

26 See my "Atheism, Theism and Big Bang Cosmology," *Australasian Journal of Philosophy* 69 (1991): 48–66, and Craig's reply to this and my reply to Craig, in Craig and Smith, *Theism, Atheism and Big Bang Cosmology* (Oxford: Clarendon Press, 1993).

27 Plantinga, *The Nature of Necessity*, 166–67.

28 Wesley Morrison, "Is God 'Significantly Free'?" *Faith and Philosophy* 2 (1985): 257–64, esp. 257–58.

29 Plantinga, *The Nature of Necessity*, 166.

30 Richard Swinburne, *The Coherence of Theism* (Clarendon Press: Oxford, 1977), 146.

31 Plantinga, "The Free Will Defence" in *Philosophy of Religion*, ed. S. Cahn (New York: Harper and Row, 1970), 56–57. (10) is Plantinga's (6'). This article was originally published in Max Black, ed., *Philosophy in America* (Ithaca: Cornell University Press, 1965).

32 John Mackie, "Evil and Omnipotence," *Philosophy of Religion*, ed. Cahn, 7–22, esp. 17.

33 Gale, *On the Nature and Existence of God*, 160.

34 Ibid., 158.

Chapter 6. Essentialist Ethics

1 Fred Feldman, *Doing the Best We Can* (Dordrecht: D. Reidel, 1986); David O. Brink, *Moral Realism and the Foundations of Ethics* (Cambridge: Cambridge University Press, 1989); Thomas Hurka, *Perfectionism* (New York: Oxford University Press, 1993).

2 Robert Adams, "Divine Command Metaethics Modified Again," *Journal of Religious Ethics* 7 (1979): 71–79. A large part of this article is reprinted as "Divine Command Metaethics as Necessary A Posteriori," in *Divine Commands and Morality*, ed. P. Helm (New York: Oxford University Press, 1981); my references are Helm's book.

3 Hilary Putnam, *Philosophical Papers*, Volume Two (Cambridge: Cambridge University Press, 1975), p. 290.

4 John Mackie, *Ethics* (London: Penguin Books, 1977).

5 John Post, *The Faces of Existence: An Essay in Nonreductive Metaphysics* (Ithaca: Cornell University Press, 1987), 255.

6 Brink, *Moral Realism*, 23.

7 Panayot Butchvarov, *Skepticism in Ethics* (Bloomington: Indiana University Press, 1989); Nicholas Sturgeon, "Harman on Moral Explanation of Natural Facts," in *Moral Realism*, ed. Gillespie, 1986 (*The Southern Journal of Philosophy, Supplement* 24); Richard Boyd, "How to Be a Moral Realist," in *Essays on Moral Realism*, ed. G. Sayre-McCord (Ithaca: Cornell University Press, 1988); Sayre-McCord, ibid.

8 G. E. Moore, *Principia Ethica*, 16–17.

9 I discuss this principle in *The Felt Meanings of the World: A Metaphysics of Feeling* (West Lafayette: Purdue University Press, 1986), 131–34, and in *Language and Time* (New York: Oxford University Press, 1993), 14–18.

10 Mackie, *Ethics*, 48–49.

11 Post, *The Faces of Existence*, see, e.g., 281.

12 Michael Pritchard, *On Becoming Responsible* (Lawrence: University of Kansas Press, 1991), chap. 3.

13 Hurka, *Perfectionism*, 18.

14 Arthur Falk, "Essay on Nature's Semeiosis," *Journal of Philosophical Research* 20 (1995): 297–348.

15 Joseph Ellin, *Morality and the Meaning of Life* (Fort Worth: Harcourt Brace College Publishers, 1995), 89.

16 See Quentin Smith, "An Atheological Argument from Evil Natural Laws," *International Journal for the Philosophy of Religion* 29 (1991): 159–74.

17 Pritchard, *On Becoming Responsible*, 2.

18 Stephen Hawking, *A Brief History of Time* (Toronto: Bantam Books, 1988), 137.

19 J. Hartle and S. W. Hawking, "Wave Function of the Universe," *Physical Review* D28, 2960–75, 2961. For further discussion, see William Lane Craig and Quentin Smith, *Theism, Atheism and Big Bang Cosmology* (Oxford: Clarendon Press, 1993), part 3; and Quentin Smith, "Stephen Hawking's Cosmology and Theism," *Analysis* 54 (1994): 236–43.

20 Ellin, *Morality and the Meaning of Life*, 306–07.

21 Ibid., 319.

Conclusion

1 Alvin Plantinga, "Pantheism," in *A Companion to Metaphysics,* ed. Jaegwon Kim and Ernest Sosa (Oxford: Basil Blackwell, 1995), 376.

2 Quentin Smith, *Language and Time* (New York: Oxford University Press, 1993), 199–204.

3 J. Hartle and S. W. Hawking, "Wave Function of the Universe," *Physical Review* D28, 2961. For a further explanation of this equation, see chapter 12 of William Lane Craig and Quentin Smith, *Theism, Atheism and Big Bang Cosmology* (Oxford: Clarendon Press, 1993), and Quentin Smith, "Stephen Hawking's Cosmology and Theism," *Analysis* 54 (1994): 236–43.

4 Quentin Smith, "An Analysis of Holiness," *Religious Studies* 24 (1988): 511–27.

5 Michael P. Levine, *Pantheism* (London: Routledge, 1994), 238–39.

6 Quentin Smith, *The Felt Meanings of the World: A Metaphysics of Feeling* (West Lafayette: Purdue University Press, 1986); John Post, *The Faces of Existence* (Ithaca: Cornell University Press, 1987).

7 The most frequent misunderstanding of the book results from readers assuming the traditional reason/feeling dichotomy the book rejects and then concluding that the book is not a true "metaphysics of feeling" because it is not a metaphysics of feeling in the traditional sense of "feeling." Traditionally, "reason" involves logical arguments (such as are associated with analytic philosophy), and a philosophy based on "feeling" consists of vague or poetically evocative statements (such as are associated with much of continental philosophy). The metaphysics of feeling developed in *The Felt Meanings of the World* rejects this reason/feeling distinction and makes the case that all modes of awareness, including logical argumentative modes, are feeling-awarenesses and ways of appreciating the world. As I indicated, Bruce Wilshire, in a long and insightful feature review in *International Philosophical Quarterly* (June 1991): 237–42, concluded that "a colleague has called *The Felt Meanings of the World* the most important book in phenomenology yet written by an American. I tend to agree." But Wilshire also criticized it for containing logical arguments. I would say the book is neither phenomenological nor analytic (I think Wilshire's own book, *Role Playing and Identity,* is the most important book in phenomenology written by an American); but because the analytic philosophy/continental philosophy paradigms dominate contemporary thinking, it is natural to read the book in terms of these paradigms. David Schenk wrote an especially insightful article about the book; see Schenk's "Smith's *Felt Meanings of the World:* An Internal Critique," *Journal of Speculative Philosophy* 7 (1993): 21–38. Chad Allen also wrote a carefully argued article, "Smith's *The Felt Meanings of the World* and the Pure Appreciation of Being Simpliciter," *Journal of Philosophical Research* 21 (1996): 69–89, in which he endeavors to introduce a moral realist theory into the metaphysics of feeling.

8 Panayot Butchvarov, Review of Quentin Smith's *The Felt Meanings of the World, Nous* (April 1989): 281–84, 281.

9 Marija Gimbutas, *The Language of the Goddess* (San Francisco: Harper and Row, 1989), 316, 317.

10 Donna Wilshire, *Virgin, Mother, Crone* (Rochester, Vt.: Inner Traditions International, 1994), 4, 12.

11 The quotes from Roethke's poems are taken from *The Collected Poems of Theodore Roethke* (New York: Harper and Row, 1968).

12 Quoted in Ronald C. Pine, *Science and the Human Prospect* (Belmont, Calif.: Wadsworth, 1989), epigraph.

13 In *The Felt Meanings of the World,* I also tried to deal with "the meaning of human life" in a detailed way but without using the familiar categories of analytic philosophy (metaethics, ethics, philosophy of religion).

Index